W9-CDB-403

Praise for the military writing of Bill Yenne

SUPERFORTRESS:
The Story of the B-29 and American Air Power
in World War II
(with Gen. Curtis F. LeMay)

"An eloquent tribute."

—*Publishers Weekly*

"This fascinating volume should be a welcome addition to any airman's library."

—*Air Force* magazine

"An invaluable statement on American airpower, as well as a fascinating history of a remarkable aircraft."

—Edward Jablonski, author of *America in the Air*

"BLACK '41":
The West Point Class of 1941 and
the American Triumph in WWII

"A uniquely vivid tapestry of an American experience."

—Michael J. L. Greene, Brigadier General,
US Army, Retired

OPERATION COBRA

★ AND THE GREAT ★

OFFENSIVE

Sixty Days That Changed the Course of
World War II

BILL YENNE

POCKET BOOKS
New York   London   Toronto   Sydney

An *Original* Publication of POCKET BOOKS

 POCKET BOOKS, a division of Simon & Schuster, Inc.
1230 Avenue of the Americas, New York, NY 10020

ISBN: 0-7434-5882-6

First Pocket Books printing January 2004

10 9 8 7 6 5 4 3 2 1

POCKET and colophon are registered trademarks of Simon & Schuster, Inc.

Cover illustrations by Bill Yenne; photos from the collection of Bill Yenne

Manufactured in the United States of America

For information regarding special discounts for bulk purchases, please contact Simon & Schuster Special Sales at 1-800-456-6798 or business@simonandschuster.com.

CONTENTS

A good battle plan that you act on today can be better than a perfect one tomorrow. . . . Nobody ever defended anything successfully. There is only attack and attack, and attack some more.

> —General George S. Patton Jr.
> commander, United States
> Third Army

As a result of the breakthrough of the enemy armored spearheads, the whole Western Front has been ripped wide open.

> —Field Marshal Günther
> von Kluge, commander,
> German Army Group B

NOTE

(1) Official military style states that arabic numerals are used to denote all units except:

(A) Allied and German numbered armies and USAAF numbered air forces, which are spelled out.
(B) Allied and German corps and USAAF commands, which are designated with Roman numerals.

(2) All Allied Infantry Divisions and Armored Divisions are identified in all references by number. All but United States divisions are identified by nationality. When reference is made to the 2nd Infantry Division or the 4th Armored Division, these are American. The 4th Canadian Armored Division is identified as being Canadian, etc. Where there is a possibility of confusion in a complex discussion of various units, United States divisions are identified as such. German Infantry Divisions are identified as such. German Armored Divisions were called "Panzer Divisions," and are so named. Any reference to a "Panzer Division" is a reference to the German equivalent of an Allied Armored Division. To distinguish corps, we use the German spelling "Korps" to identify German units.

PROLOGUE

Six weeks had passed since Operation Overlord, the Allied invasion of Normandy that took place on "D-Day"—June 6, 1944. On that day, for the first time since William of Normandy became William the Conqueror in 1066, a military force had successfully crossed the English Channel and secured a foothold on the opposing shore. Overlord was rightly heralded—then as now—as one of the greatest military achievements in the history of modern warfare.

Four years earlier, in June 1940, Germany's then-invincible Wehrmacht had stunned the world by defeating and occupying France in a matter of weeks. During the four ensuing years, German military engineers had worked tirelessly on the northern and western coasts of France to create the Atlantic Wall, the most formidable network of fortifications ever constructed. Much of the reinforced concrete poured by the Germans during those four years still survives in the twenty-first century. It is so solid that it is not economically practical to dismantle it.

The German idea was to build a wall that would make

the Allies consider an invasion of northern France impractical. Adolf Hitler himself had such great confidence in the Atlantic Wall that he assuredly referred to his empire as *Festung Europa*—Fortress Europe.

The Anglo-American Allies, of course, had other ideas.

The idea of a cross-channel invasion as the means to liberate France and defeat Germany had been agreed to in principle by President Franklin Delano Roosevelt and British Prime Minister Winston Churchill in April 1942, and it was at the Eureka Conference in November 1943 that the two Allied leaders gave the 1944 invasion priority over all other military operations that the Anglo-American Allies would undertake anywhere in Europe, the Mediterranean, or the Pacific.

On December 7, 1943, two years to the day after the United States entered World War II, US Army Chief of Staff George Marshall informed General Dwight Eisenhower that he was to be the Supreme Allied Commander for history's biggest military operation.

When Eisenhower arrived in England in mid-January 1944 to set up the Supreme Headquarters, Allied Expeditionary Force (SHAEF), American supplies had been flowing into the island nation for two years, but what had initially been a trickle now became a torrent. Nevertheless, a great deal of key materiel would not arrive until May.

To insure the success of Overlord, Eisenhower had amassed the largest force of men and war machinery that would be committed to a single operation in the history of warfare.

The 175,000 men of Operation Overlord would make the trip across the English Channel aboard more than 5,000 ships and landing craft supported by 6 battleships, 2 monitors, 22 cruisers, 93 destroyers, 250 mine sweepers, and 150 smaller fighting craft, not including motor torpedo boats and mine layers.

Overhead, the British First Tactical Air Force and the American Eighth and Ninth Air Forces committed 5,000 fighters; 3,500 heavy bombers; 1,600 medium, light, and torpedo bombers; and 700 other combat aircraft. This was not to mention the 2,300 transports and 2,600 gliders that would carry paratroopers into battle.

Overlord's landing zone would be a fifty-mile section of the Normandy coastline between the neck of the Cotentin Peninsula in the west and the mouth of the Orne River in the east. This region, in turn, had been divided into five zones or "beaches." The westernmost, Utah and Omaha, were assigned to General Omar Bradley's United States First Army, while the others—Gold, Juno, and Sword—were assigned to the British and Canadians of General Sir Miles Dempsey's British Second Army.

The troops would come ashore across the beaches. Prior to these amphibious landings, under cover of darkness in the early morning hours of D-Day, paratroopers of the United States 82nd and 101st Airborne Divisions would land behind the line of German coastal defenses overlooking the invasion beaches.

The day originally selected to be D-Day was June 5, 1944, but weather delayed Operation Overlord for twenty-four hours. The leading waves of Allied landing craft hit the beaches of Normandy at 6:30 A.M. on June 6. It was here that the British and American soldiers would get their first taste of the ferocity of resistance that the Germans would have in store for them at the Atlantic Wall.

Despite an unprecedented amount of shelling by Allied

warships offshore, the German defenders were able to put up a ruthless defense. Fire from fortified machine gun emplacements chewed up soldiers attempting to make their way through barbed wire entanglements to cross the narrow, heavily mined strip of sand that separated the cold waters of the English Channel from the Norman cliffs. Meanwhile, landing craft and tanks were hung up on obstacles, and many vehicles never made it ashore.

Losses were extreme, but as D-Day wore on, the German defenses were eventually overcome. By the end of the day, the Allies' beachhead at Utah was ten miles wide and four miles deep, and the Gold/Juno/Sword beachhead, which was twenty miles long and five miles deep, reached to within a few miles of the city of Caen. The stiffest German resistance had come on Omaha Beach, where towering cliffs gave the Germans a defensive advantage. Nevertheless, the tenacious Yanks of V Corps held on and refused to be pushed back into the sea.

The impregnable Atlantic Wall had been beached.

By daybreak on June 7, Overlord had been deemed a complete—albeit costly—success. Within a few days, a quarter million Allied troops were in France, and the Allies had installed vast prefabricated artificial harbors known as Mulberries at Omaha Beach and Gold Beach. These ingenious and cleverly designed facilities had been built the previous winter and were quickly towed into place to aid in the off-loading of supplies and troops.

The news that the invasion had been a success was greeted with enthusiastic optimism in the United States and Britain. "At last the supreme moment has come," wrote the editorial page of *The New York Times*. "The months and years of waiting are over."

❂ ONE ❂

PRELUDE

The six weeks that had passed since Overlord would not be nearly so good for the Allies as they had hoped on that heady morning-after when the cross-channel had been deemed a success. In the days that had followed, the Allies had pushed forward confidently—the British and Canadians toward the mouth of the Seine River, and the Yanks into the Cotentin Peninsula. Though the Allies cautiously reminded themselves that it would be a long march from Normandy to Berlin, the morning-after mood in the SHAEF war room had been buoyant.

Thanks to the Mulberries, personnel and supplies were pouring ashore at an astounding rate. As far as the beaches were concerned, things were going according to plan. Inland it would be another story.

The D-Day objective for the British and Canadians had been the city of Caen—the city wherein lay the tomb, albeit empty, of William the Conqueror himself. Despite a comment by Prime Minister Churchill that Britons were "fighting in the streets" of Caen, his troops had not reached the city on

D-Day. The next day, they were reported to be "just outside."

Unfortunately, a month after the invasion, on July 6, 1944—D-Day plus thirty—they were still "just outside."

For the Americans, the prize was at the end of the thirty-mile dash to the tip of the Cotentin Peninsula—the port city of Cherbourg. It was to have been the seaport through which supplies and personnel for the conquest of Festung Europa would flow. Men and heavy equipment could be unloaded in protected waters rather than pulled through the crashing waves of a beachhead or unloaded at artificial harbors.

With its long breakwater and large anchorage, Cherbourg was indeed a major port city. In the decades before the war, it had been a major transatlantic embarkation point. It was smaller than the great port of Le Havre at the mouth of the Seine, but Allied planners felt that it would be easier to capture. It was confidently hoped that this would be accomplished within a week. On June 13—D-Day plus seven—the Yanks were still about twenty miles short of the prize. In the days that followed, the Americans took the town of Montebourg, about fifteen miles from Cherbourg, but were forced out by a German counterattack. Things were not going as planned.

Five days later, the American 9th Infantry Division managed to reach Carteret on the west side of the Cotentin Peninsula, effectively isolating the Germans within Cherbourg. The city would finally fall during a round of intense fighting that would take place between June 25 and June 27. However, when the Yanks finally reached the port itself, they discovered that the extensive dock facilities had been so effectively destroyed and dismantled by the Germans that they'd not been usable for months.

In Normandy, progress had gradually ground to a halt by

the end of June. The Germans continued to hold Caen against the repeated efforts of the British and Canadians. The Americans had captured much of the Cotentin Peninsula, but as they turned and pushed south toward the interior of France, they ran into a solid wall of German firepower. They came to a stop north of the city of St. Lô, which was about thirty miles due west of Caen.

Despite the optimism in the communiques that were issued daily, the leadership within SHAEF was gradually coming to the realization that conditions in Normandy were a prescription for stalemate. The implications of this fact were not lost on those who shivered with memories of the trench warfare of World War I. This horrid bloodletting had dragged on for years—consuming young lives by the millions—with no appreciable changes in the front lines.

During the nearly five months of the Battle of the Somme in 1916, Britain had suffered more than 420,000 casualties, including 58,000 on the first day alone. When the battle was over, the front line had moved *less than ten miles*. The war dragged on for another two years with minimal changes in the front lines. In one week during the 1918 Meuse-Argonne Offensive, the United States had suffered 6,589 battle deaths.

The old memories were still fresh. In 1944, people on both sides of the Atlantic remembered statistics like these and the fact that the carnage had occurred against a backdrop of deadlock. In 1916, the Germans controlled a tiny sliver of France. Even after Overlord, they *still* controlled virtually all of France. By this logic, some pundits compared the deadlock in Normandy to the tragedy of the Somme, predicting that the Germans could hold the line indefinitely while casualties mounted.

In a July 5, 1944, memo to Army Chief of Staff Marshall, General Eisenhower categorized the three obstacles that had made progress in Normandy for the Allies so dreadfully slow—the "fighting quality" of the enemy forces, the "nature of the country," and "the weather."

The "nature of the country" to which Eisenhower alluded, included a terrain feature that the French call *bocage*, and which the Allies referred to as "hedgerows." These were not hedges in the sense of those with which the Americans were familiar at home. The hedges that these same young GIs had been trimming for spending money back home a few years earlier were benign things. The hedgerows of Normandy bore more resemblance to the impenetrable jungles in New Guinea and Guadalcanal that other young Americans had been cursing since 1942. The Norman hedgerows *were*, in fact, impenetrable jungles. They had been growing in Normandy for centuries, cultivated by farmers as wind breaks. Because of the length of time that they'd had to mature, their bases were essentially solid masses of roots and suckers that could not be penetrated. Jungles of tropical succulents could be hacked through with a machete. The hedgerows had the consistency of razor wire.

Unlike the hedges of home, the hedgerows of Normandy were the height of trees. Indeed, they *were* trees. This fact had eluded the interpreters of aerial reconnaissance photos, who saw them only from straight up and imagined them to be no taller than shrubs.

Because they were so thick and impenetrable, the hedgerows were like a maze. They were as opaque as stone walls. Driving or walking between them on the narrow country lanes, the troops found it easy to become confused and disoriented. They couldn't see what was going on behind the hedgerows that surrounded them on all sides. They couldn't see whether there was a German machine gun or another American patrol. Troops often got lost and were forced to backtrack, often getting themselves more lost.

As with most terrain features, the hedgerows favored the defenders. The Germans had mapped the hedgerows and were using them as traps. The fields that were bounded by the hedgerows became kill boxes for German gunners. An American patrol in the open trapezoid bounded by a fortress of hedgerow was like so many pins in a shooting gallery—virtually defenseless.

The third factor cited in Eisenhower's memo, the weather, had been a nightmare. June and July of 1944 were the wettest June and July that had been experienced in Northern France and on the English Channel since the nineteenth century. Relentless wind and rain made operations on the channel miserable and turned the roads ashore into rivers. The marshland of the Cotentin Peninsula became a cold and slippery bayou.

Bad weather and poor visibility also grounded the Allied tactical air armada that was proving to be essential to any gains that ground forces were able to make. Some tactical bomber units were grounded for nearly two weeks straight, and those who did manage to get to the front found targets obscured by fog and low clouds. Poor weather generally favors the defender, and this was especially true that summer in Normandy.

Just to make matters even worse, a horrific storm blew in on June 19 and raged for three days. It disrupted communications and made life miserable for the troops ashore. Meanwhile, the violent waves that it kicked up in the English Channel destroyed the Mulberry artificial harbor at Omaha Beach and severely damaged the British Mulberry at Gold Beach.

Because there were so few paved roads in this part of Normandy, moving men and materiel was a difficult task. Vehicles moved at the pace of a slug, and gridlock was constant. Of course, the only bright side was that the distances to be traveled were short because the Allies had not penetrated very far into Normandy!

Leading the Allies into Europe

As we discuss the unfolding of events in Normandy and Europe, it would be useful to provide a brief sketch of the Allied chain of command—from SHAEF to the field armies—in the summer of 1944. As noted earlier, the Supreme Commander of Allied Forces was United States General Dwight David "Ike" Eisenhower, whose headquarters was SHAEF. He held this job on D-Day, and he would continue in the post until World War II in Europe finally ended on VE-Day, May 7, 1945.

The ground forces commander for the Allied Expeditionary Force was the colorful General (later Field Marshal) Sir Bernard Law Montgomery, who had achieved notoriety—and hero status—for his decisive 1942 victory in North Africa over the German forces under the command of Field Marshal Erwin Rommel. Montgomery's 21st Army Group was composed of the two field armies mentioned earlier. These were the United States First Army, commanded by General Omar Nelson Bradley, and the British Second Army under Lieutenant General Sir Miles Dempsey, to which Canadian divisions were attached.

Offstage during Operation Overlord and the opening weeks of the Battle of Normandy were two additional armies, each commanded by lieutenant (three-star) generals. These were the Canadian First Army, under Lieutenant General Henry D. G. "Harry" Crerar and the United States Third Army, which would be under the command of Lieutenant General George Smith Patton Jr. Both would be on the ground within sixty days of D-Day.

Each of the Allied numbered field armies would be composed of between two and four corps. These would, in turn, each contain two or three—occasionally more—divisions. The corps were adaptable organizations that were assembled within the numbered field armies from whatever grouping of divisions was necessary to accomplish a given mission within the context of a given campaign. As we shall see, divisions were frequently "borrowed" back and forth by the corps as the Allied armies marched and wheeled across Europe.

The division was then, and is today, the basic building block of a ground army. There were essentially two types of divisions employed by the United States Army in the European Theater of Operations in World War II—the infantry division and the armored, or tank, division. Ideally, each American corps contained one of each, or two infantry divisions and one armored division. Airborne divisions were based on infantry divisions, but were designed to go into battle by parachute. Once on the ground, however, an airborne division functioned pretty much as an infantry division. In the US Army, they are numbered within the same sequence of numbers as infantry divisions, while armored divisions have a separate series of numbers.

In World War II, a United States infantry division was composed of about 15,000 soldiers organized into three infantry regiments, each of which consisted of three battalions. At least one regiment out of the three would be "motorized," with trucks available to carry the foot soldiers more quickly from one action to the next. However, Quartermaster Corps truck battalions could be, and often were, attached to divisions so that all the personnel could be moved quickly. There were also four artillery battalions assigned to the division and equipped with 105mm and 155mm howitzers. Infantry divisions also often had a tank battalion and a tank destroyer battalion assigned to them.

Parenthetically, German infantry divisions of the summer of 1944 numbered between 12,000 and 14,000. Prior to a reorganization program earlier in 1944, a German division had been larger, numbering about 17,000 men. The German divisions were typically superior to American divisions in terms of the number of machine gun and mortar teams assigned, but inferior to American divisions when it came to transportation. The German divisions had fewer motor vehicles, relying to a greater extent on horse-drawn vehicles and on the foot soldiers of the infantry to actually travel by foot.

American armored divisions were slightly smaller than infantry divisions in terms of head count, usually numbering about 11,000 men, with their tank crews manning more than 260 M4 Sherman medium tanks. The armored division was subdivided into three tank battalions, three battalions of armored infantry, and three battalions of self-propelled artillery. For actual tactical operations, the armored division was subdivided into three combat commands. Designated as Combat Commands A, B, and R (meaning primary, secondary, and reserve), these could contain any number of tanks and men that the division commander thought was necessary for a given operation, and were not limited to a strict regiment-size mix of people and equipment.

In addition to the combat troops within the divisions, the numbered field armies had large numbers of support troops that "worked for" other organizations such as the Quartermaster Corps, the Signal Corps, the Medical Corps, and the Corps of Engineers—rather than the combat corps that were designated with Roman numerals. Typically, a combat corps would be supported by members of these corps that numbers as many or more people than the combat corps itself.

In addition to Montgomery, who had commanded ground forces during Operation Overlord, there were the officers who commanded the sea and air components of the Allied Expeditionary Force operations in Europe during Operation Overlord. The naval forces commander would be Admiral Sir Bertram Ramsay. Technically, there was no overall air commander, but Eisenhower's deputy, Air Chief Marshall Sir Arthur Tedder of Britain's Royal Air Force performed the role of coordinating whatever air components would be assigned to the task of supporting troops in the field.

Allied air power in Europe during the summer of 1944 would perform both a tactical mission—supporting ground forces at the front—and a strategic mission—striking industrial and transportation targets within Germany itself or at other locations well behind enemy lines. The strategic mission involved the Royal Air Force Bomber Command under Air Chief Marshal Sir Arthur Harris and the US Army Air Forces (USAAF) Eighth Air Force under Lieutenant General Carl "Tooey" Spaatz.

On the tactical side, air forces were under the umbrella of the Allied Expeditionary Air Force (AEAF), under the command of Air Chief Marshal Sir Trafford Leigh-Mallory. Units assigned to the AEAF were drawn from the USAAF Ninth Air Force (especially its IX Tactical Air Command), the Royal Air Force Second Tactical Air Force, and the Royal Air Force Air Defense Command.

The air operations would be vital, but it would be the soldiers on the ground who took the chances and took the ground.

Patton and "Fortitude"

Third Army's Lieutenant General George Smith Patton Jr., who would emerge as the central figure in ground operations in France over the coming months, was a mercurial and controversial character. He had graduated from the United States Military Academy at West Point in 1909, and had been a medalist in marksmanship at the 1912 Olympic Games. He then went on to command the US Army's tank corps in combat in World War I. He was an officer with an almost obsessive sense of duty, who once commented that "the greatest privilege of citizenship is to be able to freely bear arms under one's country's flag."

In the interwar period, at a time when the US Army officially downplayed the usefulness of tanks, Patton became an outspoken advocate of armored (tank) forces, and the sort of mobile warfare that they made possible. When traditionalists thought of tanks as a minor weapon to be used only in support of infantry action, Patton advocated tanks as spearheads, commenting that "the tank must be used boldly. It is new and always has the element of surprise. It is also terrifying to look at as the infantry soldier is helpless before it."

His ideas would be professionally vindicated in 1939–1940, when the German army conquered most of Europe using fast mobile warfare based on the deployment of large numbers of tanks.

In World War II, Patton commanded armored units in North Africa and had demonstrated an uncanny brilliance as a commander of troops in combat as he rose quickly through the ranks. He also developed a reputation as a man who was ruthless with the enemy in combat. "War is simple, direct, and ruthless." Patton shrugged. "It takes a simple, direct, and ruthless man to wage it."

In March 1943, he was given command of II Corps, and in July 1943, he was promoted to command the United States Seventh Army for the invasion of Sicily. His swift capture of Messina assured his reputation for tactical brilliance. Both the Allied leadership and the German General staff recognized him as the most gifted field commander of three star or higher rank that the Allies had on the ground in Europe.

While many senior US Army officers were uneasy with Patton's aggressiveness and his flamboyance, they respected his uncanny tactical brilliance. He was an avid student of military history with an encyclopedic knowledge of military campaigns from the time of the Caesars and Alexander the Great through those of Napoleon Bonaparte and Robert E. Lee. As Patton once said, "To be a successful soldier, you must know history."

Patton's stellar career was sidetracked after a controversial incident in Sicily on August 2, 1943, in which Patton slapped a pair of shell-shocked soldiers, calling them cowards. Patton's war record made him a natural to command United States ground forces for Operation Overlord, but when the "slapping incident" was described publicly in a broadcast by reporter Drew Pearson in November 1943, the general became an official pariah.

Said Patton of the incident, "I am convinced that my actions in this case were entirely correct, and that had other officers had the courage to do likewise, the shameful excuse of battle fatigue instead of cowardice would have been infinitely reduced . . . I love and admire good soldiers and brave men. I hate and despise slackers and cowards."

Of cowardice, Patton had explained that "All men are afraid in battle. The coward is the one who lets his fear overcome his sense of duty."

In reference to Pearson and the media, he observed that "I have written more damn letters, I suppose a thousand, to the mothers of private soldiers whom I happen to know have been killed, but that never comes out. I kick some SOB in the ass who doesn't do what he should, and it comes out all over the whole damned country."

By the end of 1943, the Patton star that had shone so brightly in North Africa and Sicily, had faded. An officer who had been his junior earlier in the war was now leapfrogged over Patton to become second only to Eisenhower himself among high-ranking US Army ground leaders within SHAEF. This former Patton subordinate who became the penultimate American officer in the European Theater was General Omar Nelson Bradley.

A West Point classmate of Eisenhower's, Bradley had graduated with Ike as a member of the class of 1915. It was known as "the class that the stars fell on," because more of its graduates became high-ranking generals than any other. Indeed, both Eisenhower and Bradley would eventually rise to five-star rank, the highest possible.

Bradley had been Patton's deputy commander at II Corps in North Africa and had taken command of the corps when Patton moved up to take over the Seventh Army. With Patton out of the limelight as 1943 turned to 1944, Bradley had become classmate Ike's favorite son, and Eisenhower named him to command the United States First Army. Bradley was a skillful administrator and an excellent organizer. His reputation was forged by his ability to take on extremely complex tasks and to execute them with precision.

Of course, Eisenhower also recognized Patton for everything he was—and which Bradley was *not*. Eisenhower had known Patton for years and appreciated his capabilities. Ike even liked Patton. While Eisenhower and Bradley had that special bond that evolved from being classmates at West Point, Eisenhower knew that Patton was ideal for the role of a field army commander. In a series of memos in April 1944 to US Army Chief of Staff General George Marshall, Eisenhower had written that Patton had "demonstrated [the] ability to get the utmost out of soldiers in offensive situations."

Eisenhower also told Marshall that Patton displayed an "extraordinary and ruthless driving power . . . at critical moments."

In his memoirs of World War II, Eisenhower wrote that "for certain types of action [Patton] was the outstanding soldier our country has produced."

Ike knew that he needed Patton's skill on the battlefield. He knew that this would be essential to winning the upcoming war in Europe. He knew that he would have to bring the misbehaving general in from the cold.

Eisenhower had decided to capitalize on the German perception that Patton was the best field commander in the Allied armies, so he made Patton the centerpiece of an elaborate ruse that he concocted to confuse the Germans. Eisenhower's idea was to create the impression that the cross-channel invasion of northern France would occur, not in Normandy, but in the Pas-de-Calais region. This was logical, because only thirty miles separated this area from England. As the nearest point on the continent to England, it would be the easiest and most obvious place for an invasion, and it would be the easiest place to run supply lines to support an army *after* an invasion.

The Germans would also find it logical that Eisenhower

would choose Patton to command such an operation. The fact that Patton had recently been relieved of the command of the Seventh Army, made it certainly plausible to observers in Berlin that he had been summoned to England to assume another important command.

Eisenhower went about seeing to it that references to the invasion of France in the Pas-de-Calais were deliberately leaked to German intelligence. Through these leaks, the enemy "learned" that the invasion, code named Operation Fortitude, would be spearheaded by the newly formed "First US Army Group (FUSAG)"—which was also referred to as "Army Group Patton" to underscore Eisenhower's choice of its commander. Eisenhower went so far as to have large numbers of dummy tanks and other equipment repositioned throughout southeast England opposite the Pas-de-Calais where German reconnaissance aircraft could photograph the "invasion preparations."

The phony First Army Group (properly written as 1st Army Group) was not to be confused with the entirely distinct, and real, First Army. The 1st Army Group was apparently a formidable force, but all the evidence of troops and tanks was contrived. The 1st Army Group existed solely as an administrative unit, although its sizable staff generated the amount of paperwork that an outside observer, such as a German spy, would expect of a real army group. It would continue to exist "on paper" until October 1944, when it was finally "disbanded." FUSAG's role in winning the war was simply as a cover for the equally false Operation Fortitude. In fact, "Fortitude" was never actually an invasion code name, but the code name of the *deception*.

In the week prior to the real Operation Overlord invasion, Eisenhower had ordered a massive air campaign against the highway and rail net of northern France in order to "isolate the battlefield." A major part of this effort was directed at the area around Calais in an effort to convince the Germans that the invasion was actually going to take place there.

The Operation Fortitude ploy was an amazing success. When the actual invasion of Normandy did occur on June 6, 1944, the Germans were so completely convinced of the Pas-de-Calais ruse that they were certain that the Normandy invasion was merely a diversion. Adolf Hitler himself ordered that the tanks of the German Fifteenth Army should remain in the Pas-de-Calais to defeat Patton and he would not permit it to be redeployed to defeat the Normandy invasion. The Fifteenth Army would stand by waiting for the fictitious FUSAG until July. Even then, it was not entirely clear to the Germans that Normandy was the *real* cross-channel invasion site.

Of course, Patton *would* eventually arrive in France, but not by leading FUSAG ashore at Calais. In early 1944, Eisenhower had given Patton command of the newly organized United States Third Army which was earmarked to be sent into Normandy after the First Army had succeeded in securing a foothold in Normandy through Operation Overlord.

The Enemy

Facing the armies commanded by Eisenhower, Montgomery, Dempsey, Bradley, and Patton, the German forces in France were under the command of Oberbefehlshaber West, the German Army field command for the Western Front. Oberbefehlshaber West, in turn, answered to the German Armed Forces High Command in Berlin, the Oberkommando der Wehrmacht, which answered only to Adolf Hitler himself.

Oberbefehlshaber West contained four armies. The Nine-

teenth Army was on the southern coast of France, the First
Army was in central and western France, and the Fifteenth
Army controlled Belgium and northern France from the Belgian border to the Seine River. Facing Operation Overlord directly would be the German Seventh Army in Brittany and
Normandy. Coincidently, it had been the Seventh Army that
had spearheaded the German victory over France four years
earlier in June 1940. A key element of Seventh Army would be
Panzer Group West and amalgam of four tank corps.

General Friedreich Dollman, who had commanded the
Seventh in 1940, was still in charge on D-Day, running things
from his headquarters at a chateau near Le Mans. Owned by
the Countess du Houssoix, the flamboyant palace had, in
1918, housed General John J. Pershing, the commander of the
American Expeditionary Force in World War I.

Dollman was a controversial character around whom a
number of conspiracy theories would swirl. When he "died of
a heart attack" at the Houssoix chateau shortly after the Americans captured Cherbourg, there were rumors that he'd committed suicide, being distraught over having allowed his
command grow flabby during four years of quiet occupation
duty. There were also rumors that he had been *asked* to commit suicide.

At the time of the invasion, the commander of Oberbefehlshaber West was Field Marshal Karl Rudolf Gerd von
Rundstedt, with his headquarters in Paris. A legendary Prussian military genius, the sixty-nine-year-old von Rundstedt had
been one of the senior commanders who had overseen the unprecedented buildup of Germany's Wehrmacht during the late
1930s. He had retired in 1938, but Hitler had called him back
a year later to plan and execute the invasion of Poland that
started World War II. In 1940, he had guided the Blitzkrieg in

the West that swallowed France. In 1941, von Rundstedt had guided the unstoppable Wehrmacht into the Soviet Union and deep into the Ukraine. In 1942, as commander of Oberbefehlshaber West, he had been the architect of the Atlantic Wall.

Meanwhile, both the Seventh and Fifteenth Armies were part of Army Group B, commanded by General Field Marshal Erwin Rommel, the legendary commander of German forces in North Africa in 1942 and 1943. Rommel was to the German armies what Patton was to the Allied armies. He was regarded as an aggressive commander and a brilliant tactician. It was widely understood that the defeat of Rommel's Afrika Korps a year earlier in Tunisia had been attributable to inability of the Wehrmacht to provide the Afrika Korps with supplies, and not to Erwin Rommel's abilities as a field commander.

Rommel defended Normandy and developed plans for a counterattack utilizing the resources of the Seventh Army. He would have liked to have been able to make use of the Fifteenth Army, but Hitler, as well as many of the serious people at the Oberkommando der Wehrmacht, still believed that the invasion of the Pas-de-Calais region was going to happen soon.

Despite having had half of his forces denied him, Rommel still had several advantages. Defenders generally have the advantage in any action, and Rommel had the benefit of a terrain situation that greatly favored defense. Nor was Rommel as hampered by the weather as the Allies. His supply lines were on land rather than on the treacherous waters of the English Channel. Like the terrain, the horrible weather in June and July became Rommel's ally because, more often than not, it grounded the tactical air power upon which the invaders depended so dearly.

By mid-June through a shortage of tanks, Rommel had

clearly missed the chance to push the Allies off the beaches and back into the sea. Had he been able to make use of the Fifteenth Army and its tanks, he might have been able to defeat Overlord, but that opportunity had slipped away. Nevertheless, he had made the Allies pay dearly for Cherbourg in June, and he had succeeded in fighting them to a stalemate elsewhere.

Rommel's Achilles heel was the fact that the Allies had almost complete air superiority over the battlefield. The German Luftwaffe was able to mount only token attacks on the Allied positions, while large numbers of Allied tactical warplanes were able to roam with virtual impunity over the German positions and to range deep into France to attack Rommel's supply lines. This forced the Germans to move men and materiel mainly at night.

During July, there would be an extensive change of leadership in the West. At the top, Hitler named General Field Marshal Günther von Kluge—a tough, veteran army commander who'd served on the Eastern Front—to succeed von Rundstedt as head of Oberbefehlshaber West. Von Rundstedt had angered Hitler by suggesting that France might be indefensible, and the Führer had suggested that it might be time for the old soldier to think about going back into retirement.

Replacing the deceased Dollman at Seventh Army would be an SS general named Paul Hausser. The key component of the German Seventh Army would be the LXXXIV Korps under General Dietrich von Choltitz. Contained within the LXXXIV Korps were eight divisions, including the Panzer Lehr Division under General Fritz Bayerlin and the 2nd SS Panzer Division—nicknamed "Das Reich"—under SS Standartenführer Christian Tychsen.

Another Eastern Front tank commander, General Heinrich Eberbach, took over Panzer Group West when its previous commander had the temerity to question Hitler's authority. By the first week in July, Rommel remained as the only pre-invasion face in the upper echelon of the chain of command in the West—and *his* days were numbered.

Machines

If the Allies held a material edge in terms of their superiority in the air, the Germans had a clear advantage on the ground in terms of armor. German industry had, by 1944, created the best tanks—known in German as *Panzers*—yet seen in the history of mechanized warfare.

The standard German tank in mid-1944 was the Krupp-manufactured Panzerkampfwagen (PzKpfw) IV, or simply Panzer IV. It had been in use against the Soviets on the Eastern Front for two years. Panzer IVs weighed between eighteen and twenty-five tons, depending on the specific model, and carried a 75mm gun. The forward armor for most Panzer IV models was between 30mm and 50mm thick.

A newer tank that was first delivered to Oberbefehlshaber West units in June 1944 was the extraordinary Panzerkampfwagen (PzKpfw) V, that was best known as the Panther, a name that was reported to have been bestowed by Hitler himself. The Panthers were developed and manufactured by the industrial firms of Daimler-Benz and MAN (Machinenfabrik Augsburg-Nürnberg). Panthers weighed forty-three to forty-five tons and each carried a high-velocity 75mm gun. The armor on the forward hull varied in thickness from 60mm to 80mm depending on the specific model.

Theoretically, each German army panzer division in 1944 contained one battalion each of PzKpfw IVs and PzKpfw Vs, although there were more Panzer IVs than Panthers overall, and SS Panzer units were always favored with more Panthers than were regular army divisions.

Most feared of German tanks was the legendary Panzerkampfwagen (PzKpfw) VI, best known as the Tiger. These enormous vehicles weighed up to fifty-seven tons and carried 88mm high-velocity guns. Their forward armor was 100mm thick. Developed and produced by Henschel, the Tiger beat out a competing design by Ferdinand Porsche, who is better remembered for his postwar sports cars. Tiger tanks had first seen action on the Eastern Front in September 1942, and were widely used there by 1944. Though they equipped most SS panzer units, Tigers were still relatively rare in Normandy in the summer of 1944.

Other German vehicles that were available in France during the summer of 1944 included self-propelled guns, or "tank hunters," which were essentially heavily armored tank chassis with fixed guns rather than turrets. The Jagdpanther (Hunting Panther), which Allied troops would often encounter in Normandy, was a Panther chassis with an 88mm gun.

The 88mm gun was the ubiquitous German artillery weapon by 1944. Not only were the huge weapons used on armored vehicles, they were the standard heavy field artillery piece and the standard antiaircraft gun. To the Allied troops, the phrase "eighty-eight" became synonymous with German artillery. When German heavy guns were seen or heard, they would automatically be referred to by the Allied troops as "eighty-eights," rather than as "enemy artillery," regardless of what the actual bore of the weapon was. More often than not, however, the guns *were,* in fact, 88mm guns.

On the other side, the standard American tank was the M4 Sherman. It was also widely used by British and Canadian forces, as well as by Free French armored units. Sherman tanks weighed between thirty-three and thirty-five tons depending on equipment and had two-inch forward armor. Most of the M4s in use in Normandy in June and July of 1944 carried a short-barreled 75mm gun, but later models introduced soon afterward carried a much more effective long-barreled 76mm gun.

Nearly fifty thousand Sherman tanks were built by a number of manufacturers, including American Locomotive (ALCO), Baldwin Locomotive Works, Detroit Tank Arsenal (Chrysler), Federal Machine & Welding, Fisher Tank Division (General Motors), Ford Motor Company, Lima Locomotive Works, Pacific Car & Foundry, and Pullman Standard.

While the Sherman was the primary tank used by British forces, the latter armies also used large numbers of British-made Churchill tanks, which weighed forty tons and carried a 75mm gun. Canadian troops used a nearly indistinguishable variation on the Sherman that was known as the Grizzly.

All of the above tanks carried a crew of five. The crews of the German tanks consisted of the driver, a gunner, a loader, a radio operator, and the tank commander. Rather than a dedicated radio operator position, the Allied tanks carried a back-up driver, who also operated a forward firing machine gun that was located in the hull.

In one-on-one combat, the Shermans were no match for the German tanks. The latter were invulnerable to a forward attack from the Sherman's 75mm gun. Even from the side, the German equipment, especially the Panther and Tiger, could often survive a hit from the M4 Sherman's gun. Allied anti-tank weapons, such as the famed bazooka with its 2.36-inch rocket, were effective against the German tanks, but only with a properly aimed shot.

The Allied gunners had to surmount a long learning curve in order to find and overcome the weak spots in the German armor. Eventually, however, the Allies were able to defeat the Germans through the Sherman's superior maneuverability and by superior numbers. If the Shermans were no match for the German tanks in one-on-one combat, then the trick was to avoid one-on-one combat and use a flock of maneuverable Shermans against a smaller number of Panthers.

The numbers told a big part of the story. American industry would turn out ten Shermans for every Panther that the Germans built.

In Normandy, hedgerows were largely impenetrable to anyone's tanks, although a Tiger could often bully its way through one. The German advantage was in their knowing the lay of the land. The American advantage would come in the form of the so-called Rhino Shermans. Numerous efforts were made to develop a means of cutting through the hedgerows. Bulldozers were ineffective, because the hedgerows had to be cut rather than pushed.

Initial efforts to breach a hedgerow involved using explosives. On July 10, it was accidently discovered that a forklike device used to punch holes for the explosives could be used to lift part of the hedgerow.

The technological breakthrough came when Sergeant Curtis Culin of the 102nd Cavalry Recon Squadron invented the Rhino. It involved welding tusklike scrap steel to the front of a Sherman tank in such a way that it would cut through a hedgerow like scissors. General Bradley was so impressed with Culin's invention that on July 14, he ordered Rhinos to be mass produced, using steel salvaged from German antitank barriers that had been placed on the invasion beaches.

Forging Ahead

For Allied leaders, the deadlock in Normandy demanded a re-assessment. The German side viewed their own situation as being much more desperate than that of the Allies, but their tenacious defense gave SHAEF the impression of a force that could and would hold its own.

The Allies had expected to have broken out of the beach-head area by early July, and to be on their way to the goal of capturing additional French ports, such as Brest, that lay far-ther west on the Breton Peninsula. The Allies had also in-tended that they would have broken through the German line at Caen, and would have penetrated into the rolling hills south of the hedgerow country where they would have more room to maneuver.

None of this had come to pass.

The German defenses had far exceeded expectations. The Allies controlled only about 20 percent of the ground that they had expected to control. They needed a plan.

As many as four proposals called for variations on another Operation Overlord—amphibious landings farther to the west in Brittany. This would bring Allied troops ashore in such a way as to outflank the German defenders in Normandy. These ideas were rejected because most of the troops that had been trained for amphibious warfare were already committed to the fight. Instead, the plan would be to continue to push the German defenders on the existing front in Normandy.

The American First Army would launch an attack on the western edge of the Cotentin Peninsula, driving south through La Haye-du-Puits toward Coutances. The latter was seen as the key to the city of Avranches, which was at the neck of the Co-tentin. By capturing Avranches, the Americans would be able to outflank the German LXXXIV Korps, control the Cotentin Peninsula, and have an open door to Brittany.

By this time, the First Army consisted mainly of two corps, VII Corps under Major General Joseph Lawton "Lightning Joe" Collins with six divisions and VIII Corps under Major General Troy Houston Middleton with five divisions.

In the planned action, the First Army's VIII Corps would hit the German left flank at a point west of St. Lô. This operation jumped off during a driving rainstorm on July 3 with artillery support. There would be no air support because of the weather.

Unfortunately, Rommel had anticipated such a move and had heavily reinforced the area, and the VIII Corps attempt at a breakthrough was largely blunted. Slightly to the east, a similar attack by VII Corps was launched on the Fourth of July. They managed to secure a bridgehead across the Vire River, but this narrowed the Corps advance because the narrow bridgehead produced a bottleneck effect and by July 10, VII Corps had been stopped by the German Panzer Lehr Division.

That same day, the Associated Press quoted General Eisenhower as having said that "long and bitter fighting must be expected."

While the Yanks were attempting to push forward on the Cotentin Peninsula, the British were making a concerted effort to blast their way through to Caen with heavy support from Royal Air Force heavy bombers. In essence, the British had decided to destroy Caen in order to capture it. In the face of the attack, Rommel and Eberbach chose to withdraw south of the Orne River, which flows generally through the middle of Caen. Only on July 9 were the British finally tentatively sending their first patrols into the city—thirty-three long days after D-Day.

For the Americans farther west, the capture of St. Lô and

its pivotal crossroads remained a major goal. By mid-June, it was said that the failure to have yet captured it only served to magnify its significance in the overall scheme of things. The Germans, meanwhile, had intercepted American communications that stressed the desire for St. Lô, and they had dug in to defend it. A major effort against the city by the First Army was launched on July 11, but, as had been the case with the drive through La Haye-du-Puits toward Coutances a week earlier, poor weather prevented tactical air support. The ground forces used only artillery to pummel the German defensive positions on the hills that guarded the approaches to St. Lô.

The ensuing week saw some of the most bitter fighting that Allied troops had yet faced in Normandy. The Americans advanced, but they did so inch by inch and in the face of withering enemy artillery and machine gun fire. The Germans counterattacked with undiminished ferocity, making headway in some sectors, and wearing down the already weary Yanks everywhere.

American troops finally entered St. Lô on the afternoon of July 18, but German artillery fire would continue to rain down on them, and enemy troops mounted an attempt to recapture the city. It was only when the Germans undertook a general withdrawal from the entire sector on July 19 that the Americans could call the city secured.

The battle of St. Lô had become a symbol of American determination to overwhelm the enemy at all costs, but it had also been a symbol of German determination to make the Yanks pay dearly for every square inch of Normandy. Between them, the 29th Infantry Division and the 35th Infantry Division had suffered more than 5,000 casualties at St. Lô alone.

It had been six weeks since D-Day, and the First Army as a whole had taken 40,000 casualties. On top of this figure, cases of combat fatigue, or shell shock—later to be called post-traumatic shock syndrome—added as many as another 10,000 to the total. It was a high price to have paid considering that in the nearly three weeks preceding the capture of St. Lô, the front had been advanced by less than ten miles. As had been the case for the British at Caen, the Yanks had discovered that they had to destroy St. Lô in order to liberate it.

The comparisons to World War I were heard more often now. On July 11, *The New York Times* editorial page had commented that "The battlefronts themselves are only now beginning to approach the great battlefields of the last war, where German resistance must be expected to develop to its greatest strength."

The editorial went on to underscore the differences between 1918 and 1944 on the political and diplomatic fronts, noting that the Allies this time were demanding an "Unconditional Surrender" rather than offering Woodrow Wilson's "Fourteen Points." Within Germany, there was no sign yet of an internal civil collapse as had occurred in 1918. The editorial included the sober assessment that "Victory in this war is likely to be far more difficult and costly than it was in 1918."

On July 18, as the Americans were mopping up on the St. Lô front, the British launched their methodical three-day Operation Goodwood, a coordinated air-ground effort to widen their bridgehead across the Orne River near Caen. General Montgomery executed Goodwood so cautiously that many predicted he would be sacked by SHAEF for his timidity. Enormous bomb tonnage was dropped on the German Seventh Army lines, but Montgomery's ground forces moved slowly and methodically. On July 20, he went so far as to order Dempsey to withdraw his armor and replace it with infantry.

It was later claimed that Montgomery had no intention of achieving and exploiting a breakthrough with Operation Goodwood. In light of the reason that the Allies were fighting in Normandy, this seems odd.

Montgomery's slow progress, often characterized as lethargic and timid by those who would come to favor Patton's approach, was born of a more methodical nature and of a fear of the ghosts of the previous generation. With memories of the terrible World War I battles such as the Somme, he was unwilling to commit large forces to battles that might end in huge casualties traded for nominal ground gained.

Having spent some time with Montgomery in Normandy, *New York Times* correspondent Drew Middleton wrote in mid-July that "the cautious manner in which General Montgomery has approached his present tactical problem is not surprising. He is no slashing 'hell for leather' attacker but an extremely cautious soldier who dislikes shedding the blood of his own men needlessly and who therefore prefers to wait until he has assembled an overwhelming force."

In rebuttal to such strategy, one is reminded of Patton's oft-repeated maxim: "Success in war depends on the 'golden rules of war,' speed, simplicity, and boldness . . . We can conquer only by attacking."

As the Allies marked the forty-fourth day since D-Day, Lieutenant General Sir Miles Dempsey's British Second Army had managed to penetrate about ten miles inland from the invasion beaches, while the Yanks had captured all of the Cotentin Peninsula. In terms of objectives, the British had finally taken Caen, and the Americans had captured St. Lô—both at great cost. At this point, neither exhausted force seemed capable of breaking out and pushing south.

Things had bogged down so badly by July 10, that Eisenhower had warned during a press conference in Normandy against "rosy optimism," predicted "heavy losses," and said that the Allies would have to fight hard for every foot they gained.

Secretary of War Henry Stimson, speaking to the United States on a nationwide radio broadcast on July 25 after an inspection tour to France, commented that the end of the war in the European Theater was "not yet apparent."

Günther von Kluge had been ordered to hold the Allies, and he was doing so.

Reflecting on the battles that the Yanks felt as though they'd only just barely won in Normandy, Raymond Goguen would observe a year later in the official history of the 329th Infantry Regiment that "considering the high price in American lives, we lost."

The July 20 Plot

As gloomy as things appeared for Eisenhower and the Allied leadership during the third week of July, their troubles paled by comparison to an especially bad turn that befell the apex of the German chain of command on July 20. It would be a political turning point that would cast its shadow across German morale for the remainder of the war.

Though it was difficult for the Allies to gain ground, they *were* gaining ground, and every yard gained by the Allies was a yard lost by the Germans. The mood in Berlin was growing as dark and foreboding as the leaden overcast that was blanketing Normandy.

There were supply problems and difficulties at the front, but the nearly total Allied air superiority was a nagging reminder of a serious tactical inadequacy that the Germans simply could not adequately address. This could not have been brought into sharper focus than through a July 17 strafing attack that had critically wounded Erwin Rommel himself.

The growing dissatisfaction—even within the German general staff—was about to boil over.

Three days after Rommel was injured, Colonel Claus von Stauffenberg, a Wehrmacht staff officer, entered Adolf Hitler's "Wolf's Lair"—his Eastern Front command center at Rastenberg in East Prussia—carrying his briefcase. He left it next to the map table where Hitler was working with his staff and stepped out of the room to make a phone call. Moments later, the bomb in von Stauffenberg's briefcase detonated. Had the case not been moved a few feet by someone working at the map table, history might have taken a very different course. As it was, the explosion wounded Hitler, but did not kill him.

The July 20 assassination attempt was the culmination of an elaborate conspiracy by German military officers aimed at assassinating Hitler, overthrowing the Nazi government of Germany and negotiating an immediate end to World War II. Among the leading figures in the plot were General Ludwig Beck, a former chief of the German General Staff and General Henning von Tresckow, a former chief of staff to Günther von Kluge when the latter was on the Eastern Front.

The plan of the conspirators was that German officers in Berlin would stage the coup d'état as soon as they got word of Hitler's death. Unfortunately, they launched the coup on this faulty information and they failed.

The conspirators were rounded up and tortured to death. Though Hitler described the conspiratorial group as a "small clique of ambitious, unscrupulous, and stupid officers," it was not a "small" clique. An investigation by Hitler loyalists turned up the disconcerting fact that the plot actually involved dozens of very senior officers.

Perhaps the hardest pill to swallow for Hitler was the fact that Erwin Rommel himself was peripherally involved in tacitly supporting a coup d'état. While von Stauffenberg and others were brutally executed with meat hooks, Rommel, still recuperating at home from the wounds he'd suffered on July 17, was permitted the gentleman's way out. He was left alone in a room with a pistol.

Hitler was badly shaken, both physically and emotionally, by the July 20 plot. His arm was injured, and his hearing was seriously degraded. More important, his already obsessive paranoia became extreme. His distrust of the Oberkommando der Wehrmacht was magnified, and he simply used it as a conduit for issuing his own orders. Meanwhile, his dependence on the cruel SS as his chosen instrument to wage war increased.

Hitler had been angered by the way things were going on the Eastern Front and enraged by the July 20 plot. Very soon, the Allies would be giving him something on the Western Front that would *really* make him mad.

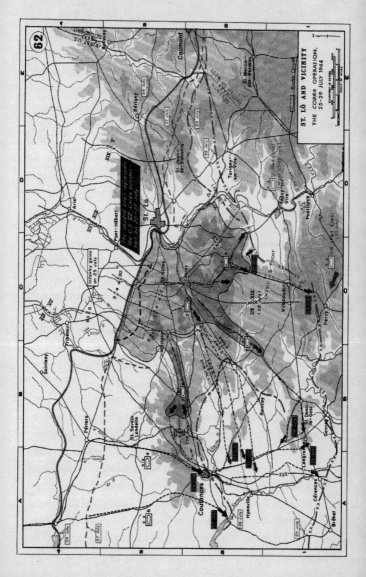

ST. LÔ AND VICINITY

THE *COBRA* OPERATION,
25–29 JULY 1944

✪ TWO ✪

COBRA STRIKES

As Montgomery's Operation Goodwood fizzled to a halt on July 21, General Eisenhower cabled Montgomery that he had been "extremely hopeful and optimistic" about its success, adding disdainfully that the hoped-for result "didn't come about."

Eisenhower told him that SHAEF was now "pinning our immediate hopes on Bradley's attack."

Even as the fight at St. Lô was raging, the planners on General Bradley's staff had been devising what would be called Operation Cobra. It was to be a major thrust south by elements of the United States First Army in coordination with a huge tactical air offensive. When—and *if*—a breakthrough was achieved, General Patton would arrive in Normandy with the Third Army and use the momentum created by Operation Cobra to capture the channel ports farther west in Brittany.

Bradley was eager to move quickly, before the Germans had an opportunity to organize a new defensive line. The more time that the Allies allowed the Germans to create such a line, the harder it would be to surmount. In fact, von Kluge did view the American sector as a defensive position, while the British sector was a place for offensive action. He ordered Seventh Army units to dig in, while he ordered Heinrich Eberbach to prepare Panzer Group West for a counterattack against the British and Canadians around Caen. Meanwhile, two armored divisions, the 2nd SS Panzer Division and Panzer Lehr, were earmarked to form a mobile fire brigade to go to the aid of any unit that came under attack.

Like Montgomery's ill-fated Goodwood, Bradley's Cobra would utilize massive air operations featuring heavy bombers. Unlike Goodwood, Cobra was designed to achieve *as well as to exploit* a breakthrough of German lines.

Sizable numbers of American troops had flowed into Normandy during July, including 8 fresh divisions, 4 armored and 4 infantry. This brought the overall total to 6 armored and 14 infantry divisions, plus the 82nd Airborne Division and the 101st Airborne Division. For Operation Cobra, Bradley would utilize 15 of his 22 divisions.

In a "textbook" offensive operation, an attacker should have a three-to-one advantage over the defender in order to be successful. The First Army would have an estimated five-to-one advantage over Hausser's Seventh Army for Operation Cobra.

While the First Army had no heavy tanks to match the relatively small number of German Panthers and Tigers, the Yanks had roughly a ten-to-one advantage in medium tanks—M4 Shermans versus Panzer IVs. By now, a growing number of the Shermans were of the newer types that carried the high-velocity 76mm guns that were more effective than the 75mm weapon with which the original Shermans were equipped.

Cobra would use massed armor spearheaded by Collins's VII Corps to drive south from St. Lô, then pivot from facing south to facing east toward Paris and Germany. The attack would drive south toward Coutances, breaking through in the vicinity of the villages of Marigny and St. Gilles. For Operation Cobra, Collins would be given control of six divisions, virtually the strength of an army. These included the 9th Infantry Division and 30th Infantry Division—both of which were veterans of earlier Normandy fighting—as well as the 1st "Big Red One" Infantry Division, the 3rd Armored Division under Major General Leroy Watson, and the 2nd "Hell on Wheels" Armored Division. Now commanded by Major General Edward Brooks, the latter had been commanded by Patton himself before the war.

Overhead, air support would be provided by B-25 and B-26 medium bombers and P-47 Thunderbolt fighter-bombers of the USAAF Ninth Air Force, and its continuant IX Tactical Air Command. The USAAF Eighth Air Force would also make about 1,800 heavy bombers—B-17 Flying Fortresses and B-24 Liberators—available for the attack.

In preparation for Operation Cobra, SHAEF had taken a further step in the Operation Fortitude deception. With Patton preparing to come to the continent, the imaginary 1st Army Group needed a new commander. This would have to be an officer of high stature who was not otherwise engaged in leading a command that was essential to the war effort. The choice, announced publicly on July 14, was one of the highest-ranking US Army officers on the staff at the Pentagon in Washington—Lieutenant General Lesley McNair, who was then serving as commanding general of all US Army Ground Troops.

Disaster on the Eve of Breakthrough

General Bradley had in mind that the ground attack portion of Operation Cobra should be launched immediately after the air attack. American forces were positioned relatively close to the German positions that were to be targeted, and air commanders recommended that they be pulled back to allow a margin of safety of 3,000 yards between friendly forces and the areas where bombs would fall. Bradley insisted on not pulling back more than 1,000 yards, but a compromise of 1,450 yards for heavy bombers was finally reached. Smaller tactical aircraft working from low altitude would fill in the margin. The attack would begin with the heavy bombers carpeting the area five miles wide between Marigny and St. Gilles for an hour. This would be followed by a forty-five-minute work-over by IX Tactical Air Command medium bombers.

To minimize the possibility of accidents, Bradley had instructed the air commanders to instruct the bombers to fly their bomb runs *parallel* to the front line. This would ensure that bombs dropped a little too soon or a little too late would fall on the German side of the line.

Most of the elements necessary for Cobra were in place by July 20, so it was just a matter of waiting for the clear weather essential for an air-ground operation of this magnitude. The SHAEF weather prognosticators predicted that the haze and ground fog present during the weekend would lift by Monday, July 24, so Operation Cobra was put on the schedule for 1:00 that afternoon by Air Chief Marshal Leigh-Mallory, the SHAEF air boss. He opted for starting in the afternoon, just to be sure that residual morning ground fog would have cleared.

The wheels whirled into motion and the troops moved into position. On the morning of July 24, the first of about 2,000 bombers began lifting off from bases in England.

Meanwhile, Leigh-Mallory himself had gone down to Normandy to observe the action. By noon, there was still heavier than expected ground cover, so he ordered that the bombers abort their mission. His message caught the IX Tactical Air Command medium bombers on the ground before they took off. Half of the IX Tactical Air Command fighter-bombers were recalled before they hit their targets, but because of radio silence protocols and communications relay problems, the message did not reach the Eighth Air Force heavy bombers.

As the heavy bombers reached the target, the majority found their assigned targets obscured by clouds, and they aborted on their own initiative. More than a quarter of the bombers, however, arrived over their targets with sufficient visibility to release their bombs. It was standard operating procedure in the Eighth Air Force for the bombardier in the "pathfinder" plane to locate and identify the target and for bombardiers in following planes to follow his lead. This meant that the target selected by the leader was bombed by a whole Bombardment Group.

In most cases, the bombs dropped on the afternoon of July 24 went where they were intended, but one Bombardment Group released its ordnance incorrectly in a major "friendly fire" tragedy that would cast a dark shadow over the ultimate success of Operation Cobra. The bombs hit elements of the 30th Infantry Division, killing or wounding more than 150 men. To complicate matters, the bombers had executed their bomb run perpendicular to the front rather than parallel to it. Bradley was livid.

Confusion was also rampant on the ground. Many ground commanders, from platoon sergeants up to General Collins himself, assumed that the ground attack would go forward, and many units *had* moved forward. Collins did not get the word until the last minute that Bradley wanted to hold off on the ground assault and efforts to recall advancing units added to the confusion.

Meanwhile, the Germans had intuited from the air attack that an American offensive was afoot. They countered with a massive artillery barrage. They also engaged the advancing Yanks and infiltrated American lines as they withdrew. Things on the American lines were a mess.

Yet within that mess men kept their heads, and there were instances of heroism and courage under fire. One such action would involve First Lieutenant (later Captain) John Ausland of the 4th Armored Division's 29th Field Artillery Battalion. He was the artillery liaison officer with the second of two infantry battalions that were making an attack against Germans dug in near the village of La Mardell. As the battle was joined, German fire severely wounded the artillery liaison officer who was Ausland's counterpart in the lead battalion.

The key to breaking the German resistance at this point on the line was to call in artillery support, but suddenly there was nobody in the lead battalion to do the calling. Nor were there means to *place* the call. In Normandy, the Americans were using land lines for communications, and the same shell that wounded the liaison man in the lead battalion also destroyed the string of telephone wires that led back to the fire direction center at the artillery battery.

As German shells rained down on the men in the two battalions, Lieutenant Ausland moved quickly to get communications reestablished and to take over for the wounded artilleryman. For the next several hours, he directed and coordinated 29th Field Artillery fire against the enemy. By the end of the day, thanks to adequate artillery support, the two infantry battalions had taken their objectives, and Ausland was being written up for a Silver Star.

When the dust settled on the evening of July 24, Bradley was left to ponder what had to have appeared to many as just the latest in a long list of monumental SNAFUs that had beset the Allies since they'd arrived in Normandy. July 24 ended with the loss of the hoped-for tactical surprise and the Germans were mobilizing for the next punch.

The only choices left to Bradley were to cancel Operation Cobra, or go again immediately.

Tuesday, July 25

What would eventually turn out to be the most successful sixty-day offensive campaign in American military history began under partly cloudy skies, and under the cloud of discouragement from the near disaster of the day before. Today, the jump-off time would be two hours earlier than on the previous day.

As twenty-two hours before, more than two thousand bombers came overhead, with about three quarters of them being Eighth Air Force heavy bombers, each with over two tons of bombs. IX Tactical Air Command Thunderbolts raked the enemy positions, went away to refuel and rearm and then came back again.

Unfortunately, just as in the July 24 version of Operation Cobra, the aerial bombardment was marred by a horrific friendly-fire incident. A pathfinder inadvertently released his ordnance too soon, and several dozen bombers followed suit. It could have been worse, but it was bad enough.

Nearly 500 men were wounded, and 111 lost their lives. Among them was Lieutenant General Lesley McNair, who had left a relatively safe desk job in Washington to command the fictitious 1st Army Group. Ironically, the unlucky McNair had been wounded in the head by flying shrapnel a year earlier while on an inspection tour of United States forces in action in Tunisia. Though the initial SHEAF communique claimed that he had been killed by enemy action, the highest-ranking US Army officer who was to be killed in World War II had died as a result of friendly fire. SHAEF would officially confirm this fact the following week.

Coincidentally, McNair's only son, Colonel Douglas C. McNair, an artillery officer with the 77th Infantry Division, was killed in action less than a month later on August 6 by a Japanese sniper near Ipapao on Guam. A formal portrait of father and son, together with their wives and Colonel McNair's ten-month-old daughter, would be the subject of *Life* magazine's Picture of the Week in the August 21 issue. In the picture, the elder Mrs. McNair has a look of prophetic foreboding on her face.

Another casualty of the incidents having occurred two days in a row was the overall notion of using heavy bombers as tactical weapons near ground troops. Eisenhower decided to forbid their use in this role in the remainder of the European campaign, but the idea would be revived with B-52s during Operation Arc Light in the Vietnam War, and with withering success, still using B-52s, during the Gulf War in 1991 and in Afghanistan a decade later.

The effect of the two days of bombing on the enemy was devastating. The first day had been bad, but the second was horrible. Though neither side would know it until later, the bombing had wiped out approximately a third of German front line troops in the area.

On the morning of July 25, the United States First Army's VIII Corps and VII Corps were arrayed next to one another, with VIII Corps to the right, on the west coast of the

Cotentin Peninsula. Between them, the two corps possessed eight infantry divisions and three armored divisions. To the east, on the VII Corps left flank, were two smaller corps, V Corps, with two divisions assigned, and XIX Corps, with a single division.

By virtue of the main force of the German LXXXIV Korps being opposite VII Corps, they would see the brunt of the fighting during the opening three days of Operation Cobra.

The ground attack by VII Corps jumped off quickly as soon as the bombs had stopped falling, securing predetermined positions as quickly as possible so that larger forces could follow. Once a channel through the German line was cut, tanks could pour through into more lightly defended rear areas.

By the time that Cobra got underway, 60 percent of the First Army Sherman tanks had been converted to Rhino configuration, and this made quick work of hedgerows which had stopped the Yanks in their tracks just a few weeks earlier.

Because they were important regional road junctions, securing the villages of Marigny and St. Gilles would be an important goal of the day for VII Corps. The east-west road between them could be used for shuttling personnel and equipment back and forth parallel to the front, while the other roads that ran through them would be important for further advances toward the south. The 9th Infantry Division under Major General Manton Eddy was assigned Marigny as an objective, and the 30th Infantry Division under Major General Leland Hobbs directed its efforts toward St. Gilles.

In some places, the Americans discovered that the German lines were in disarray, and they found the German soldiers obviously dazed. Many emerged from the foxholes in which they'd endured the air bombardment with their hands over their heads and tears streaming down their cheeks.

In other areas, however, German positions that had been so far untouched responded to the American assault with massive fire and determined resistance. As the Yanks reached their lines, the enemy fought back, ripping the Americans with heavy machine guns.

In one area, a trio of Panther tanks destroyed a like number of Sherman tanks and halted a portion of the 30th Infantry Division advance. In other places, handfuls of German machine guns with interlocking fields of fire managed to halt entire battalions.

As the American battalion commanders on the ground had earlier suspected, the Germans had interpreted the air attacks as preparations for ground attacks. However, when the Americans quickly withdrew on July 24, many German officers interpreted this as a German tactical success. They confidently assumed that they'd repelled an American attack. When the Yanks came across on the following day, they expected to throw them back once again just as easily. Those German units that had survived the second day's attack reacted as though they would force the Americans back as they had the day before. They were mistaken.

The sixty days of Allied victory that began in Normandy on July 25 would be made up of countless small actions—and countless magnificent acts of heroism. In those sixty days, there would be thousands of heroes, but there is one who stands out. Captain Matt Urban was a Buffalo, New York-born company commander who had not yet reached his twenty-fifth birthday when he came ashore at Normandy with the 60th Infantry Regiment. However, Urban was also a decorated hero of the North African campaign—with two Silver Stars—when he landed at Normandy on D-Day. Beyond that, he had already earned a Bronze Star for actions in Normandy five weeks earlier.

On June 14, Urban's company had been in action near Renouf, when they were slammed by a hail of heavy enemy small arms. Then the panzers arrived, unmercifully raking the company's positions and inflicting heavy casualties. Realizing that his company was in immediate danger of being decimated, Urban armed himself with a bazooka and worked his way through hedgerows under a continuing barrage of fire. When he and his ammunition carrier reached a point near the tanks, Urban stood up in the hail of bullets and demolished both tanks with the bazooka.

With the tanks knocked out, Urban led his company forward and succeeded in routing the enemy. Later the same day, the company was still on the attack near Orglandes, when Urban was wounded in the leg by direct fire from a 37mm tank gun. He refused to be evacuated and continued to lead his company until they moved into defensive positions for the night.

In the predawn darkness, the following morning the badly injured Captain Urban led the company in yet another attack near Orglandes. An hour into this attack, he was again wounded. Finally, having received two wounds, one of them serious, Urban reluctantly agreed to permit medics to evacuate him to England.

Because he had been written up for a Bronze Star, and badly wounded, this should have been the end of the war for Matt Urban. He would have had a high priority for a ticket to go home. However, he didn't see it that way. In mid-July, while he was recovering from his wounds, Urban learned of his unit's severe losses in the hedgerow battles in Normandy. Realizing that the 60th Infantry Regiment needed experienced leaders, he checked himself out of the hospital and hitchhiked back to his old outfit.

Matt Urban arrived at the 2nd Battalion command post at 11:30 A.M. on July 25 near St. Lô, only to find that his company had gone out a half hour earlier in the first attack of Operation Cobra.

Still limping from his leg wound, Urban caught up with his company and retook command. Even as he arrived, his outfit was under heavy German small arms and artillery fire. Of the three Sherman tanks that were supposed to have been supporting them, two had been knocked out, and the third was idle, having lost its tank commander and gunner.

Urban found a tank company lieutenant and worked out a plan of attack to eradicate the German position that was causing so much difficulty. The lieutenant and his sergeant started climbing aboard the Sherman, but were shot and killed before they could manage to get inside their tank.

Though his leg wound from five weeks earlier made even walking difficult, Urban dashed through the brutal enemy gunfire and climbed aboard the tank himself. With bullets ricocheting off the tank's hull, Urban ordered the tank driver to move forward while Urban manned the machine gun on the turret. Seeing what he was doing, the entire battalion went into action, attacking and destroying the German strongpoint.

The world had not seen the last of the indestructible captain from Buffalo. He would continue to battle his way across Europe with the 60th Infantry Regiment, chalking up the incredible series of heroic adventures that would climax in an action at Heer, Belgium, on September 3 that would lead one day to a president of the United States calling Matt Urban "the greatest soldier in American history."

The going had been slow on that bloody Tuesday, but the Yanks were on the move. Taking German resistance on a case-by-case basis, they crawled forward. As the dust settled and commanders were able to take stock of what individual units had been able to accomplish, it became clear that remaining German resistance in what had been the front line on the morning of July 25 had been overcome. The Germans had pulled back.

When the sun went down over the artillery-splintered apple orchards of Normandy that night, the gates to the roads that led to both Marigny and St. Gilles had been pried open.

Wednesday, July 26

After more than a month of the worst weather on record, sunny skies greeted the second day of Operation Cobra. When the fog had burned off on Tuesday morning, the weather had turned warm and clear. Allied tactical air power was out in force, working the entire front.

At one point on Wednesday near the village of Canisy, two miles south of St. Gilles, five German tanks surrendered to the fighter-bombers. When they saw the P-47 Thunderbolts driving toward them, the tank crews threw open the hatches and started waving white cloth. The pilots alerted a ground force nearby, who sent two scout cars to take the Germans into custody.

General Lawton Collins had made the decision that VII Corps would attack in force again on the morning of Wednesday, July 26. Late on Tuesday afternoon, it had become clear to him that German resistance was in disarray. The enemy had taken a horrible beating, first from Allied air power, and second from the United States ground troops. There were still Germans in the line, but they were isolated. Until and unless they pulled themselves together and reorganized, they wouldn't be a major obstacle to the VII Corps armor—and Collins was not about to give them a respite to get themselves reorganized.

His plan was to secure the former German lines south of St. Lô with the 9th Infantry Division and 30th Infantry Division, and then commit fresh troops to achieve a breakthrough. The 1st Infantry Division—the "Big Red One" under Major General Clarence Huebner—was to take Marigny, with this objective exploited by a stream of General Watson's 3rd Armored Division armor that would move south toward Coutances.

Meanwhile, to the east, tanks of the 2nd Armored Division would pass through the 30th Infantry Division sector north of St. Gilles and guard the overall American left flank from possible German action.

On the German side, Paul Hausser and Dietrich von Kluge were cognizant of the same facts, although neither yet had a full picture of the extent of German losses. Bayerlein's Panzer Lehr Division had, for example, lost most of its fighting effectiveness. Nor did Hausser and von Kluge realize that St. Gilles was open to an American thrust.

Thinking in the context of earlier contests in the Cotentin campaign, Hausser imagined that a determined counterattack would be the ticket to stopping the Yanks in their tracks.

Günther von Kluge, however, had a sense of the bigger picture. He had watched essential reserves diverted to meet a Canadian attack near Caen at precisely the moment when they could have been used against VII Corps. Of course, they might just as likely have been chewed to bits by Eighth Air Force bombs. The 2nd SS Panzer Division, however, was released from the Caen sector and rushed to help shore up Hausser's position and to help him prepare his counterthrust. As it went into the line with the LXXXIV Korps, the "Das Reich" Division was situated opposite the American corps boundary where it would face elements of both VII and VIII Corps.

At dawn on July 26, the Americans of VII Corps carefully moved out to recapture the momentum of the previous day. While the 3rd Armored Division and the 1st Infantry Division moved toward Marigny, the 2nd Armored Division probed toward St. Gilles with their primary mission being to be ready to defend the flank. Thanks to the work being done against German positions by the 30th Infantry Division, the 2nd "Hell on Wheels" Armored Division encountered little resistance. By early afternoon, they had not only reached St. Gilles, but had passed through the town.

Early in the afternoon, Huebner's Big Red One ran into elements of "Das Reich" north of Marigny. This slowed Huebner's advance to a crawl. Though American troops did enter the town by nightfall, it was by no means "captured" until the following day.

Collins had hoped to have captured Marigny on July 26, but instead, his forces had broken through at St. Gilles. Nevertheless, a great deal of progress had been made. A sizable proportion of VII Corps was well south of the line occupied by the Germans when Operation Cobra had begun forty-eight hours earlier. Most important, the Germans had been unable to reform a defensive line or organize a counterattack.

Though a breakthrough had not yet been achieved, the Americans on the ground were speaking in terms of the "hard crust" of German resistance having been pierced.

Thursday, July 27

Having achieved his initial breakthrough on Wednesday, "Lightning Joe" Collins would consolidate his gains with the

9th Infantry Division and the 30th Infantry Division, using mainly armored forces to exploit the breakthrough. He directed the Big Red One and Combat Command B of the 3rd Armored Division to move on Coutances, while the remainder of the 3rd Armored Division would follow a parallel route along the left flank of the other force. They would be about five miles to the south of the others, with their objective being Hyenville, a town about that same distance south of Coutances.

Farther east, the 2nd Armored Division would sweep south toward the highway that ran between Cerence and Tessy-sur-Vire. If all worked as planned, VII Corps would wind up far closer to the base of the Cotentin Peninsula than anyone—especially the Germans—had expected when Cobra began.

On the 1st Infantry Division front, Huebner's first task was to finish mopping up Marigny, which was not fully secure after an all-night battle. He knew that he dare not send his main force sweeping toward Coutances without being in control of the important crossroads at Marigny.

The 18th Infantry Regiment of the 1st Infantry Division succeeded in taking the town by noon as the 16th Infantry Regiment cut wide to the right flank to encircle it. By early afternoon, the Big Red One was on the road to Coutances—spearheaded by Combat Command B—and they were largely unopposed. In one isolated case, however, a single 2nd SS Panzer Division Panther managed to destroy three Shermans before it was forced to retreat.

Morning rain and fog gave way to the third sunny day in a row. Overhead, IX Tactical Air Command Thunderbolts were able to supply important air support to the advancing troops. The air support was extremely useful to the ground troops, but the greatest contribution of tactical air power during this week in Normandy was in harassing the Germans behind the lines. To counter the VII Corps drive, Hausser and von Choltitz needed to reinforce their front line troops quickly, and Allied air power made this extremely difficult. As had been the case since Overlord came ashore six weeks earlier, the Luftwaffe was unable either to provide regular air support for German ground troops or to defend German supply lines from American fighter-bombers.

During the afternoon, the 3rd Armored Division Combat Command B advanced four miles in four hours. To the east, meanwhile, the 2nd Armored Division made similar gains as it dashed through St. Gilles in the vanguard of the rest of VII Corps. In light of the fact that a mile in a day had seemed good during previous battles, this was a major accomplishment that buoyed American morale everywhere on the battlefront.

These American units were facing German forces that had not—and would *never*—recover from the effects of their horrible mauling they'd suffered in the sights of the Eighth Air Force heavy bombers on Tuesday. For example, the once much-feared Panzer Lehr Division had essentially ceased to exist.

Meanwhile, back near the coast of the Cotentin Peninsula, General Middleton's VIII Corps had achieved their initial objective—the capture of the east-west road through Periers and Lessay that linked St. Lô to the coast. Middleton was moving slowly and cautiously, but the "slowly" part would soon change.

Friday, July 28

Paul Hausser awoke on Friday morning to a very distressing situation. His forces had been offering stiff resistance to the

American campaign all week, but he knew this was about to end. The Allied press office in London had announced that General Bradley had estimated gains of up to twelve miles in some places, and the SS general knew that it was true. The German front on the Cotentin Peninsula was crumbling. The road between Percy and St. Lô had been cut, and the town of Périers had been lost to the Allies.

It didn't really matter whether the German Panthers could take three Shermans to their grave with them. Hausser was practically out of Panthers, and his other armored and mechanized units were being cut up by bazooka-wielding Yanks on the ground and Thunderbolts overhead. For four days in a row, the skies had been clear and the weather warm. Allied tactical airpower was out in force again.

The dash toward Coutances by Combat Command B and the Big Red One was merely the showpiece. The Americans were advancing everywhere. Nearly every German unit that still had a communications line to headquarters—and the number of these was dwindling—was reporting American patrols penetrating their lines.

Wherever he turned, Hausser saw a desperate situation. Christian Tychsen, commander of the 2nd SS Panzer Division, had been shot and killed when a Yank patrol hit his command post. Lieutenant Colonel Otto Baum of the 17th SS Panzer Grenadier Division had assumed command of both units, but communications within German units was so jumbled that many units of the two divisions did not know what had happened.

Even without the confusion, the panzer force had not been nearly as effective in dealing with Operation Cobra as it might have been. This was due to Hausser's insistence on using tanks as an integral part of his defensive lines, rather than as a mobile reserve to cut up American troops who broke through that line. As it was, the Americans who broke through were able to run circles around the infantry that Hausser did have in reserve. Instead of using tanks as armored cavalry—as Rommel would have done and as Patton would do so effectively—Hausser thought of them simply as metal pillboxes!

In the face of the quickly deteriorating situation, Hausser made the decision to withdraw the LXXXIV Korps to the east, with the idea of letting it be part of a major counterattack that Hausser knew was being planned at Günther von Kluge's headquarters.

Meanwhile, Otto Baum had been in contact with Dietrich von Choltitz—the commander of the LXXXIV Korps. Baum proposed, and von Choltitz agreed, that the remaining assets of LXXXIV Korps should be moved south—not east—to block any further American advance toward Avranches. When Hausser's orders finally reached von Choltitz, he argued the case for a southerly move.

Meanwhile on the American side, General Bradley was making some changes of his own. Most of the week's fighting had involved Collins's VII Corps, but their drive toward Coutances took them to the west. Thus they were now directly south of Middleton's VIII Corps. Late on Thursday, with this in mind, Bradley had made it known that he was going to halt the VII Corps advance on Coutances and bring VIII Corps into play—rounding the VII Corps right flank—to capture the city.

Middleton's VIII Corps had made cautious progress on Thursday. Having seized the road through Periers and Lessay to St. Lô, they were tasked with preparing to exploit any sign of a German withdrawal. Their opportunity came when a slackening of German "eighty-eight" fire signaled that the enemy LXXXIV Korps was moving back. Though they encountered only sporadic German resistance, Middleton's men discovered that the Germans had heavily mined the roads to the south, and this had made for slow going.

Friday morning found the spearhead of VII Corps—units of the 1st Infantry Division along with Combat Command B of the 3rd Armored Division—moving in on Coutances before explicit orders were issued calling for a halt. Working with the momentum they'd generated on Thursday, they were determined to roll as far as possible before the anticipated termination of their drive. Naturally, the men of these units felt that they had a right to capture the prize after all the work and sacrifice they'd put into coming this far.

Meanwhile, VIII Corps—spearheaded by the 4th Armored Division—was also on the move. Having picked their way through the minefields in and around Periers and Lessay, the corps moved faster than expected. By noon, the village of Montuchon, a few miles north of Coutances, was in American hands.

With two American spearheads crashing toward the same goal, the potential for disaster clearly existed that morning. In the fog of battle, the two might have found the two forces trading "friendly fire" in the narrow, winding streets of Coutances, each side thinking the other was German.

The vanguard of Combat Command B got the word to halt. Their Shermans were shifted into neutral within sight of the city's church spires, with some of their infantry patrols already on the edges of town.

The Germans, however, had no intention of contesting the American drive at or south of Coutances. Though the Yanks were not yet aware of it, the order of the day for their enemy had been "withdraw," even if there had been a bit of disparity over *where* to withdraw.

When Günther von Kluge had been advised of Hausser's plan to withdraw to the east—and of von Choltitz's disagreement and his suggestion to move south—he sided with von Choltitz. In fact he was irate at the idea of moving east. While Hausser saw such a move in terms of saving and consolidating forces for later action, von Kluge and von Choltitz viewed it as an abandonment of the Cotentin Peninsula.

Hausser was caught in the middle and issued orders that countermanded the orders he had given von Choltitz in the morning. As word of the change of plans reached—or failed to reach—the withdrawing German units in the field, there was mass confusion. This was, in turn, only magnified by the already chaotic interruptions in lines of communications that had been caused by the Americans. Von Choltitz received the vital second order from his boss not via field telephone, but from a bicycle messenger!

On the other side of the line, Bradley's order of the day for Friday had included the phrase "maintain unrelenting pressure" on the enemy. Both VII Corps and VIII Corps were doing so in the west, while the much smaller V Corps and XIX Corps were making modest gains against German Seventh Army units on the Vire River south and east of St. Lô.

As the 1st Infantry Division and the 3rd Armored Division were advancing westward in the direction of Coutances and the coast, other VII Corps elements, especially the 2nd Armored Division, were making a great deal of progress farther east. Driving against withdrawing German forces generally southward from St. Lô, they managed to gain about four miles across a wide front during the day. By sundown on Friday, they had reached a major east-west road southeast of Coutances. They were now crowding the right flank of the German forces retreating south of the town.

In some cases, the Yanks managed to cut off the Germans, but usually in cases where they were actually running *ahead* of the retreating Germans. In the small hours of Saturday morning, a column of German armor—led by a Jagdpanther—reached the village of Nôtre-Dame-de-Cenilly, which was guarded by two companies of Americans, including several tanks. Using its 88mm gun, the Jagdpanther managed to bully its way through the American lines. Had an American soldier not managed to kill the driver, the Germans would have broken through. As it was, the Jagdpanther became a massive road-block. A gun battle ensued that lasted until dawn. Some of the Germans managed to escape, but they took heavy casualties.

Otto Baum, shouldering the responsibilities of command for both his own 17th SS Panzer Grenadier Division and the remnants of the Das Reich Division, had succeeded in saving his troops by a bit of creative interpretation of the orders he'd received. Early on Thursday, he and von Choltitz had discussed their preference for a southerly withdrawal toward Avranches, but this order had been countermanded by Hausser who called for the two divisions to go east. Baum had responded by moving south—across the Sienne River—*before* moving east.

By crossing the Sienne (not to be confused with the larger Seine River, which is much farther east), Baum had a more stable defensive line. By the end of the day, of course, Hausser had been overruled by *his* boss, von Kluge—and Baum had been ordered to do as he had already done.

Saturday, July 29

The sun rose on a battlefield much changed in the past twenty-four hours and virtually unrecognizable from forty-eight hours earlier. More than half of all the territory captured by First Army forces in Operation Cobra had been taken in those two days.

While the 3rd Armored Division and the 1st Infantry Division had encountered a great deal of resistance, the units on both their flanks—the 4th Armored Division of VIII Corps to the right and the 2nd "Hell on Wheels" Armored Division to the left—had made a great deal of progress. Coutances was now firmly in the control of the 4th Armored Division, and the rest of VIII was close behind. By now, VIII Corps had been augmented by the addition of the 6th Armored Division, which was on loan from the Third Army, which was scheduled for activation on August 1. The 6th Armored Division operated initially on the 4th Armored Division right flank, but it would find itself in the forefront of VIII actions during the coming week.

Bradley's plan was to use Middleton's VIII Corps to keep the Germans engaged at Coutances, while elements of Lightning Joe Collins's VII Corps—specifically the 3rd Armored Division and the Big Red One—circled south of the town to sweep up and encircle the enemy.

As the 3rd Armored Division and the 1st Infantry Division swept south of Coutances, they discovered that the Germans had been there and—for the most part—had gone. The firefight at Nôtre-Dame-de-Cenilly had been repeated many times that night, but most German units had managed to slip away.

Shielded by darkness, commanders such as von Choltitz and Baum had succeeded in saving sizable remnants of four divisions—including Das Reich—from encirclement by the Americans.

Paul Hausser had awakened to disorder on Friday, and his troops had experienced a madhouse during their tumultuous all-night withdrawal that continued through daybreak on Saturday and only amplified during the day. Now, Hausser sleeplessly greeted Saturday somewhat relieved that a great deal of shifting of forces had occurred under the cover of night. His relief was short-lived.

Saturday had brought another sunny day of good flying weather, and good flying weather brought the Allied fighter-bombers out in large numbers. They raked the lines of German vehicles that were crawling away from the front, destroying valuable tanks, which in turn blocked the narrow country roads. The resulting traffic gridlock only served to make the German columns more vulnerable to air attack.

Near the village of Roncey, between Coutances and the Sienne River, the Allied airmen discovered a target of opportunity. Hundreds of retreating German vehicles were snared in a massive traffic jam like so many sitting ducks. A six-hour bombardment ensued as wave after wave of IX Tactical Air Command aircraft scoured the area. VII Corps artillery joined in and by the end of the day, roughly 400 vehicles—about a third of them tanks—were destroyed.

American troops that entered the "Roncey Pocket" Saturday evening discovered that, in addition to the vehicles that were destroyed, many had simply been abandoned. Either their crews were blocked in by damaged vehicles, or they just fled to save themselves from being pulverized by American firepower.

By the end of the day, American patrols had captured Coutances and units had reached the Sienne River near the town of Cerences. The Yanks had arrived at the seashore on the west coast of the Cotentin Peninsula at both Pont de la Roque and at Montmartin-sur-Mer.

As darkness fell, the front was plunged into confusion, characterized by desperate small-unit firefights. The Germans who were anxious to escape rather than be captured were harassed by American patrols tasked with cutting them off.

As often happens in battle, some of the worst fighting occurs after the tide has turned. Such fighting also often brings out the greatest heroism. Such was the case around midnight on Saturday. A Panzer unit with about 2,500 troops and 100 vehicles overran a roadblock near the village of Grimesnil that was manned by the 41st Armored Infantry Regiment of the 2nd "Hell on Wheels" Armored Division. The enemy force was on the verge of annihilating the Americans when the defenders were rallied by a twenty-three-year-old squad leader, Sergeant Hulon Whittington of Bastrop, Louisiana.

When his platoon leader and platoon sergeant went missing in action, Whittington took command of the platoon and reorganized the defensive perimeter. Then, under heavy enemy automatic weapons fire, he crawled between gun positions to check on his men. Suddenly, the Germans launched an assault against Whittington's line, led by a Panther tank. The sergeant jumped onto an American tank that had been immobilized and blinded by loss of its commander. By shouting through the turret, Whittington directed the tank crew into position to fire point blank into the enemy tank.

The destruction of the Panther blocked any further movement by the long column of enemy vehicles. As if his earlier actions were not enough, Whittington proceeded to lead an old-fashioned bayonet charge against the stalled German troops. Using hand grenades, bazookas, and tank fire, the Americans followed Whittington and proceeded to attack the remaining German vehicles. The destruction of the German convoy was completed as American artillery units joined in.

Hulon Whittington's own heroism did not end with the bayonet charge. When a medical corpsman was hit, the sergeant personally jumped in to administer first aid to wounded men. It was a fitting climax to the Operation Cobra offensive. For his actions that night, Whittington was awarded the Congressional Medal of Honor.

Sunday, July 30

The mauling that the German LXXXIV Korps had taken on July 29 essentially terminated their resistance to the Operation Cobra offensive. The Cobra objectives had been met and exceeded. In five days, the Americans had captured about as much ground as in the previous five weeks, and massive amounts of German equipment had been destroyed or captured. A few days before, the Sienne River had been envisioned as a German defensive line. By Saturday night, the US Army Engineers were installing a number of temporary bridges to facilitate rapid troop movements in the coming days.

The American success can be attributed to a number of factors. Certainly the superior communications, logistics, and air cover were vital, but most of the success on the line had to be attributed to the training and tenacity of the American GIs—from squad sergeants such as Hulon Whittington to the corps commanders in whom General Bradley invested a great deal of confidence and independence of action.

The British front had remained relatively static while the Yanks were rolling up acres and acres of captured ground, and General Montgomery naturally wanted some of the action and ordered the British troops to launch Operation Bluecoat against Caumont, a city east of St. Lô and south of Caen. The purpose was twofold. Montgomery also felt that Bluecoat could aid the American offensive of the Cotentin Peninsula by forcing von Kluge to keep the units assigned to Heinrich Eberbach's Panzer Group West away from the Americans.

In the long run, Bluecoat laid a blueprint for future British actions farther east. That blueprint held the premise that the general German disorganization that had been a byproduct of Operation Cobra could be exploited. And it *would* be exploited, not only by the British Second Army in the east, but by the American First Army in southern Normandy and by the soon-to-be-added Third Army in Brittany.

The ultimate success of Operation Cobra had been apparent to General Bradley by early Friday, when he issued his directive to "maintain unrelenting pressure." He had accomplished what he had set out to do. Accepted practice suggested that it was now time for a pause, but Bradley had made the decision to keep up the momentum. It was time to apply some of the First Army's "unrelenting pressure" against Avranches, where he feared that the enemy would be regrouping behind the See River.

In fact, by Sunday, the Germans had been on the run for the better part of three days, and there was little left to regroup.

Responsibility for the attack on the medieval walled city of Avranches would be allocated to the two armored divisions assigned to VIII Corps. On Sunday morning the 6th Armored Division, under Major General Robert Grow, generally occupied positions around the mouth of the Sienne River, just south of Coutances. Meanwhile, Major General John "Tiger Jack" Wood's 4th Armored Division was about eight miles farther south, and about twenty miles from Avranches.

For several days, the plan had been for Grow to follow the coastal roads, while Wood took a more direct inland route. At VIII Corps headquarters, General Middleton had originally believed that the progress of the two would be roughly equal and that it would take several days. With this in mind, the 6th Armored Division had been tasked with taking Avranches, while the 4th Armored Division would cut farther inland. However, when Combat Command B of the 4th Armored Division—under the command of Brigadier General Holmes Dager—managed to advance ten miles on Saturday, Middleton rethought this notion. General Wood was given the mission to capture Avranches, an assault that was to begin on July 30.

To no one's surprise, the spearhead for this operation would be Dager's Combat Command B. He split the command into two parallel columns, taking command personally of the western one.

The eastern column was ambushed shortly after the two sections jumped off on Sunday morning. They would eventually break through, but they lost several vehicles and were out of the picture for the rest of the day.

Dager's western column, meanwhile, met no appreciable opposition, and their Shermans had dashed ten miles down the road by midday. They were less than four miles north of Avranches when they ran into their first significant German defensive fire. Dager had stumbled across what he thought was a roadblock. In fact, it was the forward command post for the German Seventh Army—with SS General Paul Hausser himself among them. The Germans had no idea that the Americans were coming on so fast.

Hausser fled on foot, flagged down a passing Kubelwagen, and escaped to Mortain.

Dager smashed through the command post and reached the See River within the hour. After ensuring that the two highway bridges into Avranches were intact and secure, Combat Command B of the 4th Armored Division entered Avranches.

Meanwhile, the 6th Armored Division had made it about halfway from Coutances to Avranches when they ran into German resistance at the coastal city of Granville. In keeping with the general pattern, the Germans put up a fight—hoping to stall the Americans long enough to escape.

By midnight, the advance guard of the retreating Granville Germans had reached Avranches. Unaware that Combat Command B was already there, they simply drove into town as though they still "owned" it. Shots were fired, but the Germans quickly surrendered. From their new prisoners, Dager's people learned that another, larger, German force was coming down from Granville about an hour behind the first. The Americans who had come so far that day, dug in for a long sleepless night.

Monday, July 31

The German escapees from Granville ran into Combat Command B at Avranches in the early hours of Monday morning. Though the Yanks had been forewarned, they had difficulty stopping the determined and well-armed enemy. The Germans set up artillery and attempted to slam through the American defensive line.

One of the decisive factors in stopping the German advance was the determination of Private William Whitson, who single-handedly knocked out twenty German vehicles and killed roughly fifty enemy soldiers before he himself was gunned down.

Other actions during the night found several groups of 4th Armored Division artillerymen operating as infantry—but nevertheless operating quite effectively.

One of these occurred near La Haye-Pesnil, about ten

miles due north of Avranches, involving the 94th Armored Field Artillery Battalion, which was assigned to the division's Combat Command B. A lone infantryman informed Corporal Bernard Gallagher and Private First Class Lige Lewis of the battalion's Battery C that German troops were holed up in a particular house. The two artillerymen took it upon themselves to remove this threat and staged a surprise attack. Nine Germans emerged with their hands clasped behind their heads, urged along at gunpoint by Gallagher and Lewis.

Meanwhile, the main force of the 94th, 969th, and 66th Armored Field Artillery Battalions were digging in north of Avranches, preparing to help cover the river crossings that the 4th Armored Division would be using to cross the See River on Monday. Part of this effort involved setting up and manning roadblocks on thoroughfares that fed into the intersection of the main highways coming south from Coutances and Granville, as well as the equally important main highway that linked Avranches to points to the east.

During the night, the GIs manning the roadblock managed to capture a number of German vehicles that were making their way south from Granville. Some time later, a group of Germans managed to get through the roadblock using a captured American scout car. Before they were intercepted, they managed to attack a 105mm gun emplacement. They also tossed a couple of grenades into an ammunition dump, and shells exploded for several hours. This conflagration, in turn, set fire to the camouflage netting that was over a four-ton prime mover.

Four men from Battery A of the 969th Field Artillery Battalion leaped into action to save the huge vehicle. Captain Charles Temple, Captain Robert Franks, Tech Sergeant Carl Bergman, and Private John McGann worked quickly to save the vehicle by pulling off the burning net. Meanwhile, Private Miles McClelland jumped into the cab and drove the truck into a clearing to safety. He was wounded in the process. When it was discovered that McClelland had saved the life of a wounded soldier who had been asleep on top of the ammunition in the truck, he was awarded the Silver Star for his bravery.

Temporarily halted, the Germans rallied at daybreak and attacked again. The Americans responded with mortar fire, and were aided by the arrival of tactical aircraft. Basking in the warm glow of nearly a week of good flying weather, tactical air power was overhead throughout Normandy. These Thunderbolts raked the German positions as Combat Command B counterattacked. A large number of Germans surrendered, although many broke and ran, managing to escape.

By now, coordination between air and ground forces had been formed into an effective partnership. Using radios tuned to a common frequency, four-ship flights of fighter-bombers supported every armored column, working in half-hour shifts. The airmen were able to look ahead of the tanks, spotting enemy positions and attacking them wherever possible. These tactics, born and perfected in Normandy would be crucial to the ultimate Allied victory in Europe.

The eastern column of Dager's Combat Command B arrived soon after the battle with the Granville escapees ended, and assisted the rest of the command in securing the main Avranches bridges. At one point, a German artillery piece on a hill overlooking the easternmost of the bridges opened fire. An infantry assault using armored vehicles managed to reach the gun and put it out of business.

The arrival of Combat Command B of the 4th Armored Division in Avranches had come as a complete surprise to General Middleton at VIII Corps. It was great news; it was just way ahead of what he had planned. His immediate reaction was to order General Wood to push the rest of the 4th Armored Division down the road toward the city as soon as possible. He correctly imagined that a breakthrough like this would be essential to keeping the Germans off balance and thus preventing them from regrouping. He also knew that merely holding Avranches with part of one combat command was not nearly enough. To make his position tenable, Dager would have to control the high ground around Avranches. In order to make the seizure of Avranches meaningful, Dager would also have to secure as many bridgeheads as possible across the See River.

To facilitate the exploitation of the Avranches situation, General Middleton put General Dager in command of all the units in the Avranches area, including not only both columns of Combat Command B, but Combat Command A of the 4th Armored Division, as well as the spearhead of the 6th Armored Division. The latter had succeeded in punching through Granville and was coming down the coast highways on the heels of the Germans who had battled Combat Command B through the night.

When he was certain that Avranches and its two bridges were secure, Dager ordered Combat Command B to move upriver to take another See River bridge at Tirepied. He also ordered Combat Command A of the 4th Armored Division to move out and head for Pontaubault, the city commanding the bridge across the *next* river south, the Selune. There were also several dams on the Selune that were upriver from Pontaubault. If the Germans blew them up, the rush of water downstream could damage the bridges. Dager put these on the "to-do" list for Combat Command A as well.

Combat Command A moved quickly. The assumption

was that Germans understood the importance of a Selune River bridgehead to the Yanks, and that they would try to destroy the bridge at Pontaubault. As it turned out, the Germans had not destroyed the bridge. They planned to *defend* it. However, they misunderstood the speed at which Combat Command A was moving, and they weren't ready. Combat Command A was across the *"pont"* at Pontaubault and in control of the town before the enemy had a chance to set up their artillery.

If Dager's arrival at Avranches surprised Troy Middleton and Omar Bradley, it stunned Günther von Kluge. Every level of his command—from Oberbefehlshaber West to Seventh Army to the LXXXIV Korps—had been impacted by Operation Cobra. Some of his elite units—such as the Panzer Lehr Division and the Das Reich Division—had been cut up, and their parts destroyed or scattered. Communications was in a state of confusion.

Just after midnight, von Kluge had authorized a withdrawal from Granville even as the units defending that city were hurrying south toward their run-in with Holmes Dager and Combat Command B at Avranches. His order to LXXXIV Korps to withdraw to Avranches came *after* Dager's tanks were already in the city.

The field marshal ordered two infantry divisions to move into Avranches, but it was too late. Von Kluge didn't get the bad news until after 9:00 A.M. He had to find fault somewhere, so he blamed Paul Hausser for having ordered a withdrawal to the east on Friday. With 20/20 hindsight, von Kluge was sure that everything that had gone wrong over the weekend would have come out differently if not for Hausser's "mistake."

When von Kluge had countermanded Hausser on Friday,

the collapsed German communications system failed to get the word through to the front expeditiously. By Saturday, the situation had changed so dramatically that Friday's orders were no longer relevant. By Monday, the German defense of the Cotentin Peninsula—as well as the LXXXIV Korps itself—had crumbled.

In the first three weeks of July, the Americans had taken 8,000 prisoners. During the six days since the launch of Operation Cobra, the Allies were reporting that 18,587 Germans had surrendered, but that number would later be revised upward to more than 20,000. The 4th Armored Division and 6th Armored Division had taken 4,000 prisoners during their dash through Avranches to Pontaubault on Monday alone. Indeed, the initial Allied prisoner count for just July 31 would be 7,812. The official SHAEF communique on Wednesday would carry an overall prisoner count of 69,186 since the Allies had come ashore in Normandy on June 6.

Three days earlier, General Bradley had ordered the First Army spearheads to "maintain unrelenting pressure." They had, and it had worked.

Before Operation Cobra, pressure had been met with stiff counter-pressure. Now, less than a week after the Cobra strike, the tactical situation in Normandy had changed dramatically. It would be resurrected elsewhere, but the counter-pressure had crumbled in the Cotentin Peninsula.

Before Operation Cobra, Bradley had hoped to be able to launch an assault into Brittany sometime during August. Until now, he had no reason to believe that such a move could begin on the first day of the month, but on the last day of July, there was essentially nothing left standing in his way. By sundown on Monday, the 4th Armored Division was in control of four bridgeheads across the Selune River and three across the

See River. This was considered more than enough to support a move into Brittany.

For its actions in the breakthrough from the Cotentin Peninsula that would take the US Army into Brittany and beyond, the 4th Armored Division would come to be nicknamed "the Breakthrough Division."

Hausser's timid deployment of his armor contrasted with the "hell bent for leather" approach with which the Americans had used their tanks during Operation Cobra. Yet there was another American general waiting in the wings that Monday night—pacing the black Normandy dirt with his spit-polished cavalry boots—who would soon develop this approach more finely. He would mold the use of fast-moving tanks into a fine art of victory that is still praised wherever the tactics of armor in mobile warfare are discussed.

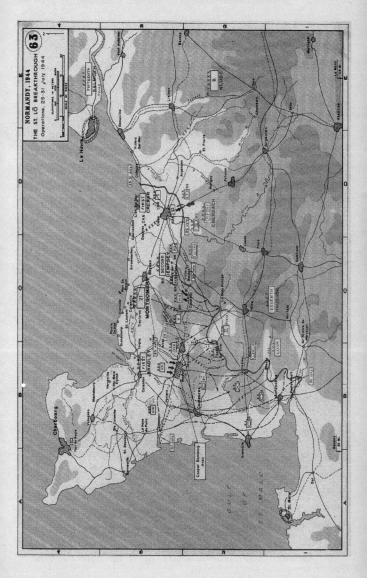

✪ THREE ✪

PATTON ARRIVES

In mid-July, General Eisenhower and his Supreme Headquarters had authorized a reorganization of the Allied command structure in Normandy. It would involve separating the Anglo-Canadian forces from the Americans into two separate army groups.

The quickly growing number of American troops in Normandy, combined with the ground gained by the United States First Army—relative to the lack thereof on the part of the British Second Army so far—would require SHAEF to undertake the reformatting of force structure. Montgomery's 21st Army Group would retain General Sir Miles Dempsey's British Second Army and gain General Harry Crerar's Canadian First Army, while the United States First Army would be peeled off and placed under the newly created 12th Army Group. Eventually, the staff of the 1st Army Group in England—which continued to busily pass paperwork back and forth to perpetuate the FUSAG myth—would be transferred to the 12th Army Group.

General Omar Bradley would move up from the First

Army to take command of the new 12th Army Group, while his former deputy, Lieutenant General Courtney Hodges, would take over command of the First Army. The all-American 12th Army Group would become operational upon the activation of the *second* American army in Normandy. General Bradley would pick the date. Even before the astounding success of Operation Cobra became apparent, Bradley had chosen Tuesday, August 1 to be that date. The new Third Army would, of course, be activated under the command of Lieutenant General George Smith Patton Jr.

If there was an apprehension on the part of certain SHAEF staff officers when they heard that Eisenhower was bringing the brilliant "bad boy" of the US Army back into the field, there was an even greater excitement among the troops that were actually *in* the field. Patton was feared almost as much by the bureaucrats of his own service as he was by the German field commanders.

On the other hand, Patton was immensely popular with the majority of the troops who served under him. They liked his "no-bullshit" style of leadership and the fact that he always backed up his words with action.

They especially liked the fact that he led his troops from the front, rather than the rear. Most officers of Patton's rank operated from command posts that were comfortably isolated from the action. Patton's command post, called "Lucky Forward," was a jeep that was usually within shouting distance of where the actual battle was taking place.

"I get criticized every day for taking needless risks by being too often right up front," Patton had said. "What good is a dead general? I say, what damn good is a general who won't take the same risks as his troops?"

In leading from the front, Patton had cast himself in the

classic mold of historic commanders such as Julius Caesar and
Stonewall Jackson, both of whom he idolized. He felt that a
leader's place was always in the lead.

"Inspiration," Patton observed, "does not come via coded
messages, but by visible personality."

By being a visible personality, Patton was to be much more
popular with his men than most World War II commanders of
his rank. After the war, veterans would proudly refer to the division or regiment with which they'd served. Those who served
with the Third Army constituent divisions and regiments often
said simply that they had served "with Patton."

Patton responded to the loyalty that he received by being
loyal to his troops in return. As he said, "The duties of an officer are the safety, honor, and welfare of your country first; the
honor, welfare, and comfort of the men in your command second; and the officer's own ease, comfort, and safety last."

As much as they hated him for how hard he made them
work, the Third Army GIs loved him for his loyalty to them.
"There has been a great deal of talk about loyalty from the
bottom to the top," Patton said. "Loyalty from the top to the
bottom is much more important, and also much less preva-
lent. It is this loyalty from the top to the bottom which binds
juniors to their seniors with the strength of steel."

The media also loved Patton. His persona as a larger-
than-life warrior king was tailor-made for the flocks of reporters covering the war. The fact that Eisenhower had kept
Patton "on ice" through the winter only added to his image as
a mysterious knight from classical mythology.

There was a great deal of speculation that Patton was involved in something very important and very big.

While Patton had, in fact, been merely cooling his heels
for much of the winter, the absence from the public eye of

someone so outspoken had clearly given credence to the rumors that swirled around the mythical FUSAG.

On the other side, the Oberkommando der Wehrmacht considered Patton the commander that they least wanted to face in battle. Hitler feared Patton. He had kept his Fifteenth Army out of Normandy because of his fear of Patton. If the American news media bought the rumors of Patton being "up to something big," the Germans had swallowed it hook, line, and sinker.

For this very reason, Eisenhower had chosen to not to make a public announcement of Patton and the Third Army on August 1. He wanted to keep Hitler and his henchmen guessing. He wanted to keep the Fortitude fable alive in the minds of those in that smoke-filled room at Rastenberg, East Prussia.

The news of the Third Army activation would remain secret for more than two weeks. Though the troops on the ground—and war correspondents at the front—knew what was going on, it would be August 15 before the news media was officially told to make it public and tell their readers: "He's back!"

Patton's first World War II battlefield in continental Europe would be Brittany, the rocky peninsula lying west of Normandy between the English Channel and the Bay of Biscay. Known in French as *Bretagne*, the remote region was inhabited by descendants of an ancient Celtic people whose language is more closely related to Welsh than to French. Brittany had maintained its native culture despite being dominated since the tenth century by Norman, English, and French conquerors.

Geographically, Brittany comprises the rugged Breton Peninsula, with its rocky and irregular coastline that is battered by North Atlantic storms. This coastline shelters several natural harbors with major port cities. In particular, these are St. Malo on the north coast of the peninsula, Brest at the tip, and Lorient and St. Nazaire on the south coast. The major city in Brittany is Rennes, which is located inland, at the center of the neck of the peninsula.

In 1940, with the fall of France, the Germans occupied the ports, established bases from which U-boats could prowl the Atlantic, and turned the cities into fortresses. In 1944, Hitler ordered his troops to defend these ports to the last man and completely destroy everything useful before they could fall into Allied hands.

In overall command of German forces defending Brittany in August 1944 was an old artilleryman named General Wilhelm Fahrmbacher. At his disposal were the 2nd Parachute Division at St. Malo, the 343rd Division in and around Brest, the 91st Division at the base of the peninsula, and three additional divisions dispersed elsewhere within Brittany.

The Allies were now in Normandy, and Fahrmbacher knew that soon the Americans would be in Brittany. The Yanks needed Brittany and its ports so as to be able to bring troops and supplies from the United States *directly* into continental Europe—rather than crossing the Atlantic to Britain and coming across the English Channel in smaller vessels.

In the summer, having the ports was a convenience. By October or November it would be a necessity. By then, the winter storms slashing against the Normandy coastline would make it virtually impossible to continue using the Overlord invasion beaches to bring supplies and troops into Europe.

St. Malo and Brest were seen as the two most important objectives because they were linked by a major rail line that led directly into the heart of France. St. Malo was also closest to American units at the base of the Cotentin Peninsula. Brest—

located in the absolute "upper left-hand corner" of France—was the closest Breton port to the United States. Brest and its excellent deepwater port facilities had served as the primary embarkation point for United States troops in World War I, and SHAEF planners wanted it back. Brest had a certain nostalgic importance to the United States as well. The American monument to its World War I naval forces had existed here until the Germans destroyed it in 1941.

The job of clearing Brittany of its German defenders, and of taking the Breton ports, was handed to General Patton on August 1.

He was ready.

In fact, he was, to use one of those equestrian metaphors favored by the former cavalryman, "chomping at the bit."

Tuesday, August 1

Patton and his Third Army staff had actually been in Normandy, studying the situation and looking at the lay of the land, since mid-July. As a student of history, Patton had done his homework. He had spent time in the area after World War I, and had paid particular attention to the roads used by William the Conqueror during his operations in Normandy and Brittany a millennium earlier. As Patton pointed out, "The roads used in those days had to be on ground which was *always* practical."

When the Third Army was officially activated on August 1, this was merely a formality. Patton knew what to do, and so did those under his command. The nucleus of the Third Army for the Brittany campaign would be General Troy Middleton's VIII Corps, whose 4th Armored Division had spearheaded the final victory on the Cotentin Peninsula along with the 6th Armored Division, which had been created in July with a predetermined assignment to the Third Army in mind. Other units, such as the 83rd Infantry Division, under Major General Robert Macon, would soon be in action with the Third Army.

Two additional corps assigned to the Third Army were XV Corps, commanded by Major General Wade Haislip, and XX Corps, commanded by Major General Walton Walker. Both had arrived in Normandy in July, but would not be committed to the Brittany operation. Instead, they would be prepared for use by the Third Army after the Brittany action. XV Corps was temporarily in support of VII Corps near Avranches. The 4th Armored Division was officially assigned to XV Corps, but because the 4th was then active with VIII Corps for the Brittany campaign, the 5th Armored Division was given to Haislip as his armor component.

Designated to supply air support primarily to Patton's Third Army would be the XIX Tactical Air Command. Like IX Tactical Air Command, it was a constituent of General Hoyt Vandenberg's Ninth Air Force. It had been organized in England as a tactical air command in April 1944 and had moved to bases in Normandy during July. Commanded by Brigadier General Otto Weyland, the XIX Tactical Air Command would come to be known as "Patton's Air Force." Over the course of the coming 281 days of combat, Patton's air force would fly more than 74,000 sorties and pummel the Wehrmacht with 35 million pounds of bombs.

Conventional strategy would have called for the United States ground forces to march methodically through Brittany, capturing the ports as they came to them. Such had been the First Army's experience with the Cotentin Peninsula. The peninsula wasn't to be considered captured until Cherbourg, and that had come six weeks after Overlord.

Patton's tactical theory was to take Brittany first, bypassing the ports and coming back to deal with them when the rest of the peninsula was in American hands. He felt that the port garrisons could be bottled up and cut off from other German units elsewhere and left for later.

Initially, Bradley, as Patton's superior, had wanted him to—at the least—capture St. Malo, the nearest port to the Third Army's jumping-off point. However, the 12th Army Group commander agreed to go along with Patton's scheme—unless and until an opportunity to grab the port quickly presented itself.

Patton intended to use his armored units decisively, hitting the Germans as hard as possible and keeping them off balance as he moved fast to capture and control bridges and lines of communications within Brittany. He would be applying his "golden rules of war": speed, simplicity, and boldness.

Specifically, General Robert Grow would lead the 6th Armored Division—followed by the Major General Donald Stroh's 8th Infantry Division—west through the center of Brittany. At the same time, General Wood's 4th Armored Division was to drive south toward the inland city of Rennes, spearheading Major General Ira Wyche's 79th Infantry Division and cutting Brittany off at the neck. Not being sent as deeply into the peninsula as the 6th Armored Division greatly pleased Wood, who was more anxious to get away from Brittany and to move east toward Paris, and ultimately Germany. This, Jack Wood correctly believed, was where the real action was going to be.

Meanwhile, Patton formed a third armored command to compliment the two armored divisions. Designated as Task Force A, it was commanded by Brigadier General Herbert Earnest. This unit was to drive west toward Brest on the road that followed the northern coast of the Breton Peninsula.

When the sun came up on the first day of August, the tank crews of the lead units of the 4th Armored Division at Pontaubault already had one foot in Brittany, as the Selune River is essentially the geographical border between Normandy and Brittany.

The 4th Armored Division jumped off toward Rennes from Pontaubault early Tuesday morning. As the largest city in the region and an important rail and highway hub, Rennes was considered an essential objective. Rennes, and the goal of cutting across the neck of the peninsula, was considered to be more essential to the immediate tactical situation than capturing the ports.

Under clear skies, the 4th Armored Division made good progress through the day, penetrating through about forty miles of Breton countryside without opposition. By afternoon, Combat Command A of the 4th Armored Division was within five miles of Rennes when they ran into a wall of German "eighty-eight" artillery fire.

Because they were about ten miles north of Avranches, and had to pass the city, General Grow's 6th Armored Division was later in getting started on Tuesday than the 4th Armored Division. Because of the massive volume of logistical traffic heading south through Avranches that morning, the city had become a traffic bottleneck.

Grow was standing at the side of the road overseeing the situation personally when Patton himself came by in his jeep. Patting Grow on the shoulder, Patton told him that he had bet General Bradley that the Third Army would be in Brest by Saturday evening. Before he drove on, Patton ordered Grow to make this happen. "Take Brest," the general said succinctly.

Grow was actually quite pleased with the opportunity to make a decisive contribution to the war, despite the fact that it meant moving an entire division two hundred miles in less than five days against unknown German opposition. Before he could undertake such a task, however, Grow would be faced with the task of getting his division through the Avranches traffic jam, so he turned his attention to a chore that would eat up most of Tuesday.

The third prong of Patton's assault on Brittany was Task Force A. Smaller than either armored division, it had the job of securing the road and rail route along the north coast of the peninsula—with its bridges intact. This route would be an essential means of transporting incoming men and material from Brest to the big rail hub at Rennes. It would not be hard for the Germans to disrupt American plans by blowing up these bridges.

As he started out on Tuesday morning, General Earnest hoped that he would be able to accomplish his mission fast enough that Task Force A would arrive at Brest simultaneously with the 6th Armored Division and thus be able to share the glory.

The excitement of being part of a Patton offensive campaign was with all three of the forces headed for Brittany that day. However, except for the 6th Armored Division, they all had the mundane chore of getting through the traffic jam at the See River and Selune River bridgeheads, and simply getting their feet onto Breton soil.

Wednesday, August 2

After moving deep into Brittany with unaccustomed speed on Tuesday, General Wood's 4th Armored Division had been halted at Rennes by resistance on a scale that they had not encountered since Coutances. The German 91st Division under

Colonel Eugen König was determined to make a stand, and to force the Yanks to pay for the city.

As Wood understood, having armored units involved in an immobile siege was contrary to both the Patton doctrine of armored warfare and the practical lessons that had been learned thus far in Normandy. With this in mind, Wood did not attack Rennes directly, but encircled it to the west so that he would be on one side, and the 8th Infantry Division—which followed the 4th Armored Division by a few hours—would be on the other.

By Tuesday morning General Grow had succeeded in his efforts to debouch the 6th Armored Division through the bridgeheads at Avranches and Pontaubault, although the 79th Infantry Division, which was scheduled to follow it, had not. Based on his specific order from Patton to "take Brest" by Saturday, Grow decided to move out on Wednesday morning without waiting. He planned to take whichever route seemed to be the fastest way to get his division to the objective. Speed, simplicity, and boldness.

Two armored columns would spearhead the 6th Armored Division drive into Brittany. Combat Command A under Brigadier General James Taylor would be on the left flank, and Combat Command B under Colonel George Read would run a parallel course, nearer Brittany's north coast on Taylor's right. A third component, Combat Command R under Colonel Harry Hanson, would follow Taylor's column.

As had been the case with the 4th Armored Division advance on Tuesday, Combat Command A was able to drive more than forty miles into Brittany without meeting any appreciable opposition. Meanwhile, however, Combat Command B encountered stiff enemy resistance at the village of Dinan, just inland from St. Malo. Read ordered his men to withdraw and bypass the town, correctly assuming that the Germans defending Dinan did not have the mobility to counterattack or give chase.

Both of the spearheading combat commands ended their day's dash near the village of Quedillac, about forty miles from Avranches. Relative to the experience of United States forces in Normandy just a few weeks earlier, the progress the division made on Wednesday was astonishing.

Thursday, August 3

The situation that the 4th Armored Division had encountered at Rennes demanded immediate action. The port cities could be bypassed because they were geographically isolated, but Rennes was different. Because it was an important crossroads for both road and rail traffic, it was strategically a key part of the whole Brittany operation. General Wood had to capture the city.

General Middleton temporarily reassigned the 13th Infantry Regiment from the 8th Infantry Division to Wood's 4th Armored Division as the unit designated to lead the urban assault on Rennes. The unit had arrived on the scene late Wednesday night. Rather than give the regiment a full day to rest, Wood insisted that momentum demanded an assault on Thursday afternoon.

Tiger Jack Wood was one of those unique commanders who understood the importance of constant and relentless action in combat. Like his mentor, George Patton, he believed that there were three essential basic maneuvers in an offensive campaign: "Attack, attack, and attack."

The celebrated British historian Basil Liddell-Hart called Wood "the Rommel of the American armored forces," and, like both Rommel and Patton, he led his troops from the head of the column rather than from a command post in the rear. From Brittany to the Lorraine, to the Reich itself, Tiger Jack would demonstrate his uncanny mixture of aggressiveness and an uncanny sense of timing that would help the United States and its Allies beat the swords and Tiger tanks of the Third Reich into plowshares and Volkswagen beetles.

The 13th Infantry Regiment attacked on Thursday afternoon, smashing their way into the northeast corner of the city. They were met by fierce German resistance, but it was clear to the defenders that a determined infantry assault, backed by an armored division was formidable.

In the face of Jack Wood's assault, a plea for permission to withdraw found its way up the German chain of command to General Paul Hausser at Seventh Army headquarters. His authorization finally came at 11:00 P.M. The defenders of Rennes were ordered to destroy everything of value and pull out to the southeast. With huge bonfires of burning fuel and materiel raging throughout the city, the beleaguered Germans skulked out of Rennes under cover of darkness at about 3:00 A.M. Friday morning.

Meanwhile, Task Force A, the third in sequence of the three components of VIII Corps, had finally squeezed through the See and Selune River bridgeheads. On Thursday morning, they ran into the same German defensive forces near Dinan that the 6th Armored Division had encountered and bypassed on Wednesday. General Earnest soon discovered that there were German defenders throughout his right flank, all across the base of the stubby peninsula on which lay St. Malo, the first of the Brittany ports that the Third Army would pass.

When General Middleton was made aware of the situation, he decided to order Task Force A to probe the defenses around St. Malo with an eye toward actually assaulting the city. After initial disarray, Earnest's men rallied and broke through the outer crust of German defenses. As they probed deeper, however, they ran into much more determined resistance. In order to complete the mission, Earnest realized that he needed backup. Middleton ordered that General Macon's 83rd Infantry Division move in to support Task Force A.

Farther north of the 4th Armored Division and deeper into the Breton Peninsula than the other elements of VIII Corps, General Grow's 6th Armored Division faced a problem of a different sort. Because they had made such quick progress on Wednesday, they had outrun their communications lines and there was a danger of their becoming overextended. Despite his sense of urgency about getting to Brest by the weekend, Grow did not want to penetrate so deeply into enemy territory that his forces would run the risk of being cut off and surrounded. With this in mind, he made the decision to wait until noon to resume the 6th Armored Division dash into Brittany.

When they got under way, General Taylor's Combat Command A headed south, ran into enemy opposition near the village of Mauron, and wheeled west, traveling overland to bypass the roadblock. Colonel Read's Combat Command B headed out at noon, following the main interior highway that snaked westward through the heart of the Breton Peninsula.

Late in the afternoon, General Grow sent orders for Read to halt his advance. General Middleton had just ordered Grow not to have his combat commands move past Dinan. Read had to have shook his head in bewilderment. Read had passed Dinan yesterday, and he had driven another thirty miles into Brittany today!

Middleton was unaware of exactly how much progress the

6th Armored Division had actually made in the past twenty-four hours, and thought that they were still close enough to the Dinan area to support the Task Force A assault on St. Malo.

Grow was on the horns of a dilemma. He had a deadline in Brest that he meant to keep, but Middleton had decided that he wanted to capture St. Malo in the meantime. Grow explained his current tactical situation to Middleton and asked to be excused from a St. Malo operation. While he was waiting for a reply, Grow decided to leave Read's Combat Command B in place where it had halted, while both Combat Command A and Combat Command R were pulled back and reconfigured for a St. Malo operation to begin on Friday.

Friday, August 4

The situation around General Middleton's order to General Grow to withdraw the 6th Armored Division for action against St. Malo took a dramatic turn on Friday morning. It was about 11:00 A.M., and Grow was at his forward command post at Merdrignac and in the process of preparing the division's Combat Command A and Combat Command R for the withdrawal to the north coast of Brittany, about forty highway miles away. Suddenly a jeep rolled into the camp bearing the stars of Third Army commander General George Patton.

Patton was enraged. He demanded to know "what the hell" Grow was doing sitting in a field when Patton had given him explicit orders to "take Brest."

Grow explained that General Middleton, the VIII Corps commander, had ordered him to halt and get ready for the St. Malo operation. Grow underscored his explanation by handing Patton a written copy of the order. Patton, who was Middleton's boss, read the order and shook his head. Patton told

Grow that *he* would deal with Middleton—*and* that Grow should follow Patton's order and go to Brest.

This incident clearly demonstrates how chaotic the communications within the Third Army had become because of the speed with which Patton's tank crews were moving. In Middleton's defense, he had not been aware of Grow's exact location when he had issued the order to participate in the St. Malo operation. Until this week, no American forces in Europe had moved so quickly. The Signal Corps—used to the nearly static front characteristic of their first six weeks in Normandy—was unable to keep pace. They raced to string phone lines, but the Sherman tanks moved faster. Though the Signal Corps would soon get their act together, the first week of August was a steep learning curve.

With the 6th Armored Division now officially out of the picture at St. Malo, Task Force A pushed toward the city with the support of advance units of the 83rd Infantry Division. By midday on Friday, they had captured the village of Dol, about five miles from the edge of St. Malo. As the attackers seemed be making quick work of taking down the German defenses, Patton ordered that the main body of Macon's division not be committed to St. Malo, but be prepared to move out to support the 6th Armored Division's westward thrust through the Breton Peninsula. However, by the end of the day, it had become apparent that German resistance at St. Malo would not be so easily overcome.

At Rennes, the 13th Infantry Regiment entered the city at dawn. Welcomed as liberators by the French citizenry, they soon learned that the Germans who had held the city for the past four years had slipped away during the night. The 8th Infantry Division came on the scene at midday, resuming command of the 13th Infantry Regiment. Together, they were

given the task of occupying the city, while the 4th Armored
Division moved on alone.

Indeed, both Combat Command A and Combat Command B of the 4th Armored Division had already moved out
at the 13th Infantry Regiment entered Rennes and they were
probing German defenses well south of the city by nightfall.
SHAEF had issued a communique declaring that the American tanks were just miles from Brest, and just thirty-eight
miles from St. Nazaire.

Saturday, August 5

On Saturday morning, General Earnest's Task Force A
mounted a major attack against the defenders at St. Malo. As
the day dragged on, it became apparent that this venture
would take a more concerted effort. Artillery was set up to begin a bombardment of the city as the 83rd Infantry Division
began to arrive in force.

By the end of the day, the Patton-induced urgency to
swallow the Breton Peninsula quickly had infected Troy Middleton to the point that he ordered Task Force A to break off
its part of the St. Malo assault. In the past forty-eight hours
this operation had slipped from the head of Middleton's
agenda. On Thursday, he had planned to throw both the 6th
Armored Division and Task Force A against the fortress of St.
Malo. Now, in a complete about-face, both of these units
would be pulled out and put back on the road to Brest. The
83rd Infantry Division would besiege St. Malo for as long as it
would need to take.

There would be no fast capture of St. Malo this week as
many had hoped, but before this day was done, the Americans
would have a port on the Breton Peninsula.

With the situation in Brittany in a state of flux, where exactly—after Rennes—to send Wood's 4th Armored Division had been one of the many other questions on Troy Middleton's plate at VIII Corps headquarters as the weekend neared. The overall plan was still for them to continue south to "cut the throat" of the Breton Peninsula. It was just a matter of how *deeply*. Should they go southwest toward Quiberon Bay, which lay between Lorient and St. Nazaire? Or should they drive south toward the mouth of the Loire River? Such a move would include St. Nazaire in the bite they took out of the Breton Peninsula.

Since both combat commands of the 4th Armored Division were already more than twenty miles south of Rennes by the end of the day on Friday, Middleton had been presented with an opportunity to adopt a combination of the above two options. He decided that having driven south, the 4th Armored Division would turn west before reaching the Loire. The division would then move on the city of Vannes, located on Quiberon Bay. Though it was a port city, Vannes was insignificant by comparison to neighboring Lorient and St. Nazaire. On the other hand, as such, it would be more lightly defended. Quiberon Bay *would* provide a useful anchorage for American ships, and taking Vannes would fulfill the 4th Armored Division mandate to cut off and seal the neck of the Breton Peninsula.

Saturday morning, Wood ordered Colonel Bruce Clarke's Combat Command A to take a direct route west to Vannes. Meanwhile, General Holmes Dager's Combat Command B was to follow Clarke's right flank, bypassing Vannes (unless Clarke needed help) and continuing toward Lorient. When Clarke had secured Vannes, he would continue west to join Dager at Lorient.

Combat Command A made fast work of the drive on Vannes, covering seventy miles in seven hours. It was a far cry from the Normandy campaign, where a mile a day would have been considered a good day's work. Clarke arrived in the city to discover that the element of surprise so valued by field commanders was on his side. The Germans had no idea that Yanks would be coming to Vannes so fast and so soon. They'd had no time to begin their demolition work on the port facilities, and Combat Command A captured these intact.

At Vannes, Combat Command A linked up with a new Allied army. This fighting force had not arrived in France through ports nor across the invasion beaches. They'd been here all along—the Forces Françaises de l'Intérieur (French Forces of the Interior).

When France had been defeated by Germany in June 1940, the French armed forces had essentially ceased to exist, and France officially accepted Germany as an occupier. However, the French military units that had escaped before the fall of France refused to accept that defeat. These were organized into the Free French Army by General Charles de Gaulle, who vowed to lead them to a victorious reconquest of France.

The former commander of the 4th French Armored Division, de Gaulle had escaped to Britain in June 1940 and had asserted himself as a prominent figure in the French exile community, and eventually as its leader. By the time that planning for Operation Overlord got underway, he had been officially recognized by the Allies as the leader of French armies outside France.

Meanwhile, within France itself, there was a growing militant opposition to the Germans that was known as the Resistance. With covert assistance from the Anglo-American Allies, the Resistance had harassed the Germans through sabotage and espionage. In turn, they aided the Allies by passing vital intelligence information to England. With the Allies now in France, the Resistance was getting bolder.

By the summer of 1944—after four long years of German occupation—the underground Resistance army was ready to begin coming *above* ground. In the wake of Operation Overlord, French general Pierre Koenig was attempting to organize the Forces Françaises de l'Intérieur as an *overt* fighting force under the umbrella of de Gaulle's command that would aid the Allies in the reconquest of France.

At a meeting in July, Koenig and his designated commander for Brittany, Colonel Albert Eon, had been briefed on Allied plans for the Breton Peninsula. Eon's troops were placed under the command of the Third Army and given the task of harassing the German supply lines and seizing key installations—such as bridges—before the Germans could destroy them.

The timetable for formally activating the Forces Françaises de l'Intérieur was dramatically condensed when the Third Army drive into the Breton Peninsula went dramatically faster than had been expected.

Colonel Eon and his staff had parachuted into Brittany by the light of the full moon in the small hours of Friday, landing not far from Vannes. Here, they had linked up with some of the Forces Françaises de l'Intérieur guerrillas on the ground. The following night, American gliders brought in jeeps, ammunition, and other equipment for the French guerrillas, and on Saturday, as Combat Command A was nearing Vannes, the Forces Françaises de l'Intérieur set out to capture the nearby airfield so that transport aircraft could land with additional supplies. The French force was on hand when the Americans arrived. Since most of the French troops knew the city from having been there—and even from having *lived* there—they were able to guide the Yanks into Vannes by the best routes.

By sundown on Saturday the French had captured their airport, and the Americans had taken the first Brittany seaport. It wasn't a large port, and it certainly was not the one that SHAEF would have predicted, but there it was. On top of this, the Americans had now drawn their battle line across the neck of the Breton Peninsula from coast to coast.

Sunday, August 6

For most of Saturday, General Middleton's VIII Corps headquarters had been completely out of touch with General Grow's fast-moving 6th Armored Division. The sketchy communications that the corps headquarters was getting from the fast-moving units were outdated by the time they were received, so Middleton really didn't know what was going on.

The first message that VIII Corps received from Grow on Sunday morning told a story of a tenuous situation. The overextended division had outrun its supply lines and was running out of gas. Grow was concerned that he could be cut off and surrounded if additional American troops were not fast in coming.

Neither Middleton nor PP knew exactly *where* the 6th Armored Division was. Rumors flew. "Confirmed" reports that the Americans had already entered Brest were countered by reports that the Yanks were nowhere near the approaches to the city. Despite it all, everyone knew that the 6th Armored Division was tantalizingly close.

In fact, both Combat Command A and Combat Command B of the 6th Armored Division had been making good progress since Friday. Grow had used the clear, warm weather and the light of the full moon for a night march on Friday that pushed them even closer to their goal. However, they had run into stiff resistance near the village of Huelgoat on Saturday, and this slowed them down considerably.

The hours slipped away, and Grow was unable to reach Brest in time to make the deadline stipulated in Patton's bet with Bradley. By the end of the day on Saturday, they were in the rugged highlands about thirty miles from the city, with advance patrols about fifteen miles out. The drive through Brittany, while it had not won Patton's arguably preposterous bet with Bradley, had been a spectacular accomplishment by a mobile, armored force.

During Sunday, Patton made radio contact with Grow. The 6th Armored Division commander told Patton that he had reached the vicinity of Brest, and that additional infantry would be needed to assault the city. Grow had no idea of the strength of the Brest garrison, but he was sure that their morale and supply situation was poor and that a successful campaign would be a short one. Though they would not reach the vicinity of Brest for several days, Task Force A had already broken off from the St. Malo assault and were working their way west along the northern coastal road.

In the meantime, Grow had been approached by the substantial Forces Françaises de l'Intérieur force that was active in the Brest area. When the battle came, it would be the first cooperative effort in a major battle between American and French troops on French soil since 1918.

Elsewhere in Brittany, Combat Command A of the 4th Armored Division spearhead consolidated their position in Vannes from the previous day. In so doing, they had to beat off a German hit-and-run attack that was launched from the

village Auray, about ten miles west on the coast road. They
struck hard at the Combat Command A perimeter defenses
and did considerable damage before breaking off contact with
the Yanks. Like a runner dashing to steal a base and then having to double back, the Germans reversed course and hurried
back toward Auray.

In order to deal with the situation affirmatively, Colonel
Clarke ordered Combat Command A to move out toward Auray. The objective was not to chase the withdrawing Germans
so much as to expand the perimeter that the command had
drawn around Vannes. At the end of the day, General Wood
contacted Patton directly, sending him an optimistic first-
name-basis radiogram stating: "Dear George: Have Vannes,
will have Lorient [Monday] evening. Vannes intact, hope Lorient the same."

Monday, August 7 (Brittany)

The week would begin with dramatic events, although these
would occur in Normandy (see following chapter) at the initiative of the Germans, not in Brittany at Patton's bidding.

The situation in Brittany had reached a turning point. In
one week, the forces of Patton's Third Army, which was, for
the moment essentially just VIII Corps, had nearly accomplished the initial goals that had been set for it. Rennes had
been captured, and an American line existed across the neck of
the Breton Peninsula. Barring the mopping-up operations, the
Americans were essentially in control of the interior and coastline of the entire peninsula aside from the ports—and capturing the ports had always been envisioned by Patton as a phase
two portion of the operation.

Monday in Brittany saw considerable movement of forces,

but little in the way of decisive action. Essentially, the Americans were drawing their forces into place for the siege of the ports. On the south coast, General Wood made good on his radiogram promise as the two combat commands of the 4th Armored Division each covered fifteen to twenty miles during the day to link up with one another opposite of Lorient.

On the north coast, the situation at St. Malo had become a static artillery dual. As had been the case in Normandy at places such as Caen and St. Lô, there would be a great deal of pounding and pummeling required to break the Germans down. It was another situation wherein the attackers were going to have to destroy the city before they could capture it. A major difference between St. Malo and the Normandy cities was that the latter were merely crossroads towns. St. Malo was specifically designed as a fortress, and it had water on three sides. While Allied naval forces would be able to join in the bombardment, it would be impossible to launch an amphibious attack to capture the fortified city. The only way in was overland.

At Brest, which was now the centerpiece of the Brittany campaign, Colonel Read's Combat Command B was in position outside the gates of the city by late Sunday. General Grow ordered him to launch a Monday morning attack on the fortified city, with the other two combat commands joining in the assault as they arrived. Unlike Colonel Clarke's fast and flawless seizure of Vannes, there was no surprise to be achieved by Grow's division at Brest. The German defenders knew the 6th Armored Division was coming, and they were prepared. Withering artillery fire greeted the Americans.

As was the case with St. Malo, Brest was specifically designed as a fortress and both had recently been reinforced, not only with steel and concrete, but with troops. Both sides at both cities knew they were in for a long siege.

✪ FOUR ✪

COUNTERATTACK AT MORTAIN

Since the beginning of June, and now, *especially* since the beginning of August, the strategic situation for Germany had unraveled considerably. On the Eastern Front, German forces had been all but evicted from Soviet territory, and the Red Army was rushing across the Polish plains toward Warsaw. In France, the Allies seemed to be piling victory upon victory at an ever increasing rate. Even in docile Denmark, there had been huge street protests against German occupation, something that would have been unheard-of only a few months before. At home, Hitler and his closest confidants were still psychologically scarred from the events of July 20.

To the Anglo-American Allies, Germany appeared to be a broken hulk. How could they hold out much longer—especially in France? Would the American boys be "home for Christmas?"

In Berlin, there was talk of withdrawing to an "inner fortress" that excluded all of France and most of Poland. The mountainous country that ran roughly along the border between France and Germany from Switzerland up through the

Ardennes highlands of Belgium to the swampy lowlands of the Netherlands presented a natural defensive line. Behind these natural features lay Germany's Siegfried Line, a formidable defensive obstacle. This would be a more natural place to stop the Allies than the fields of northern France.

However, at the highest levels of command within Germany, there was a dogged determination *not* to give ground. As far as the strategic situation on the Western Front was concerned, a pullback might make sense, but from a political perspective, it was impossible.

From Adolf Hitler's point of view, the thing to do was to defeat the Allies and to win the war. He was obsessed. If the war had been a personal concern before the July 20 assassination attempt, it now verged on mania. He would hear nothing of a withdrawal from France. To underscore his determination, Hitler gave command of the German armies to the one man who he trusted explicitly and completely—*himself.*

Strategically, the Germans had two choices. One was to withdraw to the Seine River north of Paris—still part of Normandy—and to use that as a defensive line. The other was to hold in place and counterattack to put the Allies on the defensive in western Normandy, and hold them on the line where they were now.

The latter option was the one most favored. Of course it pleased Hitler—in whose vocabulary the word "withdraw" did not exist. The option also made sense strategically. To hold France, the Germans should stop the Allies in Normandy, where the terrain was in the favor of the defenders and the defensive line was shorter. Capturing Brittany would give the Americans more territory, but to reach the rest of France—and Germany beyond—they would still have to break out through Normandy.

For the Germans to hold the Yanks in Normandy would require quick action, because both time and square yards of Norman real estate were slipping away.

After the dramatic advances made during Operation Cobra, the Allies had continued to make modest gains in Normandy. During the week that the Third Army had been swooping through Brittany, Lieutenant General Sir Miles Dempsey's British Second Army had moved about ten miles deeper into Normandy near Caen, while the American XIX Corps had pushed forward about fifteen miles on a broad front toward the Norman city of Vire. Meanwhile, VII Corps, with XV Corps on their right flank, had jumped off from Avranches and had moved east about fifteen miles to capture the town of Mortain.

At Oberbefehlshaber West, Günther von Kluge had already undertaken to carry out the will of his Führer. In fact, he had begun planning his counterstroke at the end of July, before the fall of Avranches and the American dash into Brittany had complicated things for him. This meant that recapturing Avranches—and separating the Allies in Normandy from the Allies in Brittany—was an integral part of the plan.

The concept of holding the Anglo-Canadian armies in place seemed to be working. By the first week of August, they had managed to capture less than a third of the ground that the Yanks had swallowed. The long-stated Anglo-Canadian goal of breaking through to the city of Falaise was just as elusive now as it had been a month earlier. It was beginning to take on the dimensions of a mythical quest. Clearly, the German strategy of containment was working well in the British sector. Now, all that von Kluge had to do was come up with the right balance of forces to work that sort of magic against the Yanks.

As the field marshal studied his table of organization, things were not as bad as they might have been. Sure, Paul Hausser's Seventh Army had been badly mauled by the Yanks, but elsewhere the situation was pretty good. Panzer Group West and its constituent corps had successfully held Montgomery's 21st Army Group to positions that were little changed since the first weeks after D-Day. Of these corps, the II SS Panzer Korps was the unit that was successfully holding the British Second Army near Caumont, while the LXXXVI Korps and I SS Panzer Korps were the troops preventing Lieutenant General Harry Crerar's Canadian First Army from breaking out of its perimeter around Caen.

The Canadian First Army, which had taken over the front south of Caen on July 23, was composed of the II Canadian Corps commanded by Lieutenant General Guy Simonds and the I British Corps, under the command of Lieutenant General John Crocker. The 1st Polish Armored Division (1 Polskiej Dywizji Pancernej) had been placed under Crerar's command on August 5. The latter had been organized by Major General Stanislaw Maczek, who had escaped from Poland when it had been defeated and occupied by Germany in 1939. Assembled under British auspices in Scotland from other escaped Polish soldiers, Maczek's division included the 10th Polish Armored Brigade, the 1st and 2nd Polish Armored Regiments, and the 24th Lancers, as well as the 3rd Polish Infantry Brigade and the 8th and 9th Polish Battalions.

Beginning on August 1, von Kluge reorganized his forces with an eye toward launching his counterstroke on Monday morning, August 7. Because the long-awaited Allied invasion of the Pas-de-Calais was now receding as a more remote possibility, Hitler permitted the transfer of four divisions from the Fifteenth Army. Two of these went to Seventh Army opposite the Americans, and two went to Panzer Group West, which was now to be redesignated as the Fifth Panzer Army. From Army Group G, in central France, came the LVIII Panzer Korps with two divisions, both of which were assigned to Seventh Army.

Von Kluge envisioned an offensive that would retake Avranches, separating the Americans in Brittany from their supply lines in Normandy, and cutting the United States Third Army off from the rest of the Allied front.

This would restore the line in Normandy that had existed before Operation Cobra. If all went according to the carefully crafted plan, it would be the first step in what he and Hitler hoped would be an indefinite containment of the Allies in Normandy.

Designated as Operation Lüttich, the attack would take a page out of the playbook that the Americans had used in Operation Cobra—which, of course, was a page from the "First Book of Blitzkrieg" that had served the German armies so well when had they crashed into France four years earlier.

Spearheading the attack would be the Seventh Army's XLVII Korps under General Hans Freiherr von Funck. Recently reinforced with the 1st SS Panzer Division and the 116th Panzer Division, von Funck's corps contained four of the best panzer divisions, and the 17th SS Panzer Grenadiers. These would be thrown against the American VII Corps sector.

Late Sunday, at the last minute, Hitler contacted von Kluge and promised him 140 additional tanks—including sixty Panthers—to augment the sizable number of tanks that XLVII Korps already possessed. The only glitch in this transaction was that Hitler did not realize that von Kluge planned to attack the *next day*.

Hitler told the Oberbefehlshaber West commander that he wanted to *wait* a couple of days and have the Fifth Panzer

Army launch the main part of the attack in their sector. One did not normally argue with the Führer, but von Kluge managed to convince Hitler that a Monday morning attack *somewhere* was better than a midweek attack everywhere—especially when every day of delay raised the risk that the German armored columns might get caught in the open by Allied fighter-bombers.

Hitler, who loved it when his generals talked of attacking—and hated it when they advocated delay—generously acquiesced and went back to his map room for the evening.

Off the hook with his boss, von Kluge gave the green light. Paul Hausser at Seventh Army told him to tell von Funck to get moving.

Monday, August 7 (Normandy)

Since the dramatic and successful conclusion of the Operation Cobra drive against Avranches at the end of July, the Normandy front had essentially become a sideshow to the dashing, slashing action in Brittany. At dawn, on Monday, August 7, those positions suddenly were transposed. Since Operation Cobra, the Allies had felt as though they were advancing against a stunned and demoralized defender in Normandy. These positions too would suddenly be transposed.

The powerful, armored German counterattack that Eisenhower and the SHAEF planners had feared in June, had expected in July, and had forgotten about in August would abruptly burst forth.

Von Funck had authorized no artillery preparation, assuming that the Americans, who thought that *they* were on the offensive, would not have prepared defenses. He planned to trade an artillery barrage for the equally substantive element of surprise. He would get his wish—at least with regard to surprise.

Using Mortain as an anchor point, the German tanks would strike hard and fast, mercilessly chewing up the Americans as they went. That was the plan, but the plan was getting into trouble even before it was executed.

The idea had been for XLVII Panzer Korps to move out under cover of darkness at 10:00 P.M. on Sunday night. When the hour arrived, however, von Funck soon discovered that his spearhead unit, the 1st SS Panzer Division, had only just begun to arrive at the jumping-off point. Traffic problems such as those that had impeded the earlier United States Third Army move into Brittany were by no means unique to the Yanks. As it turned out, there had also been some bureaucratic screwups in detaching the division from the Fifth Panzer Army for this operation. Obviously this fact more than displeased Hans von Funck and Paul Hausser.

Finally, shortly past midnight, in the wee minutes of Monday morning, the counterattack toward Avranches began. Ironically, the 1st SS Panzer Division made very little progress, while the units on its two flanks drove deeply into the American lines.

On the right, the 2nd Panzer Division—simple Wehrmacht troops, not the elite SS—made the deepest penetration, while on the left flank, the 2nd SS Panzer Division overwhelmed the United States 30th Infantry Division troops holding Mortain. The storm troopers captured the city and dashed several miles toward the village of St. Hilaire.

A major glitch in Operation Lüttich came when the 116th SS Panzer Division, which had been moved west of the Seine from Fifteenth Army in July, simply did not join the attack as planned. It was soon discovered that the division commander, General Gerhard Graf von Schwerin, had not issued the order. When called to task, he told Hausser and von Funck that he was afraid that his current position would not have held in the north if he attacked toward the west. For disobeying orders, von Schwerin was promptly relieved of command, effective at 4:00 P.M. on Monday afternoon. The 116th SS Panzer Division launched its planned attack at 4:30 P.M., more than twelve hours late.

Despite the fact that only two of the panzer divisions had actually made progress against the Americans, the attack was considered to have been a success. Surprise was achieved. The first inkling that many Americans had of a German attack came when they heard the rumbling sound of unfamiliar tank motors in the darkness.

American positions were swamped and overrun. The recapture of Mortain buoyed the spirits of the Germans, who were glad to feel the exhilaration of being on the offensive across a broad front once again.

However, in their swift retaking of the town of Mortain, the 2nd SS Panzer Division had omitted an important detail—they had failed to retake a piece of high ground that was known simply as Hill 317. Located just east of Mortain, the hill was so named because the elevation of its peak was 317 meters, and on maps it is labeled simply as 317. A steep, flat-topped hill, it literally casts its morning shadow across Mortain as it rises about 150 feet above the town's main street.

Mortain and Hill 317 had been captured by the United States 1st Infantry Division on August 3, and occupied by the less experienced 30th Infantry Division—commanded by Major General Leland Hobbs—on August 6 as the Big Red One moved south toward Mayenne. Most of the 30th Infantry Division did not actually reach Mortain until at around 8:00 on Sunday evening—just a few hours before the Germans attacked.

The 30th Infantry Division fought a defensive action, but was overwhelmed. The 2nd Battalion—with one company of the 3rd Battalion attached—of the 120th Infantry Regiment, were assigned to man roadblocks north and south of Mortain where roads from the east curve around Hill 317. As the situation at the roadblocks became untenable, the men retreated up the hill, where they found themselves encircled by hostile troops. Captain Reynold Erichson had assumed command of the Yanks on the hill in the absence of higher ranking officers. They had not made it to the hill when the 2nd Battalion command post in Mortain had been overrun by the Germans.

When the Germans discovered that nearly seven hundred Americans were inside his lines, von Funck ordered the 17th SS Panzer Grenadier Division to retake the hill. Though it was actually a regiment-sized unit rather than a division, the grenadiers were armed with heavy weapons and armor, and they were clearly superior in strength to the reinforced battalion surrounded atop Hill 317.

General Lawton Collins, commanding VII Corps, and his boss, General Courtney Hodges at the First Army, both reacted to the German attack with alarm. It was not hard to imagine what would happen should the Germans manage to drive deeply into the lightly defended American rear areas, capturing or destroying supplies, disrupting communications and cutting off front line units. They also saw that the advantages gained in Operation Cobra would literally be going up in smoke if the panzers punched through to Avranches.

To deal with the situation, the commanders moved quickly. Because the 30th Infantry Division had become the first line of defense, the obvious first step was to reinforce this division with armor to confront the German tanks. Combat Command B of the 3rd Armored Division happened to be in the 30th Infantry Division rear area, so this unit was quickly dispatched. Meanwhile, on Monday morning, most of the 2nd "Hell on Wheels" Armored Division happened to be passing through the 30th Armored Division sector en route south to join the 1st Infantry Division near Mayenne. This unit was also diverted.

Collins and Bradley considered pulling the 1st Infantry Division back, but decided that doing so might create another Mortain-type situation at Mayenne, so they did not. Instead, Bradley borrowed the 35th Infantry Division—commanded by Major General Paul Baade—from the Third Army's XX Corps, temporarily attached it to VII Corps and ordered it to attack east through St. Hilaire toward Mortain.

It was fortunate that the 35th Infantry Division and that the troops of the two armored divisions were nearby and uncommitted to other tasks.

Lucky too was the fact that it was another beautiful sunny day in Normandy. The perfect flying weather allowed ten squadrons from the Royal Air Force II Tactical Air Command to operate over the front, blasting the German armor and decimating their support vehicles. This was to be another classic illustration of the importance of tactical airpower in modern mobile warfare. The Germans had none, the Allies had plenty.

By noon, the German attack had come to a stop. Most of the panzer troops were in the woods spreading camouflage netting over their Panthers to hide and protect them from above.

Monday, August 7
(With the Third Army south of Brittany)

For Patton's Third Army, the Brittany campaign was its opening action, and its baptism of fire. Brittany would certainly

consume the attention of VIII Corps in the coming weeks, but
in the grand strategic scheme, Brittany would quickly become
a sideshow. The ultimate objectives, the liberation of France
and the defeat of Germany, would take place to the east of the
Normandy beachheads, not to the west in Brittany.

As VIII Corps pounced on Rennes and turned westward
into the Breton Peninsula, other elements of the Third Army
were preparing to execute a move to the east. In order to accomplish this, the Third Army would go south, flanking the
Normandy battlefront and then execute a left turn. Specifically, Major General Wade Haislip's XV Corps and Major
General Walton Walker's XX Corps would—as VIII Corps
had—drive south through Avranches and continue south,
moving on a line east of Rennes, into the Maine and Anjou regions and toward the Loire River.

Having reached the Loire, which flows from east to west
on a line about one hundred miles south of Paris, they would
turn east toward Orleans, a move that would essentially lead
to a wide encirclement of the French capital and the surrounding Ile-de-France region.

Though the political importance of Paris was being discussed at higher levels, the city possessed little tactical significance. The purpose of the Third Army drive on the
Ile-de-France and the Orleans regions was that the vast open
country afforded excellent terrain for fast-moving armored
operations. Once captured, the flatness of the region would be
excellent for locating tactical airfields. Indeed, the German
Luftwaffe had already constructed a number of large air bases
in the area, which could be dusted off and quickly put to use
by Allied tactical aircraft.

On Friday, having gotten the green light from Bradley for
a drive toward Le Mans, Patton had ordered both corps to

move out. By Monday XX Corps had reached Vitre, roughly due east of Rennes, and XV Corps was in Mayenne, northeast of Vitre. They were spearheaded by Major General Stafford LeRoy Irwin's 5th Infantry Division. At noon on Monday, Major General Hugh Gaffey, Patton's Third Army chief of staff, visited Irwin's command post and conveyed Patton's orders for the division to press south toward the Loire, specifically targeting the cities of Nantes, at the mouth of the Loire, and Angers, which was about fifty miles upriver.

Because moving toward the east was to be the next step in the overall scheme of things, Irwin decided to make Angers, the easternmost of the two cities, his primary objective, and he sent Colonel Charles Yuill's 11th Infantry Regiment in that direction. As Yuill quickly discovered, German armed presence in the northern part of the Main and Anjou regions was virtually nonexistent. As a result, the 11th Infantry Regiment was entrenched on the bank of the Loire, about two miles west of Angers, by Monday evening.

Tuesday, August 8 (Normandy)

The small hours of Monday had seen the unexpected but predictable German thrust toward Avranches. The small hours of Tuesday would witness the unexpected but predictable Canadian effort to break the long and frustrating deadlock south of Caen and get on the road to Falaise. Royal Air Force heavy bombers reprised their role from Operation Goodwood three weeks previous, slamming the German troops of the I SS Panzer Korps.

In an offensive designated as Operation Totalize, the Canadian First Army troops, in conjunction with General Maczek's 1st Polish Armored Division, jumped off at sunrise, supporting their drive with an estimated 600 tanks. Unlike the Germans and Americans, who had been achieving great success with massed armor assaults—especially when supported by air power—the Canadians and Poles had a great deal of trouble making even a few miles with their tanks.

For the Germans, this was little consolation. When Heinrich Eberbach mustered the resources of the Fifth Panzer Army to blunt the offensive, two of the three panzer divisions that he had promised to von Kluge to exploit the Mortain breakthrough had to be recalled. These were only part of the troops scheduled for the drive on Avranches that, instead, had to be diverted to meet the Canadians.

On the Mortain Front, von Funcke was unable to exploit his success of Monday. The 2nd SS Panzer Division was threatened by the United States 2nd Armored Division, while the 2nd Panzer Division—which had made the most progress on Monday—actually found itself having to pull back to protect its flanks.

Von Funck's XLVII Korps was not going to reach Avranches on Tuesday, but neither would the Americans be able to break through to Mortain to save the brave battalions of the 120th Infantry Regiment who were still trapped on Hill 317. As the 17th SS Panzer Grenadier Division launched repeated attempts to retake Hill 317, the Yanks took heavy casualties, but still resisted. As the sun went down Tuesday night, they were still holding out, but running low on ammunition and rations.

Only about five miles west of Hill 317, the United States 30th Infantry Division was engaged in a frantic pitched battle. German infiltrators seemed to have permeated their lines everywhere, ambushing patrols, cutting communications lines and generally disrupting things. Nevertheless, the Yanks responded well to the chaos and did not give ground. Instead, they managed to hold the enemy at bay and destroy a sizable amount of German armor in the bargain.

As a result of its actions around the French town that most of its personnel had never heard of before, the 30th Infantry Division—previously nicknamed after Andrew Jackson as "Old Hickory"—came to be called the "Rock of Mortain."

Tuesday, August 8 (Brittany)

In practical military operations, an offensive always takes a back seat to a defensive action. On Sunday, Patton and his field commanders had been confident that their requests for reinforcements for the Brittany action would be fulfilled as fast as SHAEF and Bradley's 12th Army Group headquarters could comply. After Monday, it became clear that they would have to make do with what they had.

At Brest, General Grow attempted to capture the city by the simplest and most direct way. At dawn, he sent a jeep into the city flinging a white flag. Grow's division intelligence officer, Major Ernest Arnold, and a German-speaking sergeant named Alex Castle drove up to the German perimeter and asked to speak to the senior officer in command of Brest.

The blindfolded Americans were taken to a subterranean command post, where Castle proceeded to read a memorandum from Grow, since none of the Germans present in the room were able to read English. The memo explained that Allied naval, air, and ground artillery were prepared to destroy Brest. Grow was offering the Germans a chance to "surrender in the face of these overwhelming forces." He went on to invite the German commander to come to the 6th Armored Division headquarters to discuss specifics.

The Germans firmly declined Grow's offer. Arnold and Castle returned to American lines.

The German offensive in Normandy had to have been encouraging to the Germans within the Brest garrison. Knowing that their countrymen were on the offensive in Normandy was good for morale, even if it was unrealistic to assume that the Germans who'd taken Mortain could break through far enough to affect the situation in Brittany.

The orders to the Brest garrison had been to defend the city to the last man, and they showed no inclination to the contrary.

Wednesday, August 9
(With the Third Army on the Loire)

South of the Mortain battlefield and far from Brittany, Walton Walker's XX Corps and other Third Army units were moving quickly and encountering little or no resistance as they drove south in order to turn east.

On Monday evening the 11th Infantry Regiment, the forward element of LeRoy Irwin's 5th Infantry Division, had reached the Loire River, just two miles west of Angers. On Tuesday, Walker had ordered Irwin to move quickly against Angers, as well as Nantes, at the mouth of the Loire. Irwin was loath to spread himself too thin, so he spent Tuesday consolidating his forces in order to deal with whatever the German defenders may have prepared for him in the cities. He was well aware of the stiff resistance that VIII Corps had faced in the Brittany cities, and he did not want to have his troops rush into Angers and Nantes too lightly armed.

By Wednesday evening, elements of the 5th Infantry Division had encircled Nantes to the north, sealing access to the city on the right bank of the Loire. At Angers, the 11th Infantry Regiment had captured a bridge across the Loire, and by the end of the day, the city was essentially surrounded by the 11th Infantry Regiment on one side and the 10th Infantry Regiment on the other.

Meanwhile, Wade Haislip's XV Corps had been on the move since the weekend, meeting little resistance as it dashed from Mayenne through Laval, to the outskirts of LeMans. As had been the case with XX Corps on his right flank, Haislip's columns moved at about the top speed of their slowest vehicles. A sizable number of Germans had been encountered, but—unlike those engaged in the fighting up north around Mortain—they were mainly in small disorganized groups that were generally more willing to surrender than to fight.

Indeed, the 90th Infantry Division, commanded by Major General Raymond McLain, swept up about 1,500 prisoners on the road to Le Mans. By the end of the day on Tuesday, elements of the 90th Infantry Division were in Le Mans and the 5th Armored Division had circled east of the city to cut off a possible German retreat.

They didn't have to wait long. Americans under Major Edward Hamilton camouflaged two Sherman tanks and several machine gun nests along a tree-lined section of the road beyond Le Mans. A column of about fifty vehicles came down the pike, oblivious to the possible presence of the GIs. Hamilton estimated that they were traveling at about forty miles per hour when the Yanks opened fire at a range of about thirty feet.

The lead truck was knocked out instantly. Suddenly there was a screeching of brakes, the crash of vehicles being rear-ended and the grinding of tank treads thrown into reverse. The Americans raked the German column with machine gun fire as the two Shermans systematically dropped 75mm shells into selected targets. Said Hamilton, "The Germans never knew what hit them."

When it was over, all fifty vehicles were destroyed, and 230 Germans straggled out of the chaos to surrender.

Thursday, August 10 (Normandy)

Adolf Hitler awoke on Wednesday at his Wolf's Lair headquarters at Rastenberg in East Prussia, hundreds of miles from Normandy. He was in a mood to exercise his penchant for micromanagement. He felt that *today* was the day for General Heinrich Eberbach and the Fifth Panzer Army to achieve the success that had been hoped for with Operation Lüttich on Monday.

The Führer saw the Fifth Panzer Army stemming the Canadian First Army advance north of Falaise, and he could still taste the sweetness of the way that Operation Lüttich had gobbled up Mortain. However, he apparently failed to fully comprehend how deeply Haislip's XV Corps and Walker's XX Corps had cut into the German left flank.

Hitler ordered Eberbach to sidestep to the south and west, cut around the American right flank and then drive northwest into Avranches. Reinforced by additional units that were dribbling in from Fifteenth Army, the I SS Panzer Korps would be tasked with holding the sector around Falaise if the Canadians continued to get pushy. The units assigned to the offensive operation would be under Eberbach's command as "Panzer Group Eberbach," while Eastern Front armored warfare veteran, Generaloberst Josef "Sepp" Dietrich, would take over the remainder of the Fifth Panzer Army.

The Führer felt that timing was the key to success, so he

reserved this decision for the person in whom he had the greatest confidence—*himself.*

He scheduled the operation for Friday, August 11. It would not take long for Eberbach to calculate that he would *not* have enough tanks on hand by Friday, nor would he have the fuel to support a breakthrough even if it could be achieved. He imagined a replay of the Mortain breakthrough, where a force that was too small for the job found itself breaking through only to become bogged down without achieving its objective.

As Hitler awoke in his smoky bunker in East Prussia, General Dwight Eisenhower awoke in a tent in Normandy.

Though the Supreme Allied Commander had visited the front a number of times in the previous two months, Wednesday had marked the official relocation of the SHAEF headquarters from London to the continent. Now that the Allies had swallowed 20,000 square miles of France, the Norman fields where the hedgerow warfare and see-saw battles of June had been fought was changing. Normandy was morphing into a sprawling Allied base complex.

Cattle munched grass amid acres of materiel dumps and busy supply depots. There were piles of truck tires and mountains of wooden crates of ration cans. Mobile vehicle repair facilities were parked beneath the apple trees and draped with camouflage netting. Tanks that had been damaged at Avranches were being rebuilt and rolled back out to rejoin the drive toward the heart of Paris.

One of the most remarkable of the facilities in Normandy was a truck factory. To save time in Detroit and space on the Liberty Ships transporting supplies to Europe, factories in the United States were packing unassembled truck parts in crates.

By the first week in August, the US Army Quartermaster Corps was rolling out 150 "assembled in Normandy" trucks each day.

Thursday, August 10 (With the Third Army on the Loire)

A funny thing happened on the way to Paris.

The dash of Patton's army across France was faster than anyone had suspected. So fast, in fact, that it was hard to keep track of it. On August 10, a strange thing happened in the dueling propaganda machines of Axis and Allies. On Thursday, SHAEF announced that the US Army spearhead was approximately 100 miles from Paris. Meanwhile, an Oberbefehlshaber West pronouncement emanating by radio from Paris itself on Wednesday night had placed the leading edge of the American juggernaut at a distance of 140 kilometers—just 87 miles. The American spin doctors were playing it more conservatively than were the Germans!

Even as Hitler was dreaming of another stab at Avranches, Patton's Third Army was securing the Maine, the vast French region north of the Loire River. Le Mans was now officially under Allied control, and Angers had been cut off from resupply from the south and it would be captured on Friday. To the north and east, the 90th Infantry Division was tightening its hold on positions in and around Le Mans. It was hard to imagine—certainly Hitler did not yet fully comprehend the significance—of the fall of the city and the palatial chateau of the Countess du Houssoix that had, so recently, served as the German Seventh Army headquarters. Just a few weeks earlier, Le Mans had been considered sufficiently far from the battlefront to still serve as the field headquarters for Günther von Kluge.

Friday, August 11 (Normandy)

Heinrich Eberbach was in a difficult situation. The Allies were pressing him from all sides, and this was the deadline that Hitler himself had set for a renewal of the Operation Lüttich offensive against Avranches. On one hand, he was encouraged by how easily the Canadians had been stopped, and he hoped that the American offensive might have been likewise nipped to a halt by the Mortain adventure. On the other hand, he had to have been worried—and worried deeply—by the Third Army penetration toward the Loire. He might have thought about the latter in a different light, but it was still yet to be acknowledged that General George Patton was in command of the Third Army.

Apparently feeling that the situation in Normandy—if not in the Maine and Anjou—afforded some breathing space, Eberbach proposed delaying the Führer's attack for more than a week, until August 20. He reasoned that he would be in a stronger position by then, and there was a prediction of bad flying weather, which would keep Allied air power away from the panzers.

As this suggestion went up the chain of command, the idea of a delay did not play well. Furthermore, von Kluge was disturbed by the advances being made to the south by XV Corps and XX Corps. He smelled an encirclement in the making, and he didn't like the odor. He felt that using the panzer divisions against the Americans south of Normandy was a better use of his resources.

At noon on Friday, von Kluge brought both Eberbach and Paul Hausser together for a meeting at which they all agreed that another attempt to break through to Avranches was not going to work, and to attempt such a gambit was a waste of the assets that they had at their disposal in Normandy. When presented to Hitler in the overall context of *preserving forces for alternate offensive action*, the plan was approved by the Führer's headquarters.

By the end of the day the general withdrawal from the Mortain area—hastened by the impending advance of the United States 35th Infantry Division—had been authorized. Meanwhile, von Kluge ordered that Panzer Group Eberbach be reoriented against XV Corps to the south near Le Mans.

Friday, August 11 (On the Loire)

Günther von Kluge's feeling of foreboding and fear of entrapment was not without justification. As Hitler had schemed another attack aimed at battle-axing through the American lines at Avranches, General Omar Bradley was doing some planning of his own, and on a much larger scale than Hitler. General Eisenhower had visited Bradley's 12th Army Group field headquarters on Tuesday, and they had come up with a plan to encircle the German forces that had broken through at Mortain.

The Third Army had built up a great deal of momentum and was poised to move eastward, debouching into the region between Orleans and Paris. The idea that Eisenhower and Bradley developed involved having the eastbound Third Army units swing *north* out of Le Mans toward the city of Alençon. This city was located roughly due east of Mortain, directly north of Le Mans and directly south of where the Canadian First Army was entrenched north of Falaise. The ideal result for Eisenhower would be von Kluge's worst nightmare—encirclement.

On Friday morning, Patton's Third Army began to implement the plan. Haislip's XV Corps turned east, and three of

General Walker's four divisions, the 35th and 80th Infantry Divisions, and the 7th "Lucky Seventh" Armored Division pivoted to the northeast from the area between Le Mans and Mayenne.

Saturday, August 12 (Hill 317)

Despite the fact that there would no further attempt to cut through the American lines at Avranches, the Germans had stubbornly held on to their gains in the Mortain sector through the end of the week. Units such as the 2nd SS Panzer Division fought relentlessly as the 35th Infantry Division attempted to push north.

Mortain itself had remained in German hands all week, and the troops atop Hill 317 remained surrounded, and still desperately resisting attempts by the 17th SS Panzer Grenadier Division to take the hill.

On Wednesday, an attempt to resupply the trapped men by air using artillery spotting aircraft failed when the planes ran into a fusillade of German gunfire. Larger transport aircraft had made a second attempt on Thursday, but much of what they managed to drop fell on the German side of the perimeter. By Thursday evening, several successful attempts had been made to drop supplies onto the hilltop by packing them into 105mm and 155mm artillery shells.

Also on Thursday, the 35th Infantry Division had shouldered its way back to the highway that ran from Mortain south toward Barenton. This accomplished, the now-exhausted 35th had the job of undertaking a frontal assault on Hill 317 to relieve the men pinned down there.

To retake the hill, General Baade had only one remaining fresh battalion, the 1st Battalion of the 320th Infantry Regi-

ment, commanded by one of the youngest battalion com-
manders in the Army. Major Bill Gillis, a 1941 graduate of the
US Military Academy at West Point, had been the captain of
Army's football team in the 1940 season.

As shells from the 35th Division Artillery filled the air
and slammed into the German positions, and as P-47s
bombed and strafed the German positions only four hundred
yards ahead, Gillis and his battalion fought their way forward.
By nightfall on Thursday, they had reached the foot of Hill
317. Throughout the night and most of the next day, the situation had remained fluid. Casualties were high, and Gillis
himself was wounded in the hand. For hours it was question-
able as to whether the rescuers were gaining ground or
whether they were themselves becoming surrounded.

Finally, on Saturday morning, the 1st Battalion broke
through the SS Grenadier lines and relieved the beleaguered
troops. The battalion received a Distinguished Unit Citation,
and Gillis received a Silver Star. Nearly half of the men on Hill
317 had been killed or wounded, but more than three hundred had survived unharmed.

The Battle of Mortain would now recede into military
history, soon to be overshadowed by much bigger things.
However, its importance—and what might have been—was
not forgotten. As General Eisenhower wrote later of the battle,
"Had the German tanks and infantry succeeded in breaking
through at Mortain, the predicament of all troops beyond that
point would have been serious, in spite of our ability to partially supply them by airplane."

FIVE

THE FALAISE GAP AND THE GERMAN COLLAPSE IN NORMANDY

Von Kluge's Operation Lüttich counterattack had almost succeeded, but the Americans had beat him back—and then some. Von Kluge was now watching his tactical situation unravel precariously. By August 13, the Yanks controlled the Loire River line from St. Nazaire to Angers. In the first two weeks of August, the Americans—mainly the Third Army—had been able to capture five times as much ground as all the Allied armies had taken during all of June and July.

By the end of the Third Army's second week in action, many things had changed. Brittany was in American hands, but even more important, a rapid advance of just a few days had secured a huge salient of the Maine region east of Rennes, north of the Loire and south of the German positions just east of Mortain.

As both Eisenhower and von Kluge now realized, this American army on the Loire—that was yet to be revealed as Patton's Third Army—had presented an unexpected opportunity for a change in overall strategy for Normandy and the Allied drive eastward toward the Seine River. As Bradley and

Eisenhower had agreed in their August 8 meeting, the Allies had a unique opportunity to surround and cut off the German defenders of Normandy.

To bite off the Germans in Normandy, Eisenhower and Bradley needed an upper jaw and a lower jaw.

General Sir Bernard Montgomery's 21st Army Group, comprising the Canadian First Army and Lieutenant General Sir Miles Dempsey's British Second Army would form the upper jaw. Their job would be to break south through Falaise toward Argentan, about twenty miles away. They had been tied down near Caen for essentially two months trying to do this, and SHAEF hoped that they'd finally be able to do it now.

The eastbound Third Army units would form the lower jaw in what was hoped to be a decisive bite into the German jugular. Patton's army would swing north out of Le Mans through Alençon toward Argentan. This drive was at least twice as far as the distance that the Canadians had to traverse, but it was reasoned that the Canadians would have a tougher time breaking through well-prepared defenses.

In any case, when the Canadians moving south linked up with the Yanks coming north, the Germans would be snared between Argentan and Mortain. Encirclement would be achieved.

If the key element of Allied operations during the second week of August was encirclement, von Kluge's plan would have to be to not permit this to happen. He could read a map as well as Eisenhower and Montgomery, and it was clear to him what the next move by the Allies would be. If they succeeded, the bulk of von Kluge's combat troops would be encircled and unable to escape from Normandy.

At first, von Kluge had agreed with Hitler and had envisioned counterattack as a means to this end. Now, but inevitably, he would turn to the practical. The best he could now hope for in Normandy was to attempt to prevent the Allies from cutting off the east-west corridor between Falaise and Alençon—the "Falaise Gap."

Elsewhere, the changes would be less dramatic in the coming days. The Battle of Brittany had changed dramatically by the end of the first week of August, from fast action to virtual stalemate. Strategically, the battle was over. The die had been cast. The peninsula had been captured and was firmly in the control of the Third Army. However, the strategic objectives, the seaports, were essentially unattainable. While the effort to capture St. Malo would go forward, Brest, Lorient, and St. Nazaire were so heavily defended that it would be impossible to capture them intact.

Of course, this was small comfort to the Germans. They could not use the ports because they were surrounded by Allied troops and naval forces. Meanwhile, there were a sizable number of German soldiers in the seaport garrisons whose fighting effectiveness was over. They would be killed or captured without ever again serving a useful function on a battlefield. The only advantage to the Germans in possessing the ports was that the Allies *didn't* have them.

Patton and many of his subordinate commanders—notably the outspoken Tiger Jack Wood of the 4th "Breakthrough" Armored Division—had been convinced early in the Brittany campaign that they were going in the wrong direction. Why, they wondered, should the Third Army be concentrating its offensive thrust toward the west when the true objectives—Paris, the rest of France, and Germany itself—lay to the east?

Indeed, Wood had advocated moving east after his division had succeeded in capturing the city of Rennes on August

4. A little over a week later, on August 13, Wood got his wish, as the 4th Armored Division was transferred from VIII Corps to Major General Gilbert Cook's XII Corps, which was being brought up to strength for the next phase of the Third Army's great offensive in the east.

From August 1 through the end of the day on August 12, the 4th Armored Division had racked up an impressive record. During that period, the division had taken about 5,000 prisoners and had destroyed or captured nearly 250 German vehicles. At the same time, the 4th Armored Division had suffered fewer than 100 men killed in action and had lost just 15 of its own tanks.

Saturday, August 12

By the weekend, the focal point of the battlefield across southern Normandy had changed. Places such as Avranches and Mortain were consigned to history. The points on both the German and Allied maps that were now getting the most attention were Argentan and Alençon. The Germans saw these as key defensive points and the Allies saw them as the key objectives. The word on everyone's lips was "encirclement." Planners on both sides agreed that when XV Corps and the Canadian First Army met at Argentan, the Falaise Gap would be closed and the Germans would be trapped.

Haislip's XV Corps was moving north from Le Mans. The corps contained the 79th and 90th Infantry Divisions, and was spearheaded by the United States 5th Armored Division and the 2nd French Armored Division under Major General Jacques Leclerc. The latter was the largest intact Free French unit within the Allied command structure. It had been formed in North Africa a year earlier from French units that

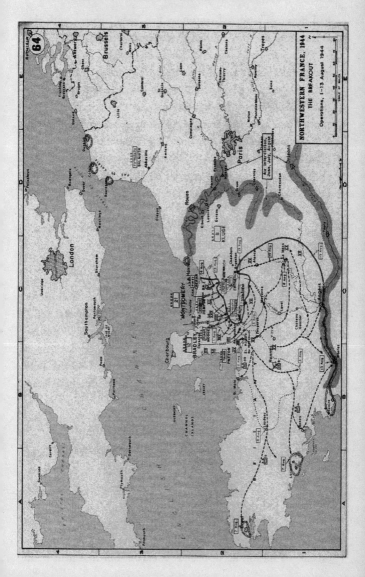

had never surrendered, and who had been fighting with the British Eighth Army in the desert war since 1941.

Though the Forces Françaises de l'Intérieur and other Resistance units had been harassing the Germans for four years, the deployment of Leclerc's division would mark the first time since the defeat of the French Army in 1940 that a conventional French division would be back in action on French soil.

As Leclerc would explain, in a radio broadcast to the French people on Monday, "We set foot again in our country at the head of French troops after having kept the French flag in the fight without interruption [since the fall of France in 1940]."

Facing XV Corps north of Alençon would be Panzer Group Eberbach, which took over the sector on Saturday. Spearheading Eberbach's group would be the 116th Panzer Division. Having gotten off to a delayed start in Operation Lüttich, the 116th Panzer had gone on to play a key role in the fighting around Mortain. Von Kluge would assign two additional panzer divisions to Eberbach, but these would not be available until at least Sunday.

On Saturday morning, the two XV Corps armored divisions pressed north, with the 2nd French Armored Division on the left and the United States 5th Armored Division on the right. Having reached the edge of Alençon on Friday night, Leclerc's command passed through the city on Saturday.

The speed with which the Allies were moving kept them one step ahead of German planners. If Leclerc was meeting and exceeding his timetable, Eberbach was behind schedule. Saturday had been a key day lost to him. The speed with which the XV Corps spearhead was moving upset the plans for defending the area. Von Kluge had intended Eberbach to attack the spearheads at or near Alençon, but that plan went out the window when the French buzzed through the city before the German armor could get into position to attack. This was a blow to German quartermasters as well as to German schedulers, because of the sizable German supply dumps in and around Alençon. Eberbach was now forced to think in terms of defense rather than counterattack.

Meanwhile, Allied planners had discussed the possibility that the Forest of Ecouves, north of Alençon on the way to Argentan, could potentially provide the Germans with a strong defensive position. It might have been, but until Saturday, Eberbach had not been thinking of a fixed defense. The French division spent most of Saturday securing the area, while the 5th Armored Division circled east of the forest.

By the end of the day, the Allies were moving into position to attack Argentan, even as Eberbach was pouring men and tanks into the city. By daybreak on Sunday morning, the entire 116th Panzer Division was in town, and advance units of the 1st SS Panzer Division and the 2nd Panzer Division were arriving.

Sunday, August 13

The day began with Haislip's XV Corps having essentially achieved its objective. The task assigned had been to push north through the rolling hills and broad meadows around Argentan and wait for the Canadians to close the Falaise Gap. Though Argentan was still in German hands, the 2nd French Armored Division was poised for the attack, and the 5th Armored Division was already east of the city, waiting for the Canadians to drive south through Falaise, about twenty miles to the north.

The obvious question was whether the 5th Armored Division should move out and accomplish the strategic goal of encirclement, or whether they should remain at their assigned objective and wait. Haislip favored the former, and his query to Patton received the predictable order to move out toward Falaise—which was still yet to be captured by the Canadians.

Patton consulted his boss, General Omar Bradley, commanding 12th Army Group. Bradley felt that the Yanks should adhere to the original tactical plan. In one of the most controversial decisions of the war, he overrode Patton's orders to Haislip and ordered XV Corps to halt at Argentan.

Bradley was concerned that the Americans meeting the Canadians at other than the predetermined place was an invitation to disaster in the form of "friendly fire" accidents. He also wished to respect the integrity of the predetermined jurisdictional boundary between his 12th Army Group and General Montgomery's 21st Army Group. Bradley made the decision unilaterally, without consulting Montgomery. The latter would later state that he would have been happy to let Patton close the Falaise Gap while the British and Canadians turned east toward the Seine.

On the German side, Eberbach was faced with a situation of two little, too late. He greeted Sunday morning with one panzer division, but just parts of the two others that von Kluge had promised. Had all three been at his disposal—and at full strength—before the weekend, he might have been able to execute what von Kluge had had in mind for him. He could have launched a decisive blow at XV Corps south of Alençon, buying time and halting the Third Army. Now, Alençon was just a memory, and Argentan was nearly surrounded.

By the end of the day, nearly all of the German commanders realized that the time to maneuver was over. It was time to retreat. Generaloberst Sepp Dietrich recommended to von Kluge that both Seventh Army and the Fifth Panzer Army be withdrawn immediately.

Monday, August 14

The week began with General Crerar's Canadian First Army—with the Polish units attached—still pushing toward the elusive objective of capturing Falaise, as they had been the week before and the week before that.

South of Caen General Montgomery's troops were converging between the Orne River and the Laize River. Bois-Halbout had been captured. From Bretteville-sur-Laize, a drive through Barbery took the troops into Moulins.

For the Yanks, the tactical situation had changed entirely. The Americans were ordered to move from offense to defense. The fast-moving spearhead of XV Corps had been ordered to halt in place. With the XV Corps advance stopped, VII Corps of the First Army moved in to cover its left flank. Meanwhile, Bradley had authorized Patton to allow elements of XV Corps to move east from Argentan, while most of the force waited for the Canadians. Patton relayed this to Haislip, who ordered the 5th Armored Division and the 79th Infantry Division to begin such a move, while Leclerc's Free French armored division took over primary responsibility of the static line at Argentan.

In the case of the Germans, there was no longer even a thought of counterattack, although the Führer's headquarters and Oberbefehlshaber West still had not officially sanctioned a withdrawal. While von Kluge favored such a move, he officially passed along Hitler's explicit orders that a withdrawal should *not* take place. It was like spitting into the wind.

When von Kluge paid a visit to Sepp Dietrich's command

post on Monday evening, he almost couldn't get through the traffic jam of troops heading *away* from the front. When he finally located Dietrich, he got the bad news—the Canadians had broken through German lines, and they were closing in on Falaise.

Adolf Hitler's own incisive assessment was that the deterioration in the German situation in Normandy was directly attributable to the failure of Operation Lüttich to reach Avranches a week earlier. This appraisal was based, as always, on his imagination, rather than the reality of the tactical situation.

Three weeks after a coterie of generals had tried to kill him, the already paranoid Führer blamed and distrusted his generals. Of course, these generals—from von Kluge down—knew that the Battle of Normandy was over and that preserving the surviving troops for the subsequent defense of Germany itself was a far more heroic thing to do than persisting in a suicidal defense of the Norman apple orchards. By now, there was only a pretense of obeying Hitler's demands for vigorous counterattacks.

Farther west within the United States First Army sector, Major General Leonard Gerow's V Corps and Major General Charles Corlett's XIX Corps were on the move, pushing from west to east into the pocket of Germans. They met little resistance, because the Germans they pushed against were withdrawing. Unfortunately, the effect was simply to push the Germans *through* the Falaise Gap. Essentially, the flow of German troops through the gap would continue like water through an open faucet. With the Third Army having been ordered to hold in place, the job of finally turning off this faucet rested with the Canadian First Army.

Having renewed their assault toward Falaise on Saturday,

the Canadians continued the effort on Monday, now supported by hundreds of Royal Air Force heavy bombers, who dropped nearly 4,000 tons of high explosives on German positions.

Tuesday, August 15

It was on Tuesday that SHAEF finally "came clean," and made the official announcement that General George Patton was—and had been for two weeks—leading the Third Army in Normandy. Quoted in the SHAEF communique, General Eisenhower commented that Patton was "where he belongs."

In Washington, D.C., the Senate Military Affairs Committee unanimously approved a permanent second star and the rank of Major General for Patton, who was already wearing the three stars and the brevet rank of Lieutenant General. (In wartime, field commanders typically have a brevet rank a grade or two ahead of their permanent rank.)

Senator Albert Chandler, Democrat of Kentucky, commented that Patton had demonstrated himself to be "the greatest tank commander in the world."

The media, who were taken with the colorful Patton, had a field day as it was finally officially revealed that the boldly successful campaigns in Brittany, Maine, and Anjou had been Patton-led Third Army operations.

In fact, most reporters in the field had been privy to this "worst kept secret" for more than a week, and were impatiently abiding by the official news embargo. *The New York Times* was finally able to report on Tuesday that "the leader of the United States Third Army, which, with the tank movements that has been the mark of General Patton's command, has run roughshod over the Germans in western France."

The New York Times editorial page would call the first two weeks of Patton's return to active command as "a brilliant page in military history." The same editorial did mention the "slapping incident" of a year earlier and General Eisenhower's controversial decision not to send Patton home in disgrace in 1943. The editorial referred to Eisenhower's having returned Patton to command of a field army. It noted that "General Eisenhower's decision would appear to have been vindicated."

When the official announcement was made, words penned in anticipation by embargoed journalists filled the newswires. An Associated Press piece by a reporter who had been in Brittany gushed that "Patton plunged on, often riding at the head of his tank columns. . . . Many military men were amazed at General Patton's audacity. His armored forces slashed through disorganized German forces for Brest, Lorient and Nantes. Frequently American units had Germans on all sides and had to send out tanks to escort their supplies. Fast mechanized cavalry detachments cut the German pockets into smaller units and spread confusion."

John McVane of NBC Radio, in a wireless report from France that was broadcast in the United States on Wednesday, reported that the officers and men of the Third Army were "100 percent behind their chief, completely confident of his qualities as a leader and are filled with almost adoring admiration for his brilliant campaign in France. . . . They swear by him, even when they're straining tired nerves and muscles to do more than they ever dreamed possible. They believe, as do many other observers here, that credit for the Brittany campaign should go chiefly to one man, General Patton."

While the action in northwestern France on Tuesday was moving closer to a climax than anyone yet realized, it was overshadowed in the headlines by events elsewhere in France. August

15 marked the *second* Allied invasion of France. This time, the objective was the sun-washed Riviera, six hundred miles south of foggy, soggy Normandy. Operation Dragoon (originally designated Operation Anvil) saw four American divisions of VI Corps and three Free French divisions of II French Corps—all components of the United States Seventh Army commanded by Lieutenant General Alexander "Sandy" Patch—come ashore at locations between Cannes and St. Tropez.

The tactical situation in the south of France could not have been more different than that which had been experienced in Normandy five weeks earlier. The weather was sensational, and the Allies faced virtually no opposition on the beachhead from the German Nineteenth Army.

In Normandy, the German positions were crumbling. The lack of ammunition and fuel was exacerbated by confusion. To make matters worse, General Field Marshal Günther von Kluge had vanished. He left Sepp Dietrich's Fifth Panzer Army field headquarters early Tuesday morning, and headed for an inspection of Panzer Group Eberbach and Seventh Army. When he did not show up, frenzied efforts were made to locate the commander of Oberbefehlshaber West. Eventually, he was located. An Allied air attack had forced von Kluge and his entourage to get off the road and under cover. In the process, their radio had been knocked out.

When he finally did make his rendezvous with Eberbach and with Paul Hausser at Seventh Army, von Kluge found that the situation report was grim. Both the United States First Army and the Canadian First Army were making steady progress against the Falaise pocket. The Allies were now breaking through at so many points that it was hard to know where to turn.

Patton's Third Army, meanwhile, presented a curious paradox. On Tuesday, August 15, it had been active for just two weeks, yet it had captured more territory than the other three Allied Armies in Northern France combined. It had achieved a momentum that made the others look as though they were standing still, yet General Bradley had ordered the Third Army to literally *stand still* at Argentan, which was arguably the most important place in Northern France *not* to stand still.

Of course, not all of the Third Army was standing still. Though much of Wade Haislip's XV Corps cooled their heels at Argentan, the 5th Armored Division, 79th Infantry Division, and 90th Infantry Division were probing toward the east toward Dreux. Patton had transferred the 7th Armored Division, commanded by Major General Lindsay Silvester, from the Third Army command to Walton Walker's XX Corps for a move directly west from Alençon toward Chartres. Meanwhile, on the southern flank of the Third Army's advance to the east, Gilbert Cook's XII Corps was pointed toward Orleans, spearheaded by the Sherman tanks of Tiger Jack Wood's 4th Armored Division.

Cook had established a temporary field headquarters for his corps in Le Mans on Sunday while the 4th Armored Division came in from Brittany and the 35th Infantry Division made its way south after its involvement in the actions at Mortain. By Tuesday, all was in order and the corps had jumped off for its drive to the east.

And what a drive it was!

During the battles in the hedgerows of Normandy in June and July, an advance of a mile in a day was considered to be an event worth celebration. The British took more than a month to penetrate ten miles from the D-Day beaches. In the three weeks before the capture of St. Lô, the front had been pushed back by fewer than ten miles. On Tuesday, August 15,

XV Corps managed to travel *eighty miles* from Le Mans to the outskirts of Orleans—despite a large number of damaged and destroyed bridges.

The 4th Armored Division's Combat Command A, meanwhile, had advanced from Nantes, at the mouth of the Loire, a distance of about *one hundred miles*.

Nightfall on Tuesday found the advance guard of Cook's corps in control of the heavily fortified Luftwaffe air base at Orleans. Though it bristled with guns, the big base was largely unmanned and virtually deserted.

At that same hour, General Silvester's 7th Armored Division tank crews had a clear view of the legendary cathedral of Notre Dame de Chartres on the not-so-distant horizon. Their rapid advance of about *sixty miles* had been facilitated by the fact that as Allied armies neared Paris, the roads improved dramatically. Slogging through the muddy ruts of rural Normandy and the narrow lanes of Brittany had given way to speeding down wide, paved highways.

While the desperate fight in and around the Falaise Pocket would continue through the coming weekend, Patton's Third Army would continue sweeping a wide arc to the south, and von Kluge's forces would continue letting ground slip away almost unchallenged. Of course, the field marshal had a lot on his plate, and a lot on his mind, in Normandy.

As Patton observed that week, "In exactly two weeks, the Third Army has advanced farther and faster than any army in the history of war."

Wednesday, August 16

General Field Marshal Günther von Kluge greeted the dawn having spent a sleepless night at Generaloberst Sepp Dietrich's

Fifth Panzer Army field headquarters in Normandy. His thoughts turned, no doubt, to the public revelation of Patton's presence in France, even though he had known the open secret for weeks.

Having inspected Seventh Army in the field on Tuesday, von Kluge had motored back to Dietrich's command post in the evening under cover of darkness. He and Dietrich had conferred until past midnight, when von Kluge phoned Generaloberst Alfred Jodl, head of operations for the Oberkommando der Wehrmacht. He explained that it was impossible for troops in Normandy to carry out the Führer's standing order to stay on the offensive, adding that "no power in this world" could defeat the Americans. Von Kluge suggested that Panzer Group Eberbach would attack at Argentan, as other units conducted a tactical withdrawal. He didn't emphasize that he envisioned such attacks as being mere covering fire to keep XV Corps occupied.

Without waiting for a reply from Hitler, von Kluge set out to design an evacuation plan for all of Paul Hausser's Seventh Army, which was the farthest west and therefore the deepest within the Falaise pocket. The idea would be for the troops to pull out at night—to avoid Allied air power—beginning Wednesday night, and continuing on Thursday night.

At 6:30 A.M., when Jodl finally relayed a response from Hitler, the Führer had assented to the notion of a tactical withdrawal of certain forces, but he insisted that Falaise be the cornerstone of a future defense of Normandy. Ironically, the word came in just a few hours later that Falaise had fallen to Crerar's Canadian First Army. The tide had turned, and it was high time to execute von Kluge's escape plan.

On Wednesday afternoon, Eberbach's Panzer Group undertook its role of providing covering fire for the evacuation through a robust attack on General Raymond McLain's 90th Infantry Division at le Bourg-St.-Leonard, about six miles east of Argentan. The Yanks had occupied the village, as well as a ridgeline nearby that would have afforded them an excellent view of the open ground to the north that was the German escape route—the Falaise Gap.

The tanks of the 116th Panzer Division and the 2nd SS Panzer Division recaptured both the town and ridge during the day, but McLain's troops counterattacked on Wednesday night.

As things were shaping up toward a bloody climax on the Falaise front, the situation to the south and east presented a stunning contrast. Having taken the nearby Luftwaffe base on Tuesday, Gilbert Cook ordered the 35th Infantry Division to surround Orleans. By the end of the day, the city was in American hands.

There was a lot of discussion going on around the issue of whether Cook's XII Corps should continue the sweep east of Orleans, but Patton ordered them to secure the American line along the Loire River. Though Patton's detractors often criticize him for moving quickly and ignoring his flanks, this instance is often cited as being illustrative of his cautious side. The German First Army south of Paris was an occupation force of minimal size compared to those forces that were arrayed in the north, but any penetration of an unprotected American rear area would have been severely problematic in the least.

On the other hand, the Allied invasion of the Riviera on Tuesday had meant that German First Army forces would certainly be called upon to move *south* rather than north to answer *that* emergency.

Meanwhile, at the cathedral city Chartres, the German First Army would present the Yanks with a situation completely different from the one they'd encountered at Orleans. One would have thought that Chartres, with its important art treasures, would not be a candidate for becoming a fortified strong point. In fact, it was. In addition to being an "art" city, Chartres was—and is—the key crossroads in the plain west of Paris, with a half dozen important highways converging upon it.

The First Army's French-surnamed commander, General Kurt von der Chevallerie, had designated Chartres as a point where units withdrawing from Normandy could reorganize and be blended with more intact First Army divisions. In fact, von der Chevallerie himself was in Chartres on Wednesday when Lindsay Silvester's 7th Armored Division prepared to attack. So was what remained of the 17th SS Panzer Grenadier Division.

When Combat Command B of the 7th Armored Division, commanded by Brigadier General John Thompson, attacked at dawn, they got more than they'd bargained for.

Thursday, August 17

The unauthorized German withdrawal from Normandy had been an open secret for the better part of a week, but von Kluge had bestowed the official sanction of Oberbefehlshaber West for everyone to flee, beginning on Wednesday night.

In general, things had gone more smoothly overnight than von Kluge might have suspected. It was as though the Americans, by halting at Argentan, had handed him the gift of precious time. In coming years, the detractors of General Omar Bradley would line up to condemn him for his fateful decision.

Eberbach's assault at le Bourg-St.-Leonard had accomplished two things. First, it fulfilled the mission assigned to him by von Kluge. It tied up American units while conveying the impression that the Germans were attempting to attack toward the south—away from the Falaise Gap. Second, it denied the Americans the use of the nearby ridge, which would have afforded a good view of the Falaise Gap. The ridge would have been a picnic ground for artillery spotters.

General Bradley responded to developments on Wednesday by ordering Patton to do what Patton had proposed—even begged—to do on Sunday. That is, Bradley ordered Patton to launch an offensive north from Argentan aimed at making contact with Lieutenant General Harry Crerar's Canadian First Army—and finally at *closing* the Falaise Gap.

Unfortunately, this change of plans came at an inopportune moment for the Third Army. On Sunday, Haislip's XV Corps field headquarters was at Argentan, along with his armored spearhead. Having been told that he would *not* be going north, and having been ordered to start moving east, Haislip had reoriented his forces. By now, XV Corps was not really in a position to do what it *could have* done earlier in the week.

Seeing that XV Corps was not available for immediate action, Bradley turned from the Third Army to the United States First Army. Without coordinating things with Patton, Bradley contacted General Courtney Hodges, the commander of the First Army, and asked him to take action. General Gerow's V Corps had moved into the XV Corps right flank and was ready for action immediately west of Argentan. Essentially, Bradley had given Hodges and Patton overlapping responsibilities without fully explaining his overall strategic concept to either one of them.

In order to accomplish what he understood as his mission, Patton ordered his Third Army chief of staff, Major

General Hugh Gaffey, to take command of a provisional corps comprised of the divisions that were immediately available for the task at hand. These included the 2nd French Armored Division, which was at Argentan, as well as the 90th Infantry Division east of the city, and the 80th Infantry Division, which was south of the city. This hastily configured new corps was ready for action by midmorning on Thursday. So was V Corps.

Gerow and Gaffey figured out the nature of the misconception under which both were operating when they ran into one another on the street in Alençon on Thursday. They discovered that they had each been ordered to establish a corps headquarters in the city for action against the Falaise Gap!

Gerow's actual corps took precedence over Gaffey's provisional one, so the latter ceased to exist and Gerow prepared to assume command for the action. The three divisions that would have made up Gaffey's provisional command were attached temporarily to V Corps. This transition was reasonably seamless, although the SNAFU had cost the Yanks the better part of a day in getting ready to move out.

By reversing his earlier order for the United States forces not to go north from Argentan, Bradley had put pressure on General Montgomery's 21st Army Group to take decisive action. Fortunately for Montgomery, the Canadian First Army had finally broken through at Falaise and was able to act. Montgomery ordered the armored spearhead of Crerar's Army—the 4th Canadian Armored Division and General Maczek's 1st Polish Armored Division—to move quickly toward the American lines that lay across the Falaise Gap.

Just as the Allied units around the Falaise Gap started to make some important progress, the Third Army forces that had moved with such blinding speed early in the week were bogging down. With Cook's XII Corps on the Loire, it was a matter of protecting their left flank and waiting for supplies to catch up to their spearhead at Orleans.

With the advance units of XX Corps—specifically the 7th Armored Division—it was the unexpected German defense of the cathedral city of Chartres. The Allies had not anticipated that the German First Army would defend this city so much more tenaciously than either Le Mans or Orleans. Perhaps it was the importance of the city as a crossroads, or as a major depot and logistical facility for the Luftwaffe. Maybe it was the fact that elements of the 17th SS Panzer Grenadier Division—veterans of excitement and disappointment at Mortain—were in town and anxious for a fight.

Friday, August 18

Friday dawned brilliant and sunny in Normandy. All things considered, Günther von Kluge ought to have been in an upbeat mood as the week neared its end. Although late in getting underway, his tactical withdrawal—or full-scale retreat, as some would have characterized it—had gone better than he had any reason to have hoped.

For two nights running, units of the German Seventh Army had slipped through the Falaise Gap en masse and relatively unmolested. The heavy rains that had occurred during the week had presented some difficulties for large numbers of vehicles trying to move over narrow, crowded roads at night, but the bad weather had kept Allied air power at bay—at least somewhat.

Eberbach's counterattack against the 90th Infantry Division by the 116th Panzer Division and the 2nd SS Panzer Division had captured le Bourg-St.-Leonard and its strategic ridge. On Friday, the Yanks had still failed in repeated efforts to take it back.

Meanwhile, the SNAFU of having had both Gerow and Gaffey primed for the attack north of Argentan had only served to delay such an attack and to buy von Kluge more time.

Indeed, Günther von Kluge might have been in a good mood Friday morning, but he had just lost his job.

Adolf Hitler, who had an aversion to bad news and a fearsome dislike for those who conveyed it, had grown weary of von Kluge's whining. The Führer's paranoid side also carried a fear that the Oberbefehlshaber West commander might be flirting with the most grievous of sins against the Fatherland—surrendering Seventh Army and the Fifth Panzer Army to the Allies.

When von Kluge had gone missing on Tuesday, there had been some speculation that he'd been at a secret meeting with Allied leaders. He may have wanted to, but he almost certainly had not been in a secret parley with the Allies. Hitler had probably entertained several thoughts of what to do with von Kluge. The gentlest was to fire him.

Late Thursday, von Kluge got the news that he was to be replaced by General Field Marshal Walther Model, who was being relocated from the Eastern Front, where he had commanded an army group. At 6:00 A.M. on Friday, Model was at von Kluge's headquarters, ready to take the reins.

Günther von Kluge left Normandy for the last time, traveling in a chauffeured car in the direction of central Germany. Somewhere near the French city of Metz, the potassium cyanide that he had taken took effect.

Von Kluge died quietly, having sent his suicide note to—of all people—Adolf Hitler.

In this last memorandum of his life and career, von Kluge recognized that he was being relieved of his command as a scapegoat for the failure of Operation Lüttich and for the collapse of the Normandy front. He went on to explain to Hitler that the "wealth of materiel" resources of the Americans was an insurmountable obstacle for the logistically starved German armies. He told Hitler that the German people had "suffered so unspeakably" that it was time to end the war, and that the struggle had become "hopeless." He closed by admitting that he had stood closer to Hitler in spirit than Hitler had dreamed, and that he had done his duty.

News of von Kluge's death would be kept under wraps until after the suicide note reached Hitler, so the Allies were not immediately aware of the change at the apogee of the opposition chain of command in Normandy. Not that it would have mattered. Model's role was hardly more than that of a caretaker of a beaten, withdrawing force. It was the Allies who were now in charge of the onrushing march of events.

The actual breakthrough from the northern side of the Falaise Gap occurred not on the highway that ran from Falaise to Argentan, but on a parallel track about six miles to the east on the road that ran from Morteaux-Couliboeuf toward le Bourg-St.-Leonard. The latter village was where the 116th Panzer Division had overpowered the United States 90th Infantry Division on Wednesday.

The 4th Canadian Armored Division—with the 3rd Canadian Infantry Division on its right flank, and the 1st Polish Armored Division on its left—had broken through at Morteaux-Couliboeuf on Thursday, and had penetrated as far as the village of Trun. They had crossed roughly half the width of the Falaise Gap. On Friday, as the German panzers withdrew, the 90th Infantry Division was able to retake le Bourg-

St.-Leonard and begin to move north into the Falaise Gap.

The 2nd French Armored Division, now attached to V Corps, was ordered to secure the area around Argentan—which was still nominally under German control—to prevent a German breakout to the south. The 80th Infantry Division pushed into the Falaise Gap just east of Argentan with the objective of encircling the city to the north and east.

In the west, the United States XIX Corps and the British Second Army made substantial progress on Thursday and Friday, dramatically reducing the size of the Falaise Pocket. By Friday evening, virtually all of the pocket was in artillery range from Allied positions. With this in mind, the shelling began. If Wednesday and Thursday nights had afforded the Germans an opportunity to move about unhindered, Friday night saw this nocturnal bliss come to a thundering conclusion.

Saturday, August 19

German forces had been withdrawing from the ever-shriveling Falaise Pocket unofficially for a week and officially for three nights. Nevertheless, a sizable number of troops—mainly belonging to Seventh Army units—were still within it. Saturday morning found the Seventh Army commander, General Paul Hausser, at work on the final touches to a plan for evacuating the balance of his command on Saturday night.

Coincidentally, August 19 was the second anniversary of the disastrous Anglo-Canadian (with a small American presence) commando raid on the French coastal city of Dieppe. Half of the 5,000 troops that went ashore were killed or captured, while the remainder beat a hasty retreat. The superiority of German defenses and the folly of Allied efforts to invade France had been clearly demonstrated. However, less than two years later, the Allies had returned to the French coast to stay. Now, exactly two years after Dieppe, it was the Germans that were being compelled to beat a hasty retreat.

As German meteorologists had been predicting for the past two weeks, the weather on Sunday was expected to include low overcast and drizzle, so Allied airpower was unable to attack the mass of slowly moving targets. It should be recalled that Sunday was the day that Heinrich Eberbach had picked more than a week earlier for the second strike against Avranches. What a difference a week had made. It is strangely ironic that the Germans had accurately predicted the weather, but had so miserably failed to predict their own fortunes on the battlefield. From planning an offensive, they had come around to planning for a retreat.

The key to the present operation would actually be in the hands of one of Hausser's subordinates, General Eugen Meindl, commander of the II Fallschirm (Parachute) Korps. Meindl's paratroopers, who hadn't seen a parachute in months, had been in action against the Americans since St. Lô, operating mainly as infantry.

Meindl proposed that his men would seize high ground in the center of the Falaise Gap and use this as a position from which to defend all of the retreating Germans as they streamed through the gap. The specific high ground that he chose was a steep line of ridges capped by a peak known as Mont Ormel, which was located directly between Morteaux-Couliboeuf and le Bourg-St.-Leonard. As such, it also lay directly between the jaws of the pincer being executed by the 4th Canadian Armored Division and the 1st Polish Armored Division on one side and the United States 90th Infantry Division on the other.

Meindl's daring operation would be covered by elements

of the Seventh Army's XLVII Panzer Korps and the Fifth Panzer Army's II SS Panzer Korps. When one says "elements," this is illustrative of the fact that by August 19, none of the surviving German units was at full strength. They were all composed of "elements." In any event, the panzers would be tasked with counterattacking against the Allies in the corridor between Morteaux-Coulibœuf and le Bourg-St.-Leonard.

It would be no easy task. By now, what was left of the Fifth Panzer Army—which had held the Canadians at bay for weeks—was suffering from the experience of having the tables turned. The 4th Canadian Armored Division reached the village of St. Lambert, while the 1st Polish Armored Division, cutting wide around the Canadian left, had actually crossed the ridge that contained Mont Ormel. As some units of the division took up positions on the hill, others moved south toward American lines. The Poles did not know, of course, that Mont Ormel was the site that Meindl had preselected as his objective for the coming evening.

Saturday afternoon, the advance units of the 1st Polish Armored Division reached the village of Chambois in the center of the Falaise Gap, where they would link up with advance units of the United States 90th Infantry Division. Technically, this represented an Allied crossing of the gap, although much of the space within the gap was yet to be physically occupied by Allied units. The contest was not over.

Sunday, August 20

Eugen Meindl would lead the dash through the Falaise Gap to Mont Ormel personally. He moved out at 10:30 Saturday night at the head of the 3rd Fallschirm Division, one of two parachute divisions within the corps that he commanded. Paul

Hausser, who recognized a competent officer when he saw one, had attached his own command staff to Meindl's. Hausser hitched his fate to a star and was off for a ride. He knew that if anyone was going to get through, it would be the tough paratrooper general.

They moved cautiously, attempting to dodge the Allied outposts that had been set up as the Allied patrols had probed their way into the gap over the past day or so. A number of firefights occurred, but by 3:00 A.M. on Sunday, the Germans had reached the Dives River, which flows north-south along the western approaches to the base of the ridge containing Mont Ormel. When the division commander was wounded in a shootout, Meindl assumed direct control of the 3rd Fallschirm Division.

The Germans were in a state of disciplined confusion—meaning that the division had become disorganized in the darkness—but were all making their way toward Mont Ormel as per the plan. Meindl was out of touch with most of his command, but he knew they were coming along.

Meindl located a place where the Dives River was shallow enough to cross and began exercising such a maneuver. As the Germans reached the eastern bank, it became clear that pockets of Allied troops were everywhere, and more firefights broke out. Thanks to the Allies' use of tracer ammunition, the Germans could identify their positions and infiltrate through the lines. At the same time, Lieutenant General Paul Mahlmann, commanding the other paratroop division in Meindl's corps—the 353rd Fallschirm Division—was executing a similar crossing about a mile away.

By first light, Meindl and the small group of paratroopers and staff officers who were with him had managed to get within about a mile of the highest point on the Mont Ormel ridge. In the gathering dawn, Meindl could see that the Allies—members of the 1st Polish Armored Division—were already there. At the same time, he could now visually identify other German units nearby. In fact, as far as the eye could see, there were large numbers of Germans, on foot and in vehicles—mainly horse-drawn vehicles. They were all adhering to the plan and streaming eastward out of the Falaise Pocket.

The objective of capturing Mont Ormel to provide cover for the evacuation remained tactically sound. Indeed, it was an obvious necessity now. Just as the high ground could be used by the Germans to protect the retreating troops, it offered a full view of the retreat that could be used to deadly effect by Allied artillery and artillery spotters. In fact, the Poles had already begun lobbing shells into the streams of German troops as soon as there was enough daylight to see what was going on.

The weather prediction had been accurate, and the low overcast and drizzle did, indeed, keep Allied airpower at bay. It did not, however, affect Allied artillery. This fire, especially that of the 90th Infantry Division Artillery battalions, would take a serious toll on the evacuation, but the situation would have been proportionally worse for the Germans with the Allies in full control of all the high ground.

The initial German assault on Mont Ormel at 9:00 A.M. was led, not by Meindl, but by a handful of tanks and exhausted troops belonging to the 2nd SS Panzer Division. The Poles turned back the SS men in several focused attacks, and Meindl's paratroopers entered the fray soon after. The fighting on Mont Ormel went on all day. While the Germans never succeeded in taking the high ground that they desired, they did succeed in keeping the Poles busy defending themselves when they could have been shelling the evacuating troops.

Meanwhile, Paul Mahlmann's troops did succeed in capturing a slightly lower nearby hill, which he successfully occupied and held throughout the day.

Slightly south and west of Mont Ormel, several German tanks backed by an infantry company attempted to cross the Dives River near the village of Cambois that was held by Easy Company of the 90th Infantry Division's 359th Infantry Regiment. In order to break through, they would have had to get past a machine gun position manned by a young sergeant from Bremerton, Washington, named John Druse "Bud" Hawk.

Hawk opened fire on the Germans at the critical moment, forcing the infantry to move back. However, an artillery shell knocked out his machine gun and wounded him in the right thigh. Still able to walk, Bud Hawk grabbed a bazooka and went after the tanks. With the help of another man who loaded as Hawk fired, he managed to force the panzers back into a forest.

Many men might have considered such an action to be a day's work, but Hawk took it upon himself to reorganize two machine gun squads that had both had their heavy machine guns damaged. With German bullets buzzing overhead, Bud Hawk supervised the disassembly of the two damaged guns, and showed the other men how to rebuild the parts into one workable weapon.

By the time that three German tanks renewed their attack on the 359th Infantry Regiment, a pair of American M10 tank destroyers had arrived on the scene. The Germans managed to use the dense woods to screen themselves from the American tankers, so effective fire was impossible. Seeing this, Hawk decided to become what would be described later as a "human aiming stake" for the tank destroyers. Dodging a hail of German machine gun fire, Bud Hawk ran up to a knoll from which he could point out the German tanks to the American gunners. When their first shots fell short, Hawk ran back down the hill to correct their range. He then ran back up the hill to continue his role as a human aiming stake.

Ultimately, two of the tanks were knocked out, and the third retreated back into the Falaise Pocket. The 359th Infantry Regiment, meanwhile, rounded up five hundred Germans who were unable to escape and unwilling to go back into the pocket.

Sergeant Hawk, though wounded, survived. For his actions this Sunday afternoon, he was awarded the Congressional Medal of Honor.

There would be many other stories about the closing of the Falaise Gap. At 11:00 A.M., Sergeant Donald Ekdahl was commanding the lead tank of a 3rd Armored Division column as it drove north on the road between Fromental and Putanges when he came face-to-face with a British reconnaissance team heading south on the same road. As they shook hands, it marked a moment that would be referred to in a wire service report as "both historic and dramatic." The Canadians and Poles had been the first, and now it was the Yanks and the Brits. A week later, the event would be permanently memorialized as the 3rd Armored Division was officially nicknamed "the Spearhead Division."

Monday, August 21

By midafternoon on Monday, the Falaise Gap was closed. Handfuls of Germans, traveling in small groups, had managed to slip through during the morning, but by 4:00 Monday afternoon, the Allies held the line between Morteaux-Couliboeuf and le Bourg-St.-Leonard firmly. No more shivering German stragglers were able to wade through the Dives River without winding up as prisoners. Canadian units had finally relieved the men of General Maczek's 1st Polish Armored Division, who'd been essentially surrounded atop Mont Ormel for forty-eight hours.

One of those brutal rainstorms for which Normandy is well known moved in late on Sunday and remained overnight, making the climax of the German escape from the Falaise pocket a miserable affair. It had also made Allied interdiction of the final stragglers difficult, and had allowed additional German troops to escape to fight another day.

It is estimated that more than 20,000 Germans had escaped through the Falaise Gap over the weekend. General Meindl escaped, as did General Hausser, although he had been seriously wounded. An estimated 50,000 were taken prisoner. Of these, the United States 90th Infantry Division captured 13,000. Another 10,000 Germans were determined to have been killed in action.

Though many thousand troops got out, the conditions of terrain and weather meant that most of the German equipment that had been located in the Falaise Pocket could not be brought through the gap. Between them, six panzer divisions escaped with 2,000 men and only 62 tanks. The 90th Infantry Division alone had bagged 220 German tanks, nearly 1,000 artillery pieces, over 5,000 motor vehicles, and 2,000 horse-drawn wagons. Field hospitals and mobile communications centers had been simply abandoned intact.

Despite the staggering losses suffered by the Germans, the fact that so many survived to fight later is a controversial point in Allied military history. In retrospect, it seems obvious that the Americans could have closed the Falaise Gap on their own on or about Wednesday, August 16, had General Bradley not ordered a halt. As General George Patton said, "This halt was a great mistake as I was certain that we could have entered Falaise and I was not certain that the British would. As a matter of fact, we had reconnaissance parties near the town [Falaise] when we were ordered to pull back."

Bradley is chastised by countless armchair tacticians with 20/20 hindsight for being overly cautious. Those who share his assessment point to his fear of allowing troops to get so deeply committed that they might become cut off and surrounded. Bradley wrote in his memoirs that he halted XV Corps at Argentan because having a "solid shoulder" there would be better than a "broken neck" at Falaise.

To Patton, who thrived on fast movement, Bradley was painfully slow to act. Patton's dislike for what he saw as timidity in Bradley is well known. "Bradley is too conservative," Patton once observed. "He wants to wait until we can all jump into the fight together, by which time half of our men will have the flu or trench foot. I wish he had a little more daring."

In any case, the Battle of Normandy was finally over, and with it, the battle for all of France north of the Loire River and west of the Seine River—except for the Brittany ports, which were surrounded and under siege.

While the rest of the Allies were chasing the German armies in the north toward the Seine, the Third Army was in the west and southwest. Patton's divisions held a solid north-south line about fifty miles west of the longitude of Paris. Haislip's XV Corps captured Dreux on Wednesday with only token resistance, while XII Corps had secured Orleans the same day with little difficulty. In the middle, Chartres had proven more difficult for XX Corps.

Chartres was defended by a sizable force of stragglers from the Normandy front, including the storm troopers of the

17th Panzer Grenadier Division. Taking the city was problematic. American artillery was hindered by a desire not to damage the cathedral and its famous mismatched towers dating from the twelfth and sixteenth centuries. It was not one of those places like Cherbourg or St. Lô where anyone wanted to destroy the city in order to capture it.

Combat Command B of the 7th Armored Division, which entered Chartres in two prongs from the northwest and southwest, found the narrow streets difficult for their Sherman tanks. As the battle at the Falaise Gap reached its pitch on Friday, the 11th Infantry Regiment of General LeRoy Irwin's 5th Infantry Division was sent into Chartres to take the city in house-to-house fighting.

By Sunday, the skirmish was finally over, and the 5th Infantry Division was processing a catch of about 2,000 prisoners. The major portion of the German garrison had, however, fled long before the battle. As they scurried away, they had cut off the electricity and water lines into the city, and had looted what they could carry. At the Hotel de France, the Germans took nearly 250 bottles of Scotch whisky, but the proprietor managed to save one bottle, which he shared with the American soldiers.

The French citizens of the cathedral city, meanwhile, began rounding up and executing fellow citizens who had collaborated with the Germans. Even before the GIs had finished rounding up all the storm troopers, three Frenchmen who had been on the Gestapo payroll to the tune of 3,200 francs a month were taken by their countrymen into a narrow alley near the town hall and shot.

Meanwhile, French citizens shared a story with an American reporter about an incident a few days earlier in the neighboring town of Nouville la Mare, in which the entire populace was forced out by the Germans to watch a mass execution of French Resistance fighters. There would be no more of those in these French towns.

Seven long weeks after the Overlord invasion of Normandy, the Allies had won their first great protracted campaign in northern Europe since the Anglo-French defeat of 1940. Now it was on to Paris and points east.

✪ SIX ✪

PARIS

By the time that the breakout achieved by Operation Cobra had occurred at the end of July, the focus of everyone studying a map of northern France had been Paris. Whether the map was on a dining room table in Highmore, South Dakota, or on the hood of a jeep in Le Mans, there was one point on the map that stood out.

For at least two centuries before the eve of World War II, the French capital had been the cultural capital of Europe. In the half century before the war, the impressionists had flocked there, the surrealist movement was born there, and the expressionists had been flourishing there. Pablo Picasso still lived there.

New Yorkers and Londoners had aspired to emulate Parisians. Charles Lindbergh had not made history with an epic transatlantic flight to London or Berlin. The "City of Lights" was accepted by many as an embodiment of—or at least the pinnacle of—everything that mattered to Western Civilization.

With a prewar population of nearly three million, Paris

was larger than Rome and Madrid combined. In continental Europe, only Berlin was larger, and Berlin's most notorious resident—Adolf Hitler—coveted Paris as a crown jewel of his empire. In June 1940, the Führer had gotten his wish. The only known film footage of Hitler dancing a jig was shot during his triumphant visit to Paris during that victorious summer.

In 1940, the City of Lights had gone dark. It had seemed to Parisians that the Paris they had known was suddenly gone forever. Paris was not even the capital of France any more. The new capital of France was in the nondescript town of Vichy, best known previously for its famous bottled mineral water. As a figurehead for the government of this greatly truncated new France, the Germans and their French collaborationist comrades had chosen General Henri Philippe Pétain, the dottering octogenarian who had been France's hero in World War I and who still commanded a great deal of sympathetic respect.

When the Allies had occupied the French colonies in North Africa, the Germans had abandoned the pretext of two Frances and had occupied the whole country. Pierre Laval, a professional politician who had served briefly as French prime minister in 1935–1936, was brought in by the Germans in 1942 to serve as a puppet premier. He ruled by decree, with the decrees being whispered to him by the Germans.

Located in the heart of German-occupied France, Paris became a de facto German city, with German troops on every street and German-language signs on every corner.

Now, just four years after the German jackboots had thundered into town, the Allies were coming. Since the early part of August, American and British newspaper articles about the Allied advances across northern France were peppered with the phrase "the road to Paris." Just as the thrust of the Allied advance had seemed to be Paris for newspaper readers in the United States, so too it seemed to Parisians.

To many political leaders—especially *French* political leaders—the liberation of Paris from the Germans was seen as an obvious and essential goal of the war effort. General Charles de Gaulle, who commanded the Free French forces fighting with the Allies, spoke of the imminent reestablishment of the French Republic with its capital in Paris.

Having been recognized officially by the Allies as the leader of the Free French armies, de Gaulle now sought recognition by the Allied governments as the political leader of France itself. He wanted his Comité Français de Libération Nationale to be recognized as the provisional government of France. He met personally with both British Prime Minister Winston Churchill and President Roosevelt. In fact he had just traveled to Washington in early July to call on Roosevelt at the White House. Yet neither leader was comfortable with the arrogant and abrasive de Gaulle, and *political* recognition had not been forthcoming.

De Gaulle was not entirely motivated by a lust for personal power. Prewar French politics had been a madhouse of squabbling political parties, and he could see that chaos would ensue without strong leadership. Already, there were squabbles erupting between the underground resistance organizations, and de Gaulle knew that the only groups that were strong enough to rule France were his own Comité Français de Libération Nationale—or the communists. De Gaulle was as staunch an anticommunist as there was. He would do everything possible to prevent their coming to power.

At the moment, de Gaulle had the military support of the Allies for his Free French army—spearheaded by Leclerc's 2nd French Armored Division with their fresh supply of brand-

new American-made Sherman tanks. Within France, he had
the loyalty of most of the Forces Françaises de l'Intérieur and
of the powerful underground resistance committee, the
Comité National de la Résistance.

The communists, meanwhile, controlled the rival underground resistance groups, the Comité Parisien de Libération
in Paris and the Comité d'Action Militaire, both of whom
were well represented within the members of the Forces
Françaises de l'Intérieur. In fact, within Paris itself, the Forces
Françaises de l'Intérieur leader, Henri Tanguy, who went by
the code name "Colonel Rol," was a communist.

De Gaulle needed a plan. De Gaulle had a plan.

De Gaulle's plan—obvious in retrospect—was to simply
recapture Paris and allow himself to become the leader of
France by popular acclamation. Of course, the first step was to
actually *recapture* Paris, and the only way to do that was with
the help and support of the Allied armies.

However, to General Dwight Eisenhower, the Supreme
Allied Commander—and to most military officers within the
Allied leadership—capturing Paris was seen as an unnecessary
deviation from the goal of defeating the German armies.
Eisenhower had calculated that the logistics of supplying the
civilian population of Paris would severely sap resources that
were needed to support Allied armies in the field. It would require an estimated 37,500 tons of food and medical supplies a
month to take care of Paris—not to mention the logistical requirements involved in trucking the supplies in from the
makeshift Allied ports in Normandy.

Eisenhower was also wary of having to get embroiled in
street fighting. Paris was the last city in France that any Allied
leader would want to destroy in order to capture. Eisenhower
had wanted to simply bypass the City of Lights and let the

German will to defend it die on the vine. Soon, however, events would be out of Eisenhower's control.

Within Paris itself, the newly arrived commander of the German garrison in the city had his hands full. On the job for less than a week when the Falaise Pocket collapsed, General Günther von Choltitz, the former commander of the German Seventh Army's LXXXIV Korps, had been sent in by the Oberkommando der Wehrmacht to replace General Hans von Boineburg-Lengsfeld. The latter, a cultured music lover, had been perfect for the post when Paris was a quiet, occupied, cultural mecca. He fit in well at a formal reception in an eigteenth-century chateau or ordering wine at the best Parisian restaurants, but times had changed. Northern France was now a war zone, and the German army needed a tough, no-nonsense combat commander who could get the job done.

The job to be done was simply this: Adolf Hitler had decreed that the cultural capital of Europe would not be captured intact by the Allies. If the glamorous City of Lights could not be defended, it would be destroyed. That was the job, and Dietrich von Choltitz was the man. He had a reputation for accomplishing his mission and showing no mercy in the process. Commanding troops in Holland in 1940, he had ordered the complete destruction of Rotterdam, and it was done. He had pounded Sebastopol into rubble and submission two years later.

There were a lot of art lovers within the German officer corps who would be sad and unwilling to damage the City of Lights. With von Choltitz, this would not be a problem. By picking von Choltitz as commandant of the city, Hitler had signaled that Paris would, in fact, be destroyed.

Upon his arrival in Paris, von Choltitz had been briefed personally by Günther von Kluge at the subterranean Oberbefehlshaber West bunker in St. Germain-en-Laye, near Paris. General Günther Blumentritt, von Kluge's chief of staff, had outlined plans for the immediate and systematic destruction of factories, power plants, train stations, telephone exchanges, and other facilities that would be vital to the functioning of the city. Demolition charges had already been placed on all of the more than four dozen bridges that crossed the Seine River within greater Paris.

On Wednesday, August 16, as von Kluge was in Normandy preparing to authorize its evacuation, von Choltitz met with Major General Hubertus von Aulock, who commanded the western defenses of Paris to discuss the possibility of Paris serving as the defensive strongpoint that would stop the Allied advance. Nobody yet wanted to say "no" to any notion that might sound defeatist to a Hitler appointee, so von Aulock—whose brother, Colonel Andreas von Aulock commanded the German fortress at the Brittany port of St. Malo—simply outlined the resources he had, and what he would need to do the job. In general, they discussed a defense of the city along the lines of the numerous major highways for which it served as the hub.

The following day, as von Kluge was anguishing over his suicide note to Hitler, he had also penned a memo to von Choltitz, ordering him to begin the systematic destruction of Paris.

Friday, August 18

Friday morning dawned bright and sunny in Paris. Parisians greeted the day with a sense of uncertainty tempered by a nervous excitement that change was in the warm summer breeze.

Events were moving quickly. At the same moment that the trickle of escaping German troops from within the Falaise Pocket was turning into a rivulet, so too was the trickle of Germans departing Paris. Those who'd been lucky enough to be posted to Paris had been in heaven. It had been like a wonderful dream. Now it was time to wake up and go home.

German administrative staffs and nonessential personnel were starting to leave the city even as additional combat troops were starting to move in. The Germans still controlled Paris with an iron fist—as they had for four years—but it was clear to the average Parisian that the Germans were jittery and that the Resistance organizations were growing increasingly restless.

Dietrich von Choltitz greeted the day with a new boss. As the old boss cruised through Paris en route to Metz and a rendezvous with a potassium cyanide capsule, new boss General Field Marshal Walther Model ordered the commandant of Paris to turn the city into that defensive strong point that von Choltitz had discussed with von Aulock on Wednesday.

The collaborationist mayor of Paris, Pierre Charles Taittinger, began his day with a visit to the lavish office of Dietrich von Choltitz at the Hotel Meurice on Rue Rivoli, just a couple of blocks from the Louvre. Taittinger may have been about as pro-German as a Parisian could be, but he was still, first and foremost, a Parisian. He complained about the demolition charges being placed throughout his city, and about the preparations for street fighting in Paris. The German commandant shrugged and told him that as a former military man he must certainly understand that certain measures had to be taken to "defend" Paris.

Pierre Laval would not greet the new day in France. At 10:00 P.M. on Thursday, Laval had officially designated the

Prefecture of Police in Paris to represent his government. Shortly before midnight, he was driving out of Paris, heading east under German military escort.

Saturday, August 19

As though to mirror the mood of the people of Paris, the weather was turning dark and moody. The same weather front that would be hindering Allied air power over the Falaise Pocket had moved over Paris.

If von Choltitz still imagined himself as the master of events in Paris, he was about to get a rude wake-up call. Henri Tanguy and his cohorts had decided that today was the day for the Forces Françaises de l'Intérieur to begin a popular uprising within the city. Such an uprising would directly contravene the orders of General Pierre Koenig, the acknowledged commander of the Forces Françaises de l'Intérieur, and a de Gaulle loyalist.

However, Koenig was not in Paris and Tanguy was. The show would go on. The plan was simple. Agents of the Forces Françaises de l'Intérieur throughout the city would go on a simultaneous shooting spree, killing German personnel wherever they saw them, and hopefully capturing weapons.

Buoyed by the news that the Yanks were already in Chartres—just fifty miles away—the Parisians agreed that now was a good time for an uprising. They hoped that the Allies would take notice and rush into the city. Unlike most Parisians, however, Tanguy and the communists *didn't* want the Allies in Paris, at least not until *after* the insurrection had been successful. They had in mind that Paris should have a communist government as a fait accompli when Paris was liberated. That was why they were so anxious to get their uprising underway.

At around 7:00 A.M., the word went out to begin the revolt, and within two hours shots were heard throughout Paris. The uprising spread quickly, taking the Germans—as well as the Comité National de la Résistance—by complete surprise. By noon, the Resistance fighters were in control of the police headquarters and several other government buildings around the city. Von Choltitz had sent tanks and troops to surround the Prefecture of Police building. He had ordered his troops to systematically retake the occupied buildings and round up the Resistance fighters wherever they could be found. He ordered the Luftwaffe to begin air attacks on the Prefecture of Police at first light on Sunday.

The Swedish Consul General, Raoul Nordling, met with von Choltitz at the Hotel Meurice on Saturday afternoon. For several weeks, Nordling had been intervening with the Germans—with some success—to help save civilian prisoners from execution and deportation. Now he was back to help save two of France's most important inanimate objects. Within a couple of city blocks of the Prefecture of Police were the Cathedral of Notre Dame de Paris, and the church known as Sainte-Chapelle—the Holy Chapel. Notre Dame, which French geographers use as the "zero point" for maps of their country, was arguably the most magnificent of the great Gothic cathedrals built across Europe in the late middle ages. Sainte-Chapelle, with its awe-inspiring stained glass windows, was built by King Louis IX—later *Saint* Louis—as a reliquary for what he believed was the Crown of Thorns that Jesus Christ had worn on the cross. Nordling explained to von Choltitz that an air attack on the Prefecture of Police would almost certainly damage—if not destroy—one or both of these extraordinary landmarks. If that happened, Nordling explained, von Choltitz would have anarchy.

Nordling's solution to the dilemma was for the Germans to declare a cease-fire. Dietrich von Choltitz would not hear of it. He had to deal with the Resistance from a position of strength. Nordling suggested that he would speak to the Resistance leaders and negotiate. Then, von Choltitz could *agree* to the cease-fire that was offered and thus save face. Von Choltitz said he would go along with the idea.

Now that he was coming face-to-face with the reality of destroying Paris, the hard-nosed general was starting to get cold feet.

By 10:00 Saturday night, an uneasy truce was in place. The first phase of the insurrection was over.

Sunday, August 20

Like an actor arriving on stage for a dramatic scene, General Charles de Gaulle arrived in France on the morning after the Paris revolt. He had come to meet with General Eisenhower at the Supreme Commander's field headquarters on the Cotentin Peninsula in Normandy.

The timing of the insurrection had caught de Gaulle, like nearly everyone else, by surprise. Events within his beloved capital were taking on a momentum of their own, a momentum that de Gaulle could not control. To the French leader, this made it even more imperative that the Allied armies—and de Gaulle himself—get into Paris as quickly as possible.

Eisenhower was unmoved. He did not want to allow Allied armies to be sidetracked from the vital mission of chasing and destroying the German armies in France. Eisenhower had made up his mind with the concurrence of his staff and his commanders. Bradley opposed going into Paris at this stage of the war. Patton understood that one of the motives of the uprising had been to compel the Allies to intervene. When he heard about it, he had quipped that if the Forces Françaises de l'Intérieur had begun their revolt on their own, they could finish it the same way.

De Gaulle still had an important card to play in his dealings with Eisenhower. This was General Jacques Philippe Leclerc and his 2nd French Armored Division. De Gaulle had agreed to his Free French army being integrated into the Allied command structure, and Leclerc's division had been assigned to an American command, first to XV Corps, and then to V Corps under the command of General Leonard Gerow. However, Leclerc was a Frenchman and de Gaulle's orders would take precedence over those of Gerow or Eisenhower. If de Gaulle was willing to risk his entire relationship with the Allies—and perhaps Allied support for his Comité Français de Libération Nationale as the next government of France—he could order Leclerc to break ranks and go into Paris. Obviously, Leclerc understood this as well. So too, did Eisenhower.

In Paris, the cease-fire was spreading across the city on Sunday morning just as the fighting had spread on Saturday. The skirmishing had not ended abruptly, it was simply tailing off. The Germans would kill 106 Resistance fighters on Sunday, only a shade fewer than the 125 that were killed on Saturday.

Monday, August 21

Rain from the fringes of the storm that was battering Normandy made the morning grim and miserable in Paris. For von Choltitz, it was past time to begin executing his orders to demolish Paris. Yet still he hesitated.

In the streets, although the truce remained in effect, there was still sporadic gunfire. Panther tanks patrolled the wide boulevards, and tension hung in the air.

Henri Tanguy and his fellow communists were impatient. They wanted to get on with the insurrection. To combat the Germans, they also needed more heavy weapons. There had been some ongoing discussions between the Allies and the Forces Françaises de l'Intérieur about an airdrop of mortars and machine guns into Paris. Tanguy decided that it was now time to call such an operation into play. As a selling point, he would suggest that such an operation would allow the Allies to be seen as doing *something* about Paris without that something involving an actual incursion into the city.

Tanguy had boldly decided to send Major Roger Gallois of the Forces Françaises de l'Intérieur to sneak through the German lines and get a message to Eisenhower. Late Monday afternoon, Gallois succeeded in reaching the Third Army lines near the village of Pussay, fifty-six miles from Paris.

Just as Tanguy had his ideas about what should be done, so too did Gallois. He had decided that instead of asking for an arms drop, he would invite Eisenhower to bring his armies into Paris. The American patrol that picked up Gallois at the front took him behind the lines. Gradually, he was passed farther and farther to the rear, until, at around midnight, he was taken to the Third Army field headquarters. Gallois had accomplished his mission. Roused from his sleep, George Patton listened to Gallois and agreed to send him deeper into Allied lines to speak to Eisenhower.

Tuesday, August 22

At dawn on Tuesday, Roger Gallois found himself face-to-face with the Supreme Allied Commander attempting to explain that for the Allies *not* to enter Paris would be to invite a blood-bath of monstrous proportions. In the meantime, Eisenhower had been having some second thoughts. After having turned de Gaulle down on Monday, Eisenhower was ready to say "yes" to Gallois.

As Eisenhower would write in his memoirs, "I was hope-ful of deferring actual capture of the city, unless I received evi-dence of starvation or distress of its citizens. In this matter my hand was forced by the Free French forces inside Paris."

Eisenhower passed the word down to Bradley, who reluc-tantly agreed with Eisenhower that the Allies should go into Paris. They also agreed that the first Allied unit to enter the city ought to be Leclerc's 2nd French Armored Division.

De Gaulle had gotten his wish. In fact, he'd gotten several. The Allies would go into Paris now rather than later, *and* Leclerc would lead them in. In the meantime, the Allies had decided *against* the airdrop of heavy weapons that Tanguy had wanted. It was seen as a risky operation that would almost certainly re-sult in most of the weapons being captured by the Germans. However, de Gaulle had opposed it because he feared that most of the weapons would fall into the hands of the communists.

Wednesday, August 23

By midweek, the situation in and around Paris was fluid and confusing. Radio, newspaper, and wire service war correspon-dents were waiting breathlessly, each hoping to be the first to report the monumental news that Paris had been liberated. This would, they reasoned, be the biggest news story since D-Day and, if linked as an extension of D-Day—which was, after all, the operation that led *directly to* the liberation of Paris—it would be the biggest story since Pearl Harbor.

Actually, the first report of the liberation would be a deliberate fabrication that would start a chain reaction that would send dominoes tumbling around the world.

Colonel André Vernon, a staffer at the London office of the Forces Françaises de l'Intérieur, had been following the action and he was concerned about the way that SHAEF seemed to be waffling on the issue of when and whether the Allied armies were going to liberate Paris. Not knowing that Bradley had already tasked Jacques Leclerc with driving into the city with all deliberate speed, Vernon decided to take matters into his own hands. He decided that he would *force* SHAEF to liberate Paris. He figured that if the BBC broadcast the news that Paris *had been* liberated, then SHAEF would be compelled to make that a reality.

On Wednesday morning, Vernon sent a "news flash" press release to the BBC, claiming that it had been cleared verbally by SHAEF censors, as news flashes often were.

Meanwhile, another news report of the liberation of Paris had already been recorded. Charles Collingwood was a correspondent covering the war for CBS Radio from General Bradley's 12th Army Group field headquarters. On Tuesday night, in preparation for the historic event, he had turned on one of two early-model tape recorders that the network had sent to Europe and had recorded an announcement of the liberation. The idea was that the moment the news really *did* come through, Collingwood would have already taped the report for immediate broadcast. Regardless of where he was, the voice on the historic broadcast would be *his*. Collingwood then sent his tape to the CBS broadcast center in London.

Having been passed along by SHAEF censors who had no way of actually decoding the confounded reel of tape, Collingwood's announcement arrived in London on Wednesday. When Richard C. Hottelet, staffing the CBS desk in London, heard Vernon's bogus news flash broadcast by the BBC, he immediately aired Collingwood's pretaped report.

By the end of the day, it was "the flash heard round the world." London newspapers carried it, as did the late edition papers in New York and San Francisco. A crowd of 20,000 swarmed into Times Square to join French pop diva Lily Pons in singing the French national anthem.

However, in Paris, Dietrich von Choltitz was still very much in control of a very *unliberated* French capital. To the Parisians, the news that the world was celebrating their deliverance while jackbooted storm troopers still lurked about must have seemed like a cruel joke.

But not for long. The inevitable tide of history was flowing, and it was flowing against Dietrich von Choltitz and his garrison.

It was a week for exfiltrating through the German lines. Just as Roger Gallois had done on Monday, Rolf Nordling managed to do on Wednesday. The brother of the Swedish Consul General had reached American lines and had been granted an audience with Omar Bradley at the latter's field headquarters. His message was much the same as that which Roger Gallois had carried, except that his carried a great deal more urgency. He explained to the 12th Army Group commander that he had met with von Choltitz, and had sensed that the destruction of Paris was imminent. He explained that von Choltitz had been dragging his feet, but that direct pressure from Hitler was about to tip the scales. Paris was on the eve of destruction.

Bradley conveyed the new sense of urgency to Leclerc, who needed no coaxing. Bradley also ordered the 4th Infantry Division, commanded by Major General Raymond Barton and attached to VII Corps, to participate in the assault on

Paris. He wanted to be sure that there would be adequate force to subdue the Germans as quickly as possible. He knew that a prolonged fight within the city greatly raised the risk of the substantial damage that everyone wanted to avoid.

The two divisions numbered a total of about 20,000 men, roughly equal to the total number of German troops in Paris. Leclerc would enter from the southwest, through the Porte de St. Cloud, as well as from the south through the Porte d'Orleans and the Porte de Gentilly. Barton would come in from the southeast, on the right flank of Leclerc's three-pronged assault, entering Paris by way of the Porte d'Italie. They would be accompanied by a 12th Army Group technical intelligence group. There was also some discussion of a detachment of British troops who would be present to underscore the international complexion of the Allied forces, but they would not arrive to be part of the operation.

Within the city, final preparations for destruction of the city were under way. Even the Eiffel Tower was slated for annihilation. As Nordling and Bradley were in conversation, German engineers were standing beneath Eiffel's masterpiece calmly calculating where to place the demolition charges that would topple the tower.

The cease-fire that had been negotiated by Raoul Nordling officially ended at noon on Wednesday, and the gunfire that had been heard around Paris during the truce continued after its expiration.

Thursday, August 24

The tanks of Jacques Leclerc's 2nd French Armored Division greeted the damp and drizzle of the day near Rambouillet, just twenty miles from Paris. Crowds of excited French citizens had already come out to cheer the liberators of their capital. The closer that Leclerc would drive, the larger and more excited the crowd became. French flags were flying. Bottles of wine and champagne were handed out, and young women competed to kiss the most French soldiers.

As the Leclerc columns rolled near enough to see the Eiffel Tower on the distant horizon, however, they began to run into German resistance. Hubertus von Aulock's antitank guns began exacting a toll on the Sherman tanks in the vanguard of the 2nd French Armored Division that were still decked with flowers tossed on them by delighted civilians an hour before. During the day, the French would lose thirty-five tanks, and seventy-one French soldiers were killed.

Within the city, the French Resistance fighters were in full scale revolt. Von Choltitz had ordered his Panther crews to show no mercy. The city was in chaos, with cannon fire slamming into buildings and monuments throughout the arrondisements. Yet von Choltitz had still not given the order to detonate the explosives.

As darkness fell, the Parisians who had hoped for liberation on Thursday, as well as the Germans who were prepared to prevent liberation on Friday, went to bed—if not to sleep—still under the swastika and with the sound of gunfire clearly audible on the western approaches to the city.

Suddenly, through the darkness, came the sound of church bells from across the city. It was a sound that had not been heard for four years.

Though Paris was not to be liberated until Friday, a small 2nd French Armored Division combat team under the command of Captain Raymond Dronne managed to slip into the city after dark using side streets. By midnight, they were within sight of the Paris City Hall, the Hotel de Ville.

Friday, August 25

After several days of rain and heavy overcast, Friday dawned bright and sunny in Paris. By daybreak, French and American troops were in the periphery of the city in force and moving toward the center.

Again, as the day before, civilians formed large crowds to cheer the advancing liberators. French tricolors, long saved for just this day, were brought out and displayed in apartment windows and waved at the French troops. An occasional, often handmade, stars and stripes was also seen. By noon, a huge tricolor was waving atop the Eiffel Tower.

There would be isolated firefights all day—some of them determined and bloody—but von Aulock's defensive lines had been broken on Thursday and there was little the Germans could or would do to halt the onslaught.

One of the more interesting encounters involved a French tank commanded by Paul Quinion. Part of Leclerc's western-most column, Quinion's tank had reached the Place d'Etoile, whose centerpiece in the Arc du Triomphe. From there, he could look down the gently sloping Champs Elysées to the Place de Concorde. Quinion spotted a German Panther tank at the Place de Concorde. It was part of a strongpoint that the Germans had arranged to interrupt Leclerc's advance into the heart of Paris.

Quinion ordered Robert Mady, the gunner, to fire on the Panther, estimating its distance at 1,500 meters. A trivia buff, Mady recalled having read in a prewar almanac that the distance from the Place d'Etoile to the Place de Concorde was exactly 1,800 meters. He set the range for this distance and fired. A 75mm shell slammed into the Panther, which began to burn.

By about 10:00 A.M., the 4th Infantry Division's 102nd Cavalry Group had reached the Cathedral of Notre Dame in the heart of Paris. At about the same time, Colonel Pierre Billotte, commanding the easternmost of Leclerc's columns, penetrated deeply into the city along the broad Boulevard St. Michel.

Having made contact with the Swedish consulate, Billotte asked them to take a surrender ultimatum to von Choltitz. The German commander refused the ultimatum, but replied that the honor of a man such as himself would be preserved if he was forced to surrender to a significant show of force. In a roundabout way, he had told Billotte to come and get him—and how.

One of the last messages that von Choltitz would receive at his Hotel Meurice headquarters came in at dawn from Oberkommando der Wehrmacht. They wanted to know whether the demolition operation was under way. Hitler had thrown a monumental tantrum, in which he had made his famous query of Generaloberst Alfred Jodl, head of operations for the Oberkommando der Wehrmacht—*"Is Paris Burning?"*

Not only was it not, the only man who could make this conflagration a reality was ignoring his Führer and dictating the conditions of his own surrender, and that of the German garrison in the city that Hitler wanted burned.

It was around 3:00 P.M. when Henri Karcher, one of Leclerc's soldiers, reached the Hotel Meurice. The building was crowded with Germans who stumbled over one another to surrender. Finally, he was taken upstairs to the office of General Dietrich von Choltitz, who promptly surrendered. Sporadic fighting continued until all German troops had been informed of the surrender. Paris had been captured with the loss of just 42 French soldiers. There were 127 civilians killed on Liberation Day. German forces had suffered 3,200 killed or wounded in the defense of Paris.

At 4:30 P.M., General Charles de Gaulle reached the city, passing north through the Port d'Orleans. A few hours later, he addressed a vast crowd from in front of the Hotel de Ville.

It had been a good day for a liberation. Friday was the feast day of St. Louis, the sainted King Louis IX, who was the patron saint of France. Now Charles de Gaulle was beginning the process by which he would become France's newest leader.

Saturday, August 26

The tactical reality of the situation in Paris called for Allied troops to move *through* town quickly to the eastern approaches of the city and to secure these against the sizable German forces still arrayed on that side of the city. General Gerow—who had entered Paris on Friday more than four hours ahead of de Gaulle—issued orders to this effect, but was told that the 2nd French Armored Division was not available.

For Charles de Gaulle, time stood still after Liberation Day. Paris was liberated, and everything else could wait. For him, it was time to celebrate Liberation, Paris, France, and, of course, de Gaulle.

The general was about to do the most tactically foolish thing imaginable. He was going to make himself, General Koenig, General Leclerc, and the Comité Français de Libération Nationale leadership into sitting ducks for any German sniper left in Paris. He was about to surround the 2nd French Armored Division with a million defenseless civilians. He was going to hold a parade. Announcements of this fact had been made on the radio all night long, and banners were everywhere by Saturday morning.

An exasperated Leonard Gerow tried to stop the parade, but failed. Gerow was understandably nervous about permitting a major element of V Corps combat effectiveness—Leclerc's 2nd French Armored Division—sidelined for a day to be in a *parade*.

De Gaulle explained to Gerow that he had "lent" Leclerc to the Allies in the first place, and all he wanted was to "borrow him back for a day." Under the theory that if you can't beat them, you might as well join them, Gerow authorized a regiment of the 4th Infantry Division to take part in the parade.

De Gaulle was born for politics. Like any true politician, he understood the importance of symbols. To him, the symbolic importance of the parade greatly outweighed any of the risks, including the risk that he himself might be shot by a sniper.

The pessimists within Allied intelligence were sure that the Germans would find the parade of sitting ducks to be a target too tempting to resist. However, the German forces in the area had either surrendered or were too busy worrying about getting away to be concerned with attacking a parade. In fact, it was later learned that the Oberkommando Wehrmacht was unaware of the parade until it was over. Otherwise, Hitler would certainly have ordered a major attack. As it was, there would be trouble, but on nowhere nearly the scale that the pessimists had feared.

The show began symbolically, with General de Gaulle arriving at Place d'Etoile, where he placed a wreath on the grave of France's unknown soldier, and ceremonially relit the eternal flame beneath the Arc de Triomphe. He then turned to salute

Leclerc and to inspect a strong showing of vehicles from
Leclerc's division.

At 2:00 P.M., de Gaulle began marching down the
Champs Elysées at the head of the 2nd French Armored Division to the cheers of a million French civilians. After a week
marked by rain and overcast, the weather was warm and
sunny. Civilians crowded the sidewalks and waved from every
balcony. The red, white, and blue of the French tricolor could
be seen everywhere in a city that had been dominated for four
years by the red, white, and black of the German swastika
banner.

General Jacques Leclerc marched on foot alongside General Pierre Joseph Koenig of the Forces Françaises de l'Intérieur. Representatives of the Comité Nationale de
Resistance, the Comité Parisien de Libération in Paris, and the
Comité d'Action Militaire were also on the boulevard, taking
the cheers of the crowd. However, all eyes were on the man
who walked several paces ahead of the others, the man whose
six-foot-five-inch frame allowed him to stand literally head
and shoulders above the rest—Charles de Gaulle.

As the procession reached the Place de la Concorde, a
couple of shots rang out. The crowd surged back and many
people ducked into the side streets. However, when they saw
that de Gaulle had ignored the sound, they cheered and
surged back. He remarked later that he had interpreted the
shots as having been celebratory shots fired in the air.

At the Place de la Concorde, de Gaulle climbed into a car
for the drive to the Ile de la Cité, where a mass was to take
place at Notre Dame Cathedral to mark the Liberation. As at
the Place de la Concorde, shots greeted the general's arrival. It
was virtually impossible for those marching with de Gaulle to
ascertain the origin of the shots, although several French sol-

diers were seen to return fire to the upper reaches of the towers of the cathedral itself. Lieutenant Burt Kalisch, a US Army photographer, later reported that he had looked up and had seen the muzzle flash from three rifle barrels high above him in the north tower.

De Gaulle casually debarked from his car at the entrance to the Notre Dame's main portal. He accepted a bouquet from a pair of young girls and casually strode into the crowded cathedral. More shots were heard after the general entered the building, but these were almost certainly shots being fired outside.

During the mass, many of the dignitaries sang along with the choir, and de Gaulle's own booming voice could be heard singing the *Magnificat*.

A later investigation failed to specifically identify the Notre Dame snipers, although both German and Vichy snipers were rounded up elsewhere in Paris on Saturday and over the coming days. Three "suspicious" civilians were cornered by the crowd outside the cathedral shortly after de Gaulle's arrival. One was beaten to death, but the other two were not charged with a crime.

Far from disrupting de Gaulle's grand parade, the shots that were fired on Saturday afternoon only served to underscore the general's heroism, which certainly enhanced his popularity with the future French electorate.

By the end of the day, elements of the 2nd French Armored Division were back on track and executing Gerow's orders to move east toward Aubervilliers and St. Denis.

De Gaulle had admitted to Gerow's liaison officer that Gerow was right about the foolhardiness of the parade from a military standpoint, but he added that it "is going to give France political unity."

He was right.

The parade would also define de Gaulle's future. He would serve as president for the next two years, returning to the post for a full decade in the 1960s, and he would remain France's leading political figure for as long as he lived.

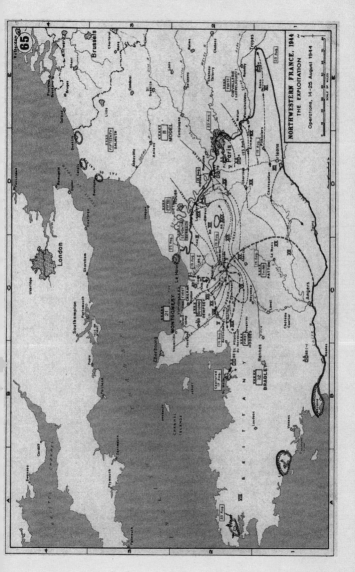

NORTHWESTERN FRANCE, 1944
THE EXPLOITATION
Operations, 14–25 August 1944

✪ SEVEN ✪

FARTHER AND FASTER

By August 22, as Eisenhower reluctantly directed Bradley to order Leonard Gerow to take Paris, the Battle of Normandy was over, and a new phase in the crusade to liberate Europe had begun. Though it was covered by the media as a milestone of world history, the liberation of Paris was merely a sideshow in the context of the grand strategy of liberating Europe.

After Paris, the liberation of Europe now seemed much closer than anyone—on either side—would have predicted on June 6, or even on July 25. The original plan had been to try to reach the Seine by late autumn and to wait for supply stockpiles to catch up with the field armies. Many planners assumed that the campaign east of the Seine would not be under way until early 1945. Here it was August 1944, and decisions had to be made. The momentum had to be exploited. Eisenhower had already decided that the Allies would capitalize on the successes enjoyed thus far and push east expeditiously—rather than reverting to the pre-D-Day plan of pausing at the Seine.

More than any other organization in the Allied juggernaut, General George Patton's Third Army epitomized the
success of Allied power since the Operation Cobra breakout
on July 25. The Third Army was clearly poised to continue
what it had been doing in Normandy, Brittany, the Maine,
and the Loire—that is, to paraphrase the general's own words,
"to advance farther and faster than any army in the history of
war."

The Third Army was demonstrating what officers such as
Patton had theorized before the war, and what the Germans
themselves had demonstrated in the Blitzkriegs of 1939 and
1940. Blitzkrieg, or lightning war, is a good term—certainly
the "sexier" term than the one the US Army coined a generation later, the more antiseptic "Air-Land Battle Doctrine."

By whatever term one uses, the doctrine calls for essentially three things: First and second, there should be complete
air superiority over the battlefield, combined with fast and aggressive armored operations on the ground. Third, there
should be a close integration of the actions of tactical air
power and ground forces. It was working for Patton in France,
just as it would work against the Iraqi army in 1991 and 2003.

Patton was one of the greatest advocates of air power
among the US Army's ground commanders. He understood
its value and necessity, but also its limitations. He would often
put airmen in their place with the comment: "Aviation cannot
take prisoners nor hold ground." Holding ground was the job
of the ground army, and the Third Army had so far done a
better job of it than any other American army in history.

The vast area liberated by the Third Army was in marked
contrast to what had been accomplished by the other three
armies. Patton had taken more than twice as much in about
half the time. Granted, Patton had not faced the German

armies at the peak of their strength, and much of the region of
the Maine and the Loire Valley had been lightly defended, but
Patton's success was a major contribution to both the morale
of the Allies and to accomplishing the goal of liberating Europe.

At the beginning of the week leading up to the liberation
of Paris, the Third Army was west and south of the city. By
Liberation Day, they had completely encircled the city to the
south and east, and were the first Allied units to cross the
Seine. However, Patton was a poster child for Allied reluctance
to capture Paris. As such, he was only too happy when Bradley
designated components of his own former command—the
First Army—to take the city.

After Paris, the final defeat of the German armies in
northern France was the next step. Beyond this lay Germany
itself. Those armies included the German Seventh Army and
Fifth Panzer Army, both badly beaten ghosts of their former
selves that were dragging eastward after escaping the meat
grinder at Falaise. Generaloberst Sepp Dietrich still commanded the Fifth Panzer Army, while General Heinrich Eberbach, the tough panzer commander whose task force had been
so effective in Normandy, had taken over as commander of
Seventh Army when General Paul Hausser was wounded during his escape through the Falaise Gap.

The Normandy veteran armies were supported by the
German First Army, which was largely unbloodied in battle,
but badly depleted by having been repeatedly harvested for replacement units for other armies.

The most intact German army in northern France was
the Fifteenth, which had been guarding the area northeast of
the Seine River since the Allies had come ashore at Normandy
on June 6. It too had seen its strength gradually chipped away

through the release of units to be sent to aid the armies fighting in Normandy. In retrospect, it is almost comical that, even after the fall of Paris, the Führer and Oberkommando der Wehrmacht still harbored fears of the phantom FUSAG coming across from England in the Pas-de-Calais region. This only goes to show the power of deception.

Flowing north and west through Paris, the Seine River snakes across the plains of Normandy in gigantic switchbacks—that literally remind one of a sidewinding snake—before terminating at LeHavre, the largest port in northern France. The Seine constituted the last remaining major natural defensive line in the north of France.

However, General Field Marshal Walther Model, commanding Oberbefehlshaber West since the eve of the suicide of Günther von Kluge, wanted to save the Seine for later. Model's initial idea was to establish a defensive line west of the Seine, and use the river as a fallback position only if the new line failed to hold.

On August 20, during the final hours of the withdrawal through the Falaise Gap, Model placed operational control of both the Seventh Army and Fifth Panzer Army under Sepp Dietrich, and ordered him to consolidate his panzer forces in the vicinity of the city of Evreux, which was about fifty miles northwest of Paris and about ten miles west of the Seine. This meant organizing what was left of six divisions into the I and II Panzer Korps.

It would be the following day before a sufficient amount of personnel and equipment had dragged itself into the Evreux area for Dietrich to take an inventory of what he really had. What he found was appalling. He discovered that the number of tanks was less than a quarter of what they ought to have been for a single full-strength panzer division. Within the II

Panzer Korps, the 9th Panzer Division had about two dozen tanks, while the 116th Panzer Division had half that number. At least one of the six divisions had no tanks left.

After a survey of the battlefield in Normandy, SHAEF analysts calculated that the Germans had lost more than 1,300 tanks between June 6 and August 25. Meanwhile, estimates of German personnel losses ranged between 400,000 and 450,000 men killed, wounded, or captured. Of that number, two thirds had come after the Allied breakout on July 25.

Southeast of Paris, the crossing points on the Seine were guarded by two somewhat stronger divisions, the 26th and 27th SS Panzer Divisions. These had originally been earmarked by Oberkommando der Wehrmacht to be part of the defense of Paris, but the situation within the city had changed before the two divisions arrived from Germany.

Facing Model's battered armies, the Allies were arrayed parallel to the Seine on a line that ran diagonally from northwest to southeast, beginning about fifty miles east of the June 6 Overlord beachheads, bisecting Paris and continuing southeast of the city for about sixty miles.

Sir Bernard Montgomery's 21st Army Group—who had made relatively little progress in the weeks since the invasion—occupied the northern 25 percent of the line. Courtney Hodges's United States First Army occupied the 30 percent of the line below that controlled by the 21st Army Group. The remainder represented the leading edge of that vast swath of France that had been captured by Patton's Third Army in the three and a half weeks from the time it was activated on the first day of August until the liberation of Paris twenty-five days later.

As Model and Dietreich were preparing to defend what remained of Germany's empire in France, the SHAEF leadership was consulting its own battle maps and considering its

✪ From left to right, General Dwight Eisenhower, the Supreme Allied Commander, confers with American Lieutenant Generals George Smith Patton Jr. (commanding the US Third Army); Omar Nelson Bradley (commanding the 12th Army Group); and Courtney H. Hodges (commanding the US First Army).

✪ General Charles de Gaulle, the commander of the Free French army and head of the Comité Français de Libération Nationale, speaks from a balcony at the city hall in Cherbourg, France, in August 1944. The Americans had recently liberated Cherbourg from the Germans.

✪ Recently captured by American GIs, a group of dispirited German soldiers awaits transfer to a POW facility.

✪ A US Army artilleryman grimaces as he unleashes a round at the Germans near Carentan, France, in July 1944.

✪ GIs of a motorized regiment pause for a lunch break during the US Army's dash across France in August 1944.

✪ The German Panzerkampfwagen (PzKpfw) VI tank, best known as the "Tiger," weighed up to 57 tons and carried an 88mm gun. The one pictured in this August 1944 photo had been recently knocked out by American troops. Note the US Army truck passing in the background.

✪ A group of American infantrymen dashes through a burning town, supported by an M4 Sherman tank.

✪ GIs of the 60th Infantry Division stay close to an M4 Sherman tank as they move through a Belgian town in September 1944. Each man carries an M1 carbine, except the one at the left, who has a Browning automatic rifle (BAR).

✪ A US Army lieutenant and a member of the Forces Françaises de l'Intérieur (French Forces of the Interior) pause warily, watching for German activity during a firefight in a French city in the summer of 1944.

✪ A group of American GIs that has just been ambushed by Germans somewhere in the Netherlands takes cover and prepares to return fire.

✪ A group of GIs working its way through southern Belgium takes cover after encountering heavy German fire.

✪ On August 20, 1944, this group of GIs posed proudly with a captured German flag in the French town of Chambois in the Falaise Gap.

✪ ABOVE With Paris's Arc de Triomphe framed behind them, the men of the US Army's 28th Infantry Division march proudly down the Champs Elysées on Tuesday, August 29, 1944.

✪ LEFT A US Army M8 Greyhound armored car passes near the Arc de Triomphe in Paris in late August 1944.

US Army paratroopers descend into the Netherlands during Operation Market Garden in September 1944.

This panorama of the Netherlands city of Nijmegen was taken after the bitter September 1944 battle in which Allied paratroopers captured it from the Germans. The primary objective, the big bridge across the Waal River, is seen in the background. It was captured intact.

own future actions. After France and Belgium, the next phase of the assault on Adolf Hitler's Thousand-Year Reich would be Germany itself.

The question was where.

The broad approaches to Germany from the North Sea to the Swiss border can be divided roughly into three geographical segments. On the left, as viewed from the west, is the wide, open plain of Flanders (the Flemish-speaking provinces of northern Belgium), the Netherlands, and north Germany. This is the so-called traditional invasion route between Germany and France. Napoleon fought the Battle of Waterloo here in 1815, and the German armies used it in both World Wars.

The topography here is flat, although it is criss-crossed by numerous canals and rivers. Germany's great Rhine River flows into the North Sea here, but not as a single river. It breaks into a vast delta that dwarfs that of the Mississippi south of New Orleans. There are the Oud Rijn (Old Rhine), Neder Rijn (Lower Rhine), and Waal, and these are just the three main rivers forming the delta. In addition, there is the parallel Maas River that flows through Belgium and France as the Meuse River.

To the right, as we view the approaches of Germany from the west, are the rolling hills of Alsace and Lorraine. This region, especially Lorraine, has also been used as a "traditional invasion route." The Germans had used it to attack France in the Franco-Prussian War and in World War I. After the latter conflict, France had invested millions of francs to construct the vast Maginot Line to prevent this from happening again. The Maginot Line was an incredible and "impregnable" mass of concrete bunkers and gun emplacements that was created to effectively deny access to the Alsace and Lorraine to the

Germans. In 1940, the Germans had simply bypassed the Maginot Line. A couple of weeks after the Maginot Line had silently faced its first test, it was captured without a shot—from behind—and Alsace and Lorraine were now part of Germany.

It was Lorraine that was about to become the latest battleground for George Patton's Third Army. Known in German as Lotharingia, Lorraine had been the kingdom of Lothar in Charlemagne's empire, and hence the German name. As a student of military history, Patton could recount the origins and history of the region via military conflict as though he had been there. Actually, he *had* been here—during the First World War.

Geographically, Lorraine is surrounded by Luxembourg on the north, the Vosges Mountains to the south, the Moselle River on the west, and the Saar River on the eastern, German side.

In the center of our view of Germany from the west are the sprawling Ardennes highlands of southern Belgium, Luxembourg, and the westernmost parts of Germany. Here, the terrain is mountainous and difficult to traverse quickly. Before World War II, this area had never been a "traditional invasion route." For this reason, it was not seriously fortified or defended by France in the spring of 1940. Thus it was here, that von Rundstedt and the German Oberkommando der Wehrmacht had chosen to launch a major portion of its invasion of France.

Of course, the Germans too had a fortified line. Named for the great hero of the Germanic Nibelungenlied epic, the Siegfried Line dwarfed the Maginot line in scale. Constructed by the Germans in the years immediately before World War II, it extended as an almost unbroken mass of impediments from the Swiss border to just opposite Nijmegen in the Netherlands.

Four times the length of the Maginot Line, the Siegfried Line, or "Westwall," was not really a wall at all in the traditional sense. It contained fortresses, such as those at Pruem and Istein, but for the most part it was a defensive zone miles wide that was filled with barbed wire, mine fields, and reinforced concrete tank traps known as "dragon's teeth." These zones were, in turn, covered by pillboxes containing artillery and machine guns. This provided for defense in depth.

North of Karlsruhe, a secondary line of Siegfried defenses lay along the Rhine, fifty miles or more into Germany. This provided a very deep defensive line. The Siegfried Line also made use of natural terrain features, such as rivers and mountains. Naturally, the potential of the Ardennes as a difficult invasion route was taken into consideration.

From the Allied perspective, going through the Ardennes would be unnecessarily difficult, so it became a matter of whether to go to the right or to the left.

Going left was seen by SHAEF as optimal because that would take Allied armies directly into the German industrial heartland, the Ruhr Valley. Capturing the Ruhr meant taking out a sizable portion of German industry. To the right lay the Saar region, which was an industrial center, but of lesser importance to the German economy.

The British favored a left thrust toward northern Germany by way of Belgium and the Netherlands. The Americans, especially Bradley, wanted to attack toward *both* north and central Germany simultaneously. The plan adopted by SHAEF would be a *primary* left hook, and a *secondary* right jab.

The two armies of General Montgomery's 21st Army Group, as well as the United States First Army, would go left, while Patton's Third Army would go right. Ironically, this choice left the Allies' most aggressive—and arguably most capable—army on the right and relegated to having the Saar as its objective.

General Harry Crerar's Canadian First Army would have a fifty-mile swath of France and Flanders, with the English Channel on their left flank and the English army on their left. Crerar's army contained two corps, and for operations east of the Seine, each would have a distinct mission. The I British Corps would hook north and west of Rouen to besiege the port city of Le Havre. Meanwhile, the II Canadian Corps, commanded by Lieutenant General Guy Simonds, would move east, with the objective of securing the English Channel ports of Boulogne, Calais, and Dunkirk in France, and Ostende in Belgium.

The English on Crerar's right flank would be, as had been the case since they moved west from Falaise, General Dempsey's British Second Army. On the British right was the demarcation line between the 21st and 12th Army Groups and, across the line, the United States First Army.

The First Army would have a front that was about one hundred miles wide. It would be divided between—from left to right—Major General Charles Corlett's XIX Corps, Major General Lawton Collins's VII Corps, and Major General Leonard Gerow's V Corps. On the First Army's right flank would be Patton's Third Army. The demarcation line ran generally from the bridgehead at Melun—which the Third Army had captured from the Germans—to the southern border of Luxembourg. The First Army would assign a single corps, V Corps, to the Ardennes salient, while Patton's Third Army would circle south into the Reich by way of Lorraine.

Lorraine was the most direct route between France and Germany, and many, including Patton himself, had anticipated that the Lorraine would be a walkover, just as the several-hundred-mile dash from the Loire to the Marne had been. As the Third Army prepared to enter Lorraine, the German forces there were practically nonexistent. Patton had more tanks in an infantry division tank battalion than the Germans had in all of Lorraine. However, this was changing. German reinforcements were pouring in from northern Italy and southern France. Patton's new nemesis, Army Group G commander General Johannes Blaskowitz, was getting set to give Patton's Shermans a run for their money. Patton would also soon be facing a revitalized Fifth Panzer Army.

At SHAEF headquarters, it seemed that Lorraine, like the Ardennes, would be a minor footnote to the coming actions on the Western Front. However, in Lorraine, as in the Ardennes, the Germans would have some nefarious tricks in store for the Allies. From this standpoint, it was very lucky for Eisenhower and his entourage that men such as Tiger Jack Wood and George Patton would be on hand where and when it counted.

Monday through Friday, August 21 through August 25

While Paris grabbed the world's headlines that week, Patton was focused on his great Blitzkrieg to the south and east. The idea was to have two corps—XII Corps east of Orleans and XX Corps south of Paris—moving abreast of one another in a rapid sweep to the Seine.

On Monday, August 21, Walton Walker's XX Corps had moved southeast from Chartres with the objective of taking a bridgehead or two across the Seine between Melun—which is about thirty miles southeast of Paris—and Fontainbleau, which is ten miles south of Melun.

Patton understood that the key to the war east of Paris was getting across the Seine. As he had once observed, "Throughout history, campaigns and wars have been lost due to an army stopping on the wrong side of a river."

He was determined that such a mistake wouldn't be made on his watch.

The attack toward Melun would be led by two combat commands of General Lindsay Silvester's 7th "Lucky Seventh" Armored Division. With Combat Command B left behind to hold the approaches to Paris by way of Dreux, Combat Command A and Combat Command R were tasked to move out on Monday. While Combat Command A circled to the north of Melun, Combat Command R would drive straight in from the west to seize the bridgehead as quickly as possible. The latter command had reached the city on Tuesday, and had found the bridge partially intact. However, it would take the better part of the week to get across the Seine at Melun.

Spearheading the drive against Fontainebleau would be General LeRoy Irwin's 5th Infantry Division, which had been essential to the capture of Chartres over the weekend. Irwin moved quickly on Monday, not encountering any significant German opposition until his division got within about a dozen miles of Fontainebleau on Tuesday afternoon.

On Wednesday morning, the 11th Infantry Regiment of the 5th Infantry Division broke through the German resistance, and the division was rolling through Fontainebleau by midday. The 11th Infantry Regiment reached the Seine, near Fontainebleau at about the same time that the 10th Infantry Regiment reached the Seine at Montereau, a few miles upriver. Both regiments found that their respective nearest bridges had been destroyed by the Germans. With the help of a Forces Françaises de l'Intérieur unit that had taken Montereau, the 10th Infantry Regiment located a ford, and managed to get across the Seine. They secured the eastern shore and waited for engineers to arrive to install a prefabricated treadway bridge.

Meanwhile, an 11th Infantry Regiment battalion commander, Lieutenant Colonel Kelley Lemon, spotted five small boats on the eastern shore, swam the river, tied the boats together, and rowed them back. Using the boats, the 5th Armored Division managed to secure a place on the east side of the Seine for the engineers to anchor a treadway bridge. By Thursday, United States vehicle traffic was flowing across the Seine both at Montereau and near Fontainebleau.

Having taken Orleans on the Monday before Liberation Day, XII Corps—where General Manton Eddy had taken over command on Sunday from General Cook—would strike out toward the Seine first thing on Monday morning. Spearheaded by Tiger Jack Wood's remarkable 4th "Breakthrough" Armored Division, the corps had advanced about seventy miles on Monday. By Tuesday morning, they were in control of the city of Sens, about fifty miles southeast of Paris, with its bridges across the Yonne River.

The Combat Command A commander, Colonel Bruce Clarke, had made his move in the sort of quick, bold thrust that had become the trademark of Third Army operations. His command moved ninety miles in twelve hours and took down the German defenders of Sens with a decisive blow. Having accomplished their mission, the GIs sat down to a welcome treat—a hot chicken dinner, courtesy of French citizens of Sens.

On Tuesday—supported by the guns of the 66th Armored Field Artillery Battalion—the tanks moved out. Clarke intended to take on the SS Panzer units that had hoped, but failed, to reach Sens before him. With the aid of P-47 Thunderbolts from General Weyland's XIX Tactical Air Command, Clarke's Combat Command A was able to break the back of the SS force.

On Wednesday afternoon at around 3:00, it was the turn of the Luftwaffe to engage in air support of the German ground troops. Fortunately, Combat Command A had dispersed its vehicles, and the air attack was ineffective. The command's own antiaircraft gunners succeeded in knocking down nine of the fifteen attacking German aircraft, mainly Messerschmitt Bf-109s. Some P-47s that were nearby intervened to destroy four more of the Messerschmitts.

On Thursday, the II Canadian Corps reached Lisieux, about halfway between Caen and the Seine. The city had seen the last stand of the British Army in France in 1940. On June 14 of that year, eight British tanks and a battalion of infantry had held off a German panzer division for seven hours—until, having suffered 70 percent casualties, they were finally smashed into surrender.

By August 25, as the bridges of Paris fell into Allied control, Patton had captured four bridgeheads on the Seine south of the French capital. Meanwhile, Major General Ira Wyche's 79th Infantry Division, attached to Wade Haislip's XV Corps, had seized a Seine bridgehead at Mantes-Gassicourt, about twenty-five miles northwest of Paris and were closing in on one at Vernon, about fourteen miles downstream from Mantes-Gassicourt.

The Third Army had the momentum to the south, but the battles to the north and south of Paris were still just shaping up.

Friday, August 25

In Paris, Friday was Liberation Day. For those who saw the City of Lights as the ultimate symbolic prize of the campaign that had begun on the Normandy Beachheads, Friday was the climactic moment. For the GIs who were still taking and returning fire beyond the edges of the city, however, Friday was just another day in the string of days that formed the relentless offensive against Hitler's legions.

On the XII Corps front to the south and east, Combat Command A and other units of Tiger Jack Wood's 4th Armored Division had reached the Seine River at the city of Troyes about seventy miles east of Paris by Friday morning. The 4th Armored Division would battle the 27th SS Panzer Division for control of the city all day long in one of the fiercest battles since Normandy. Troyes was significant as a bridgehead across the Seine River, but it was also important as a rail hub and as an industrial center. Colonel Bruce Clarke of Combat Command A had managed to envelop the German defenders by putting a task force across the river north of the town to strike from the east, while the rest of his command came in from the west.

During the battle on Friday, there was an especially sizable number of actions by 4th Armored Division personnel that warranted either the Silver Star or the Bronze Star for heroism.

Among these was Captain Crosby Miller, who led the M4 Sherman tanks of the 35th Armored Tank Battalion's Charlie Company on a three-mile dash into the heart of Troyes. Despite—or perhaps *because of*—the heavy German artillery fire, Miller kept the tanks in motion, never halting for a moment until they'd penetrated to their objective within the city's *cen-*

tre ville. Even when they encountered an antitank ditch that the Germans had prepared, they kept moving. Because it was hard to see all of the tanks under his command with his hatch buttoned up, Miller remained exposed to enemy fire atop his turret through the entire action. Once Charlie Company had secured their objective, Miller spent the night monitoring their situation and preventing a German counterattack. For his bravery and attention to duty that day, he was awarded his Silver Star.

Another Charlie Company Silver Star went to Second Lieutenant Rufus Stillman, who led the company's reserve platoon in action at the German antitank ditch. The idea behind this ditch was to stop or slow down the American tanks, which would make them more vulnerable to the German antitank guns that were covering this position. Stillman's task was to secure the flank of the ditch, while the enemy guns were systematically destroyed. Having done this, Stillman personally took over the job of directing the company's Shermans through the ditch and leading his platoon into Troyes. As was the case with Crosby Miller, Rufus Stillman refused to button himself inside the relative safety of his tank turret.

The essential mission in the battle for Troyes on Friday was to secure bridgeheads across the Seine River and the parallel Seine Canal. Conducting a reconnaissance of the canal bridges was a small patrol led by First Lieutenant Stanley Lyons. The first three bridges that they located had been dropped by the Germans, so when the GIs found a fourth still intact, there was naturally an urgency to keep it that way. In order to secure the bridge before German engineers could destroy it, the GIs first had to fight their way through a German patrol that was there to see that they didn't.

Once the American patrol was on the bridge, Lyons and a

young corporal named Joe Ham would work through the night to locate the explosives that the Germans had placed. They found and disarmed two large bombs and a number of smaller charges. These would certainly have destroyed the bridge if the Germans could have set them off. Early Saturday morning, a half dozen German vehicles towing a total of five 105mm guns crossed paths with Lyons's patrol. The Yanks managed to knock out several of the vehicles and all the artillery pieces. For their actions that night at Troyes, both Lyons and Ham would receive a Silver Star.

Also leading a unit tasked with securing Seine Canal bridges on Friday was Second Lieutenant Julian Newton. His company entered Troyes under potent German small-arms and artillery fire. Newton had to split up his company in order to both guard a disarmed bridge that he found, and take out nests of German snipers in the nearby area. With his command divided, Newton had to move about a great deal to stay in contact with everyone, so he was compelled to expose himself the enemy small-arms fire constantly throughout the day. For this, he received his Silver Star, which was awarded in addition to a Bronze Star he had earned earlier.

Silver Stars would also go to Tech Sergeant LeRoy Cook of the 10th Infantry Battalion, and to Captain John Shea, the battalion's operations officer. For most of Friday, Cook and Shea had crisscrossed the battlefield, directing artillery fire and helping to coordinate the actions of various dispersed units. At one point, they came across the battalion commander and several others that were involved in a firefight with a German force that included a pair of antitank guns and numerous heavy machine guns. Cook grabbed his rifle, entered the fray, and managed to kill about a half dozen Germans. After dark, Cook and Shea worked through the night to develop plans to resist a German counterattack. Their bravery was soon written up for the medals, but Cook's would be posthumous. Saturday morning, exhausted from lack of sleep, he would inadvertently step on a German land mine.

The executive officer of the 10th Infantry Battalion would also be a recipient of a Silver Star for his bravery at Troyes that day. Even though he was cut off from the rest of the battalion, Major Leo Elwell decided to continue his attack into the city with a pair of tank platoons and two armored infantry platoons. Despite being outnumbered in the face of stiff German resistance at nearly every street intersection, Elwell's men broke through numerous obstacles to reach their objective near the center of Troyes. They then established a perimeter and held it until other 4th Armored Division units arrived.

A key part of the action had been artillery support from the 94th Field Artillery Battalion, which had taken up positions on the hill three miles northwest of Troyes on Friday. It would not be an easy day for the gunners, as their position soon came under fire from German artillery. Artillery observer Lieutenant Lewis Dent, who was killed by machine-gun fire as he was directing artillery, was posthumously awarded the Silver Star. Three artillerymen would be awarded Bronze Stars in the defense of the battalion's position. Each did what he had to do, despite having been wounded. Technician Fifth Grade Lawrence Craggy, the Battery B first aid man and Sergeant Porter Snyder of Battery C were each cited for assisting casualties under fire, while Technician Fifth Grade George Wilds was commended for dousing a fire in a loaded ammunition trailer.

An artillery observer with the 94th Armored Field Artillery Battalion, Second Lieutenant Albert Hoffman was tasked with coordinating all the observers who were spotting for the battalion's guns during the Troyes attack. As he was doing his work, he came under fire, and a tire and wheel were blown off his jeep. He grabbed an M3 machine gun and counterattacked against a cluster of German antitank guns. For his bravery, and for destroying one of these enemy guns and several German soldiers, Hoffman was awarded a Silver Star.

Meanwhile, First Lieutenant Thomas McDonald would earn a Silver Star while hitchhiking with a 94th Armored Artillery Battalion observer. When McDonald's jeep had been hit as he was making his way toward the head of his infantry company, he hitched a ride with the observer. A short time later, this jeep came under German heavy machine-gun fire and the observer was critically wounded. McDonald jumped off the jeep and counterattacked against the machine-gun nest, destroying it with a hand grenade. In addition to his Silver Star earned at Troyes, McDonald had also been written up for a Bronze Star for his leadership and courage under heavy enemy fire dating back to July 17.

As the artillerymen worked the Germans from their dangerous hilltop, the tough street fighting within Troyes saw several other Silver Star actions. One such medal went to Second Lieutenant James Field. Not only did he destroy an enemy ammunition carrier and a number of machine-gun positions, he helped other GIs knock out additional enemy gunners. By intentionally exposing himself, he made himself an irresistible target. When the Germans fired at Field, they betrayed their own positions to American gunners, who were ready to shoot back.

Staff Sergeant George Chapman was wounded in action as his unit made its way through Troyes, but he stayed with the other men and became a rallying point. When they were later pinned down by German snipers, the injured Chapman reacted by attacking the building from which the snipers were operating. He was able to take down the enemy position with hand grenades, although he was wounded again in the process. For his bravery, the sergeant earned a Silver Star. Also wounded in action inside the city, and earning a Silver Star, was Second Lieutenant William Lovell. Though injured, he continued to lead his platoon for more than three miles into and through Troyes.

Another second lieutenant earning a Silver Star in the street fighting was Carlton Price, whose platoon had been ordered to take out a pocket of German defenders who were preventing the Americans from penetrating the center of the city. Price's platoon quickly found themselves in a bloody hand-to-hand brawl, in which bayonets became a weapon of choice. When the dust had settled on this fierce battle, as many as fifty Germans had been killed. Several machine guns and two antitank guns were also out of action.

At about that same time, Staff Sergeant Isaac Van Ee and his squad were entering Troyes when their half-track got stuck at an antitank ditch. Van Eé ordered his men to scramble out of this sitting duck and counterattack. After they'd successfully knocked out the German positions, the sergeant flagged down another half-track to pull their original vehicle out of the ditch. The two half-tracks rejoined the rest of the company and Isaac Van Ee was awarded the Silver Star.

As would often happen during World War II, medics were among those whose bravery under fire warranted commendation. Two such medics in action at Troyes, both privates, were Roderick Bishop and William Devine. In the course of the early part of the battle, the main element of their medical detachment was stalled by enemy action and could not get into the city. Bishop and Devine found themselves under fire, and the *only* medics to have reached the center of Troyes. All day, and into the night, the two men cared for dozens of wounded GIs, as well as a sizable number of French civilians. For their exhausting devotion to duty over more than twenty-four sleepless hours, both men would be awarded the Silver Star.

Another Silver Star awarded to a medic during the Battle of Troyes went to medical aid man Private Anthony Scarpa. During a firefight, Scarpa became separated from his platoon while he was attending to some wounded soldiers. When the Germans overran his position, Scarpa was captured. Recognizing that he was a medic, the Germans took Scarpa to a field hospital to help aid wounded Germans.

Private Scarpa worked through the night at the German hospital with the aid of a Wehrmacht soldier who spoke English. Meanwhile, he carried on a running conversation with the Germans by way of his "translator." Scarpa casually explained to the Germans defending the site that included the hospital that their position was hopeless. He told them that it was only a matter of time before they were captured. By Saturday morning, he had convinced roughly one hundred German troops to stack their arms. He then delivered his "prisoners" to the surprised GIs of the 53rd Armored Infantry Battalion.

Anthony Scarpa's reputation as a poker player was never again in doubt.

The bitter urban warfare within Troyes on August 25 would also result in Bronze Stars awarded to First Sergeant Raymond Bell, Second Lieutenant George Casteel, First Lieutenant Thomas Donnelly, Staff Sergeant Harold Edmonds, Tech Sergeant Charles Graham, Staff Sergeant Robert Kenny, Tech Sergeant Herbert Morris, and Tech Sergeant Francis Pascucillo.

Earning an Oak Leaf Cluster to his Bronze Star for his heroism on Friday was a plucky First Lieutenant from New York named Abraham Baum. His unique contribution to the 4th Armored Division victory at Troyes was to work with Free French troops to locate maps of the city—which had been unavailable before the attack—and to ascertain where the German strongpoints were.

Baum would later become well known for leading the most controversial action undertaken by the Third Army during World War II. Exactly seven months later, on the night of March 25–26, 1945, he would lead his Task Force Baum on a dangerous dash deep into enemy territory aimed at rescuing American prisoners held at the German prisoner-of-war camp designated as Oflag (Offizierslager) XIIIB. This camp was located near the city of Hammelburg, due east of Frankfurt in Germany.

The mission had been conceived by General Patton against the advice of XII Corps commander General Manton Eddy and General William Hoge, who was, by that time, commanding the 4th Armored Division. Though he would later deny it, Patton's enthusiasm for the raid was said to be driven by the fact that his son-in-law, Lieutenant Colonel John Knight Waters, was being held at Oflag XIIIB. He had been captured in North Africa in 1943, and had recently been relocated from Oflag 64 in Poland. Through intelligence channels, Patton knew of the presence of Waters at the camp, but he insisted that the raid was initiated, not in a grandstand play to rescue a family member, but because of his fears that the American officers might be murdered by the Germans.

Though Patton favored using an entire combat command, Eddy convinced him to use a smaller task force. The sixteen tanks and 293 men would be under the command of

Abraham Baum, who was by then a captain. Task Force Baum penetrated sixty miles behind German lines, encountering increasing resistance as they went, and losing about half their fighting strength along the way. Baum reached Oflag XIIIB by midafternoon, and the prisoners were naturally overjoyed. However, their jubilation was misplaced. There were 4,700 prisoners, more than triple the number that Baum had expected. Baum realized that it would be impossible to evacuate this many sick, half-starved men sixty miles through German territory, especially now that the enemy was fully aware of the situation. Though they made a valiant effort to escape, only fifteen men from Task Force Baum made it back to American lines. Captain Baum was himself captured, and both he and Colonel Waters were wounded. In his memoir, Patton would describe the Hammelburg raid as the only mistake that he made during the Third Army's advance across Northern Europe.

Only about seventy-five Americans, including Colonel Waters, remained at Oflag XIIIB when it was finally and permanently liberated by Combat Command B of the 14th Armored Division on April 6. Waters went on to a lengthy career with the US Army, retiring as a four-star general—the same rank that Patton held in 1944–1945. Abraham Baum received the Distinguished Service Cross for his bravery in the failed rescue mission. In 1948, he went to the Middle East, where he fought alongside Moshe Dayan in the Israeli War of Independence.

By midnight on Friday, the Yanks of the 4th Armored Division had managed to wrest most of the city from the 27th SS Panzer Division. Across the Seine River, the Combat Command A flanking attack on the east side of Troyes was a resounding success. The American tank crews took the 51st SS

Brigade by surprise. Despite a bitter firefight, the Yanks managed to overcome a superior number of Germans. By Saturday morning, the German defenders who had still not surrendered found themselves surrounded.

In addition to the numerous Bronze Star and Silver Star actions during the bitter Battle of Troyes, one man earned the Congressional Medal of Honor on Friday, August 25.

While the heavy fighting was taking place at Troyes, the German 48th Division was fiercely counterattacking against a bridgehead that was held by the 5th Infantry Division about twenty-five miles downstream at Montereau, near where the Seine River is joined by the Yonne River. Casualties were being evacuated to the south bank of the river in assault boats rowed by litter bearers from the division's 5th Medical Battalion.

As one boatload of casualties reached midstream, a German machine gun suddenly opened fire upon it from high ground on the northern bank at a range of about one hundred yards. All of the men in the boat immediately jumped into the water—except a man who was so badly wounded that he couldn't get up from the stretcher. Two other injured men, who were unable to swim because of their wounds, clung to the sides of the boat.

Private Harold Garman of Albion, Illinois, a medic with the battalion's Company B was working on the south shore, carrying the wounded from the boats to waiting ambulances. Seeing the extreme danger of the men in the water, Garman plunged into the Seine. Swimming directly into a hail of machine-gun bullets, he reached the assault boat, and then towed it back to the southern shore. It was no easy task, to move the heavy assault boat with two men clinging to it while German gunners were trying to kill everyone, but Garman succeeded, and the three wounded men survived. It was men like Harold Garman that had inspired George Patton to observe: "It is a never-ending marvel what our soldiers can do."

Garman's heroism inspired a number of others on the south bank to pitch in to help in the effort to evacuate the wounded—and it earned Garman the Congressional Medal of Honor.

Saturday, August 26

The morning after Liberation Day was a day for parades in Paris, but George Patton's Third Army had already taken the battlefront of the European Theater well beyond the city. As de Gaulle, Leclerc, and the Comité Français de Libération Nationale dignitaries were strolling down the Champs Elysées in Paris, American GIs of the Third Army were hurrying across the Seine River on four brand-new treadway bridges, all of them located well east of the longitude of Paris.

In the north, the 7th Armored Division's Combat Command R had been tasked with a frontal assault on Melun to take the bridge at that city. However, they had become bogged down on Wednesday in a firefight with troops of the German 48th Division. Combat Command A, meanwhile, had circled a few miles north of Melun and had seized a bridgehead near the village of Tilly a few miles downstream. Despite German opposition, the US Army Engineers had managed to get a bridge constructed at Tilly before Combat Command R had managed to reach the river at Melun. General Walker himself arrived on the scene and pushed Combat Command R to capture what was left of the Melun bridge. By Friday night, Melun was in American hands and the 7th Armored Division was moving across the Seine at Tilly.

The 5th Infantry Division, meanwhile, had finally secured bridgeheads a few miles apart at both Fontainbleau and at Montereau, the scene of Harold Garman's Medal of Honor action on Friday. The engineers had gotten treadway bridges in service at both locations by the weekend.

Patton and his commanders were clearly poised to move farther and faster. Essentially, the breakthrough that Patton had achieved south of Paris had been accomplished by two corps with just two divisions each. Walton Walker's XX Corps contained the 7th Armored Division and the 5th Infantry Division, while Manton Eddy's XII Corps had the 4th Armored Division and the 35th Infantry Division.

Wade Haislip's XV Corps was still assigned to the Third Army, but had not participated in the actions south of Paris. The Third Army's other corps, VIII Corps commanded by Troy Middleton, was still hundreds of miles away in Brittany besieging the tenaciously held ports.

To facilitate the exploitation of Patton's breakthrough in the east, Bradley authorized the assignment of two additional divisions to the Third Army to attach to the corps south—and now *east*—of Paris. Major General Horace McBride's 80th Infantry Division was transferred from the First Army to XII Corps, while Raymond McLain's 90th Infantry Division—which had recently been attached to corps in both the First Army and Third Army—was assigned to XX Corps.

As Patton's corps were moving east, the Allied leadership was moving into Paris. General Dwight Eisenhower arrived in the city on Saturday on an inspection tour. General Omar Bradley and his 12th Army Group headquarters staff had already arrived to set up shop.

It was also on Saturday that Oberbefehlshaber West's General Field Marshal Walther Model made the fateful decision to move eastward across the Seine. A lot had happened in the week since he had formulated his plan to use the city of Evreux as a strongpoint for his panzers to defend the Seine. Not the least of these blows had come on Wednesday when General Leland Hobbs's 30th "Rock of Mortain" Infantry Division had captured the city with hardly a fight. The Seine was less than five miles away.

With the Allies in control of Paris and so many other Seine bridgeheads, and with the Third Army's powerful flanking action south of the city, it was clear to Model that making a stand west of a natural defense like the Seine was no longer a tenable option. Of course, by having waited so long, he was facing a situation such as that faced at the Falaise Gap—escaping intact. As with the Allies, he too needed bridges—in order to *escape* across the Seine. By this last weekend of the month, few of these remained.

Sunday, August 27

As Walther Model was struggling to withdraw what was left of his Oberbefehlshaber West command across the Seine, the Allies were steaming toward the river north of Paris. In contrast with Patton's "slash and burn" Blitzkrieg, the Canadians and British moved cautiously and methodically.

The first bridgehead cities north of Paris had been captured by the Yanks. The 79th Infantry Division had taken the bridgehead at Mantes-Gassicourt late in the week. Meanwhile, the 30th Infantry Division, who had captured Evreux, were moving toward Louviers. On Friday, elements of Major General Norman Cota's 28th Infantry Division and the 2nd "Hell on Wheels" Armored Division, commanded by Major General Edward Brooks, had taken Elbeuf. Another Seine bridgehead, it was only fifty miles from the mouth of the river and practically a suburb of Rouen, the largest city in the region north of Paris.

Meanwhile, V Corps commander Leonard Gerow began sealing off the approaches to Paris in the north and northeast. On Sunday, just one day after they had participated in de Gaulle's parade down the Champs Elysées, General Jacques Leclerc's 2nd French Armored Division moved out from Paris to accomplish the mission earmarked for him late in the week by Gerow. Leclerc's troops had taken Le Bourget airport northeast of Paris, and had occupied the suburbs of Aulnay-sous-Bois, Blanc, Mesnil, Dugny, Pierrefitte, and Mont-morency.

Monday, August 28

The week began with the Third Army sweeping forward across the Seine toward the next great terrain feature beyond Paris, the Marne River. The Marne flows generally on an east-to-west line east of Paris, emptying into the Seine on the southern edge of the French capital.

It was on the Marne line that the French managed to halt the first great German World War I Offensive in September 1914. A second attempt by the Germans to breach the Marne came in 1918, and again it failed. This time, the victory was due in part to the presence of United States forces. Though the Seine is a more formidable barrier, the Marne had a great deal of historical significance to the troops fighting here in 1944. Indeed many of the higher-ranking officers on both sides in 1944 had served near there three decades earlier.

Backed by the 35th Infantry Division, the 4th Armored Division jumped off Monday morning from Troyes, crossed the treadway over the Seine, and raced toward Vitry-le-

François, hoping to capture a Marne bridge intact. Meanwhile, the 80th Infantry Division also moved out from Troyes with its sights on Chalons-sur-Marne, about a dozen miles north of Vitry-le-François.

By the end of the day on Monday, Sherman tanks of the 4th Infantry Division's Combat Command A of the 4th Armored Division were in Vitry-le-François and had crossed the Marne. Having secured a Marne bridgehead, the 4th Armored Division turned north to aid the 80th Infantry Division in taking Chalons-sur-Marne on Tuesday.

North of Paris, General Charles Corlett's XIX Corps was taking over from General Wade Haislip's XV Corps as the First Army assumed control of the sector. On Monday, the centerpiece of this sector was the Seine bridgehead at Mantes-Gassicourt that had been captured during the preceding week by General Ira Wyche's 79th Infantry Division. It had been held against determined fire from German "eighty-eights," and unlike the bridgeheads south of Paris, it was yet to be used as a springboard for operations across the river.

This delay in exploiting the northern crossing gave Oberbefehlshaber West some breathing room. Had the Allies chosen to move across quickly, as the Third Army was doing at its bridgeheads south of Paris, they would have executed a left hook, driving north on the east bank of Seine toward Rouen and LeHavre, catching what was left of the German Seventh Army and Fifth Panzer Army and pulling them out of action. As it was, the Allies would not cross the Seine north of Paris until multiple bridgeheads were available. General Field Marshal Walther Model used the extra few days that he'd been handed to execute a withdrawal farther to the east.

Far to the south of Paris came more good news—for the Allies. The United States Seventh Army, which had come

ashore on the French Riviera thirteen days earlier, announced
on Monday that they had succeeded in capturing the great
French ports at Toulon and Marseilles.

While the Oberbefehlshaber West forces in Brittany were
continuing to tightly clutch the northern French ports, the defensive preparations that had been made by the German Nineteenth Army in the south were paltry and comparatively easy
to surmount.

Tuesday, August 29

On Monday, Combat Command A of the 4th Armored Division had taken the bridgehead across the Marne at Vitry-le-
François, and on Tuesday, they'd coordinated with the 80th
Infantry Division to capture an additional bridgehead across
river at Chalons-sur-Marne.

At the same time, Walton Walker's XX Corps divisions
were racing through the vineyards of France's Champagne region toward the cathedral city of Rheims. Walker used Lindsay Silvester's 7th Armored Division as a spearhead, flanking it
with LeRoy Irwin's 5th Infantry Division on the left and Raymond McLain's 90th Infantry Division on the right. As with
XII Corps, one of the important things on Walker's mind was
to capture bridges across the Marne wherever possible. Such a
bridge was captured at Dormans on Monday, and a number of
Yanks managed to get across the Marne here before German
LXXX Korps artillery finally knocked out the bridge.

Irwin's division then split left and right at Dormans to go
after two key bridgehead cities. Combat Command B went
upstream, toward the city of Epernay, a name that was familiar
then, as today, to champagne connoisseurs. Moving with that
lightning speed that was now characteristic of the Third Army

operations, they reached the town, secured it, and immediately brought up the engineers.

Since most bridgeheads that had been encountered thus far on the Seine and Marne had been captured without their bridges intact, it had quickly become standard practice for Corps of Engineers bridge builders to race along behind the armored spearheads and to be ready to throw in a treadway bridge within a matter of hours after a bridgehead was secured.

Meanwhile, Combat Command A and Combat Command R of the 7th Armored Division went downstream toward another city that would have been vivid in the memory of most Americans in 1944. Twenty-six years earlier, Château-Thierry had been the site of the month-long World War I battle that was the point at which the Allies began to take the American Expeditionary Force seriously as an effective fighting force, and the Germans found the United States troops to be a force to be reckoned with.

The battle is alternately referred to by the name of the city or by the name of the nearby forest—Belleau Wood—where it actually had taken place in June 1918. The American units involved in that battle had been attached to the 2nd and 3rd Infantry Divisions, and had included the 4th US Marine Corps Brigade along with the Army personnel. Despite determined German resistance and the worst casualties suffered by American forces since the Civil War, the Yanks prevailed, and they captured Belleau Wood.

On August 29, 1944, it was once again a matter of American troops fighting to dislodge Germans at Château-Thierry. Much had changed. In 1944, there were no doubts about the effectiveness of American troops, and the prospect that the action might take the better part of a month was quite improbable.

The Germans had constructed a defensive perimeter at Château-Thierry, but the Sherman tanks of the two combat commands overwhelmed the obstacles, wiped out the defenders and quickly reached the Marne, accomplishing as much in a day as their fathers had in that terrible month during World War I. To their surprise, the men of the 7th Armored Division discovered that more than one bridge remained intact in Château-Thierry.

In the city of Château-Thierry, the Yanks paused at the remnants of the twin-columned monument to the 3rd Infantry Division, which had been erected by the United States after World War I. Heavily damaged in the fighting between French and German forces in 1940, it had neither been repaired nor torn down completely. Now it would be time for the former, but with new purpose to the memorial. Some French women who came out to greet the tank crews explained that all through the German occupation, they had placed bouquets at the monument on each Fourth of July, and on each Armistice Day (November 11). They told the Americans that the German garrison had quickly removed the flowers each time, but that the women had kept sneaking them back to honor the fallen doughboys of that earlier generation.

Outside Château-Thierry, at the American cemetery of World War I casualties, the huge Aisne-Marne Memorial that was constructed in the 1920s had remained undamaged by either the 1940 campaign, or by the four years of German occupation.

By the end of the day on Tuesday, Walton Walker's XX Corps had managed to get across the Marne in three places spanning a front of about twenty-five miles, and were spilling across and moving east rapidly. Patton had said of Walker that he was "always the most willing and most cooperative. He will apparently fight anytime, anyplace, with anything that the Army commander [Patton] desires to give to him."

From his new vantage point in Paris, General Dwight Eisenhower was thinking politically as well as militarily. Indeed, his job as Supreme Allied Commander in Europe contained as much of a political dimension as a military one. For the past year, he'd found himself massaging the egos of such strong personalities as Winston Churchill and Charles de Gaulle—not to mention George Patton and Sir Bernard Montgomery—as often as he found himself planning strategy and tactics.

Eisenhower had arrived in Paris as the streets were still littered with the detritus of de Gaulle's Saturday parade, in which a million Frenchmen and Frenchwomen had watched de Gaulle himself "capture" the City of Lights. From a political vantage point, Eisenhower decided that he wanted the Parisians to catch a glimpse of reality. Paris had not been liberated by Charles de Gaulle, but by the force of arms of the Allied armies—and by late August 1944, the preponderance of personnel within these armies were Americans. Eisenhower was determined that the French people—especially the Parisians—should see this.

If Saturday was a good day for a parade, so too was Tuesday. If anything, Tuesday was even better—for making a point. This was because, by Tuesday, Paris had been invaded by a mighty armada of the world's media.

As these thoughts had been running through Eisenhower's mind, he was also reviewing practical matters such as routine troop movements. Among these routine troop movements were a sizable number of divisions that were being transferred from Normandy to the new battlefronts to the east. Among these was Norman Cota's 28th Infantry Division, which was due to be transferred from XIX Corps to V Corps. In order to make the move, the men would have to pass through Paris. It was a good day for a parade.

Instead of simply driving through town in trucks, the 15,000 men of the 28th Infantry Division and attached units assumed parade formation and marched through the Place d'Étoile. With the Arc de Triomphe framed behind them in the viewfinders of countless newsreel cameras, the division marched proudly down the Champs Elysées. For most of the men of the 28th Infantry Division, this was all they would ever see of the City of Lights. They marched straight through Paris, out the other side and toward combat. The pictures, however, would remain as a permanent part of the French—and American—memory of August 1944.

However, Tuesday was more than a day for parades. General George Patton viewed August 29 as a turning point.

At the time, he had made the comment that "Our chief difficulty is not the Germans, but gasoline. If they would give me enough gas, I could go all the way to Berlin!"

In reflecting upon this day in his after-action report—written after the war ended—he called the day "one of the critical days in this war." He observed that "It was evident that at that time there was no real threat against us as long as we did not stop ourselves or allow ourselves to be stopped by imaginary enemies. Everything seemed rosy when suddenly it was reported to me that the 140,000 gallons of gasoline which we were supposed to get for that day did not arrive. I presented my case [to General Bradley] for a rapid advance to the east for the purpose of cutting the Siegfried Line before it could be manned. It is my opinion that this was the momentous error of the war."

Patton went so far as to say that the Third Army—if adequately supplied—could capture the German city of Trier by the middle of September.

Trier lies at the eastern side of the Ardennes highlands at the head of the broad Moselle Valley that leads straight to Coblenz in the heart of the Rhineland.

As any tactician knows, the Moselle Valley east of Trier is a key route for essentially cutting western Germany in half. Having studied military history all his life, Patton was fascinated by Trier, which had served as the anchor of the Roman Empire in the Rhineland. Founded by Caesar Augustus himself in 15 B.C., the city had served as Rome's capital in Gaul and was often visited by succeeding emperors. As Patton knew, its capture by the Franks in the late fifth century was a turning point in the collapse of the Roman Empire.

Patton wanted to see himself playing a parallel role in the collapse of Adolf Hitler's empire. He would, but not in September 1944.

Eisenhower and Bradley would not be taking Patton up on his generous offer to capture Rome's capital in Gaul during September. The strategic plan was not, as we have seen, aimed at cutting western Germany in half through the Moselle River Valley, but at diving into northern Germany and capturing the Ruhr River Valley.

From Patton's point of view, SHAEF was throwing away an opportunity to utilize its fastest-moving army in an effort to smash all the way to the Rhine before the autumn leaves turned in the Ardennes. From Bradley's point of view, the SHAEF high command had decided that the Ruhr was the objective, and that was that. Bradley was also repeating the caution he'd shown two weeks earlier when he'd halted Patton's drive at Argentan. He feared what might happen if Patton's army became overextended.

On August 29, Bradley might have paraphrased his earlier comments by saying that he would rather have a "solid shoulder" in Flanders than a "broken neck" east of Trier.

Of course, one issue upon which Patton and Bradley were certainly in agreement was that the chief difficulty facing the Allies at the end of August was not the Germans, but gasoline.

It was estimated that it took about a quarter of a million gallons of gasoline to move a corps fifty miles. At the end of the previous week, the Third Army had less than half that amount on hand, and was making do with captured German fuel supplies. Indeed, on the preceding Wednesday, as the Third Army spearheads reached the Seine, Patton's legions passed the milestone of receiving less fuel than they had consumed for the first time since the Army had been activated.

The Rhine River was one hundred miles and a million gallons of gasoline away.

Wednesday, August 30

By Wednesday morning, the First Army was moving toward a bridgehead across the Aisne River near Soissons. The Third Army had secured a sizable number of Marne crossings and was pressing the attack toward the east with great speed. Having captured the Marne bridges at Château-Thierry on Tuesday, the 7th Armored Division raced to encircle Rheims to the north.

Like Chartres, Rheims was considered an important art treasure because of its great Gothic cathedral. For this reason, there had been some apprehension on the part of Allied planners that the cathedral and other sites might suffer irreparable damage if the Germans resisted and an artillery duel ensued. As it played out, however, the German lackluster defense melted quickly, and the 5th Infantry Division had the city secured by nightfall.

Farther north, in the First Army sector, progress had also been swift. Lightning Joe Collins's VII Corps made use of two Third Army bridgeheads in a move east of Paris. Having taken over the Seine bridgehead at Melun from the Third Army, they utilized the Château-Thierry bridgehead that had been captured on Tuesday by Combat Command A and Combat Command R of the 7th Armored Division. By the end of the day on Wednesday, VII Corps was at Laon, another cathedral city north of Rheims.

It had been at Laon in late May 1940 that Charles de Gaulle's 4th French Armored Division had counterattacked against the invading German armies, successfully pushing them back—for two days. It was the best that the French army could do against the Germans in 1940. Now, the Germans had surrendered Laon with less a bang than a whimper.

On Collins's left flank, General Gerow's V Corps was arrayed immediately east of Paris. It included Major General Lunsford Oliver's 5th Armored Division in the spearhead, as well as Raymond Barton's 4th Infantry Division. In keeping with General Omar Bradley's post-Paris plan of supplementing each vanguard corps with an additional division, Gerow had received the 28th Infantry Division, which had marched through Paris on Tuesday to join him east of town.

About fifty miles north of the city, General Charles Corlett's XIX Corps was preparing for action to exploit the Seine bridgehead at Mantes-Gassicourt.

Still farther north, Wednesday found the 21st Army Group beginning to make its big move. By now, the British and Canadian troops were in possession of seven Seine bridgeheads—including several that had been handed over by American forces—between Elbeuf and the mouth of the Seine. During Wednesday afternoon, the crossings would begin in earnest. Also on Wednesday, General Guy Simonds's II Canadian Corps marched into the great city Rouen, securing it against sporadic opposition.

As the month drew to a close, Allied leaders could take stock of what had been accomplished. June and July had come and gone with the Allies barely off the D-Day beaches. In the final days of July, Operation Cobra had offered the promise of a breakout; advances were still measured in distances of less than ten miles in a day.

During August, Patton's Third Army had captured nearly all of Brittany, as well as all of northern France between the Loire River and the latitude of Paris, from the Atlantic Ocean to the Marne River, advancing farther and faster than any army in the history of war. Between them, the Allies had destroyed two German armies and vast stores of irreplaceable equipment. Paris had been liberated, and the Seine River bridged. Meanwhile, the Seventh Army had come ashore in southern France and was making rapid progress.

At the beginning of August, the Germans had controlled nearly all of France, as they had for the four years' worth of Augusts before that. At the end of August, they controlled nearly none. Coincidently, all of France that now remained in German hands was roughly that portion that they had occupied in World War I.

❂ EIGHT ❂

OLD BATTLEFIELDS

Ghosts and exorcism are not solely the property of devotees of the occult. Military men are often haunted by ghosts of past battles. They are haunted by the ghosts of lost soldiers and the ghosts of blunders and lost opportunities. In early 1991, American military men deliberately strove to exorcise the ghosts of mistakes of Vietnam. A dozen years later, they would seek to exorcise the ghosts and demons left over from 1991. In World War II, military leaders sought to not repeat the mistakes of World War I. Just as the officers of 1991 had been the soldiers of Vietnam, so too had the officers of World War II been the soldiers of World War I. They had been there. They remembered.

By the end of August, the lessons learned had been lessons applied. The doctrine of mobile warfare—vociferously advocated by men such as Patton before World War II—had eliminated the horrors of the static front and trench warfare.

In World War I, Patton had been the first brigade commander of the Tank Corps of the American Expeditionary Force. During the St. Mihiel offensive in September 1918,

Patton fielded a total of 144 Renault light tanks with American crews, and he had seen their potential as armored cavalry. He had then watched in disgust as the postwar Army disbanded the tank corps and officially "forgot" the lessons of World War I. It would take his old and future nemesis, the Germans, to exorcise this mistake.

While the German army of the late 1940s had totally embraced the use of tanks and mobile warfare within their Blitzkrieg doctrine, such tactics were generally ignored elsewhere until after the Germans revealed in 1939 what was possible.

Among the prewar exceptions outside the Wehrmacht were Charles de Gaulle in the French army and George Patton in the US Army. A voice crying in the wilderness, Patton would eventually be one of the tireless advocates of mobile warfare that had gotten armored units restored to the US Army in time for the American entry into World War II. The efforts of men such as Patton had helped save the United States from at least *some* of the ghosts of World War I.

While the doctrine of mobile warfare had been vindicated, its champions were still outcasts. Both de Gaulle and Patton were now back in action, both on the same front and both still on the "bad boy" list in the minds of the Allied high command.

As August was giving way to September, it was hard to ignore other ghosts, the ghosts that always inhabit the places where blood had been spilled in such huge volume. Closer to home, one still senses ghosts at Gettysburg and Antietam. In Europe, in the late summer of 1944, the Yanks were now treading on ground that had been baptized by the blood of their fathers.

On August 29, the Americans had come back to

Château-Thierry, and in the coming days many other place-names would be carrying a familiar ring. As the Allied armies advanced toward the German border, they were fighting battles for the same ground, the same cities, and the same bridge-heads that had consumed the great armies of World War I.

Patton crossed the Marne, the Vesle, the Aisne, and the Meuse, all of which had once run red with American blood.

Thursday, August 31

On Thursday, it was time for the British to borrow a page from the American experiences earlier in the week at Château-Thierry. Having crossed the Seine near Vernon, the British XXX Corps reached and occupied the city of Amiens, the key city in the region of Picardy. Like Chartres and Rheims, Amiens is one of France's great cathedral cities, where the building itself dates to the thirteenth century. Like Rheims, the city would be relinquished without the street fighting that the Americans had to endure in Chartres.

More memorable to British troops than the city was the river that flowed through Amiens. The valley of the Somme River was the scene of one of the most terrible campaigns of World War I, and one of the worst in British military history. The campaign had begun on July 1, 1916, as an attempt to break the stalemate of trench warfare that had existed on the Western Front as the war neared the end of its second year.

The Somme campaign was also an effort to coax the Germans into moving troops away from Verdun, where the French were taking a terrible mauling. French troops would be involved at the Somme, but the majority would be British.

The British assault that began the Battle of the Somme was met by such determined German resistance that the

British lost more than 58,000 casualties on the first day alone. By the time that the "Meatgrinder of the Somme" wound to a close on November 18, 1916, the British had suffered 420,000 casualties—later characterized as "the flower of British manhood"—and the French had lost 200,000.

Thoughts of this horror were certainly on the minds of the British troops who crossed the Somme late on the last day of August, twenty-eight years later.

Friday, September 1

By Thursday night, the United States 7th Armored Division was within sight of the place where the biggest battle of World War I had taken place. Located on the Meuse River and guarding one of those "traditional invasion routes" from Germany through Lorraine toward Paris, Verdun had naturally evolved into a fortress city long ago. Once occupied by the Romans, Verdun had become one of the most important cities in Lorraine by the Middle Ages. One of the counts of Verdun was Godfrey of Bouillion, who became one of the heroes of the First Crusade in the eleventh century. Napoleon later constructed numerous fortifications here to defend his empire.

During the First World War, the location of Verdun and the numerous fortresses located on the hilltops surrounding it drew the attention of German military planners. In 1916, the chief of staff of the German Imperial Army, General Erich von Falkenhayn, made the decision to attack Verdun knowing that defeating the fortresses was probably impossible. His tactical plan was not necessarily to capture Verdun, but to force the French to defend it. He was looking not so much for a victory, but a war of attrition. Verdun could not be defended without a sizable commitment of manpower, and von Falkenhayn correctly understood that these troops would have to be diverted from elsewhere. The idea was to compel a reduction of French forces on the Western Front in anticipation of possible action there. In the process, he hoped to "bleed the French army white."

A million Germans attacked Verdun on February 21, 1916. In four days, the defenders had been pushed back from the outermost defenses, and the Germans were practically in the city. General Henri Philippe Pétain, later to disgrace himself by figureheading the Vichy government during World War II, was assigned to command the Verdun garrison. Under Pétain's leadership, the initial German advance was halted. The battle continued, largely as a brutal stalemate that was a microcosm of World War I itself.

German forces managed to advance again in May and June, but this effort ground to a halt. German troops had to be relocated to the Somme later in the summer to fight in a British-initiated battle of attrition. Ironically, the Germans had hoped to force the French to withdraw troops from the area around the Somme, and now it was the Germans who were forced to make transfers.

By the time that the battle at Verdun had officially ended in December 1916, the Germans were estimated to have incurred 337,000 casualties. The French had suffered 377,000 casualties, including 162,000 dead or missing. One of the survivors was a young soldier named Charles de Gaulle. Henri Pétain became a hero for preventing the Germans from capturing Verdun, and he would remain as a generally sentimental figure even after he took his walk on the dark side in 1940.

In June 1940, the Germans tried again, using tanks and mobile units—and no thought of waiting around for a long siege. In World War I, the fighting at Verdun consumed most of 1916 and cost nearly a quarter of a million casualties. In 1940, a handful of panzers accomplished in less than a day what a million German infantrymen and hundreds of siege cannons had failed to do in ten months.

Now, four years later, it was the turn of the Americans.

The jeeps, tanks, and half-tracks of the 7th Armored Division approached Verdun from the west. Traveling at about thirty-five miles per hour, they cruised through rolling terrain scarred by countless trenches. The trenches and earthworks were still clearly visible where they had been cut in the chalky, light-colored soil by that previous generation of soldiers. Lieutenant Colonel Edward McConnell led the first column of tanks into Verdun, not knowing what to expect. He would find little to remind him of war, other than hillsides that were covered, as far as the eye could see, by white crosses on neatly tended lawns.

The 7th Armored Division tank crews paused a moment in the ghostly shadow of Fort Vaux and Fort Souville—where so much blood had been spilled in 1916—and moved on.

Across the globe, at Walter Reed Army Hospital in Washington, D.C., General John J. Pershing, the man who had led the American Expeditionary Force into that earlier war, celebrated his eighty-fourth birthday on September 1 as the Americans drove through Verdun.

When asked for his thoughts, the old general told reporters that the day he had looked forward to had finally come. He remarked about the Allied victories in Europe, and told the journalists that he was in France again—in heart and spirit if not in body. He said that he saw General Eisenhower "pressing the battle now, as we pressed it in the fall of 1918.

"To shorten the war in Europe by a single day means now, as it meant then, the loss of fewer soldiers' lives."

He recalled how the war had ended in 1918 "a month before winter closed in," and wished the same for Eisenhower in 1944.

Neither could have predicted what was to come. Neither could have predicted what lay in store for the optimistic Americans in the snowy Ardennes during December 1944.

For now, it was only the beginning of September. The leaves had not even started to turn in the Ardennes, and the next objective for Walker's XX Corps after Verdun would be Metz, in the heart of Lorraine, the fortress city that had been the Verdun of the Franco-Prussian War.

If 1944's dogs of war were nostalgic for the Verdun bloodbath of 1916, they would not be disappointed with what lay in store for XX Corps at Metz. Metz would be the Third Army's Verdun.

✪ NINE ✪

THE APOGEE OF THE GREAT OFFENSIVE

On the last day of August, the Allies marked the eighty-fifth day since D-Day. General Eisenhower held a press conference to say that the Allied armies were five days ahead of schedule. He might have said that by the old pre-Overlord timetable they were at least five *months* ahead of schedule.

At Christmas 1943, the Supreme Allied Commander had said that the war against Germany would be over by the end of 1944 if those on the battlefronts and home front did their duty. Reminded of this prophetic statement, Eisenhower confidently announced that he still "stood by" his remarks of eight months before.

Did this mean, to paraphrase Pershing, that there would be an end to the war in Europe "a month before winter closed in"?

Did this mean that "the boys would be home for Christmas"?

It seemed to.

Euphoria was in the wind on those warm late summer days. References were being made in the media to Horace

Walpole's comment about the England of William Pitt, when it had been necessary to ask each morning about the day's new victory, for fear of missing them all. Comparisons to 1918 were made, but with the reminder that in 1918 the German army had still been well organized. The German army of 1944 was seen as being in disarray. Therefore, there seemed to be no apparent basis for comparison.

By the beginning of September 1944, that great offensive that General Eisenhower consistently referred to as a "Crusade," was in full swing. The Seine was in Allied hands, with men and materiel flowing briskly eastward across bridges both north and south of Paris.

Beyond the Seine, the Allies had vaulted all of the old stumbling block rivers of World War I. On the southern wing of the Western Front, Patton's Third Army had crossed both the Marne and the Meuse. On the northern side, both British and American troops were crossing the Somme. In the south, the Germans were in full retreat up the Rhone River Valley toward Lyon, and Allied air power was tearing the enemy columns apart.

As Eisenhower had formally relocated the headquarters of SHAEF from England to France, so too had the tactical air forces supporting the Allied ground war—the British Royal Air Force and the USAAF Ninth Air Force, parent of the IX Tactical Air Command—also relocated their headquarters to the Continent. Meanwhile, SHAEF had activated, but not yet committed, a new army to complement the British, Canadian, and two American armies that had been fighting in northern France since the first of August. Commanded by United States Lieutenant General Lewis Brereton, the First Allied Airborne Army was to be primarily a paratroop force that would be assigned to the 21st Army Group, commanded by Sir Bernard

Law Montgomery, who had just been promoted from General to Field Marshal.

The Germans were withdrawing just as quickly as the Allies could advance, pausing here or there to fight a holding action. The Fifth Panzer Army had attempted such a maneuver at Soissons, but had soon fallen back. General Heinrich Eberbach, commanding the German Seventh Army, tried another delaying action against the Americans, but in the process, he himself was surrounded and captured on Thursday, August 31.

By September 1, Allied tactical aircraft harassing the Germans behind their lines reported almost nothing but streams of withdrawing troops. Allied pilots reported that tanks were virtually absent from the mix of vehicles that they observed in their strafing runs—and they were correct. The Battle of France was all but over.

General Field Marshal Walther Model realized this as well. His job, as August gave way to September, was, as it had been since Falaise, to save what he could of his armies until they could get into a safe defensive posture and rebuild themselves.

Model and his legions were retreating from France, but every step that the beaten Germans took to the east, made the supply line to support them at their next stopping point one step shorter.

The Red Ball Express

As the German supply lines grew shorter during the early days of September, those of the Allies were lengthening perilously. In the first six or eight weeks of the Battle of Normandy, Allied advances were minuscule and supply lines were short and manageable. Suddenly, in mid-August, the Americans—especially Patton's Third Army—were pushing the front lines back by a dozen or so miles every day.

In September, nearly all of the supplies for a rapidly growing land armada were *still* coming in across the original invasions beaches in Normandy yet most combat units were between two hundred and three hundred miles from there and moving away rapidly.

In the beginning, much of the fuel for the Allied armies arrived prepackaged in five-gallon "jerry cans." It doesn't take a professional efficiency expert to tell you that this is not a very practical way to deliver half a million gallons—or more— a day.

Napoleon once said that an army "travels on its stomach," which is certainly true. A modern mechanized army *also* travels on its voracious appetite for fuel. As noted above, Patton's Third Army was already experiencing critical gasoline shortages by the time that it reached the Seine River south of Paris in the third week of August. Average daily consumption for the two United States numbered armies had nearly tripled from 300,000 gallons to 800,000 gallons.

"My men can eat their belts," Patton was overhead telling Eisenhower at a conference in the field on September 2. "But my tanks got to have gas."

At SHAEF, General Eisenhower had anguished about the problem as he fielded desperate pleas from field commanders. He saw the quartermasters' dilemma as a campaign analogous to those being fought by the combat troops. In his memoirs, he spoke of "strangulation on movement," and referred to the problem as "the battle of supply."

Ernie Pyle, the famous World War II war correspondent, wrote that the situation in the European theater at the end of August was "a tactician's hell and a quartermaster's purgatory."

Before the invasion, the Allied logistical planners had projected the supply requirements, but their calculations were way off. The rapid advances in the six weeks after the Operation Cobra breakout had come at a much faster pace than Allied planners had expected, so fuel and other supplies were now scarce. They had hoped to use the French railroad network, but Allied air power, French Resistance sabotage, and the "scorched-earth" policy of the retreating Germans had combined to literally destroy the rail system in northern France. Meanwhile, an idea to install a continuous six-inch-diameter pipeline from Cherbourg to Paris had to be abandoned when the facilities in Cherbourg were found to have been obliterated by German sabotage.

In few other instances in World War II was the problem of quartermasters keeping pace with the field armies more acute. Rations, fuel, and ammunition supplies were being consumed and used up at an incredible rate. At the same time, the logistical pipeline for a million-man army led from a narrow bottleneck on the Normandy beaches across a network of narrow roads to a battlefront constantly in flux. By the beginning of September, they had still not captured a French seaport that was in anything approximating usable condition.

Air transport was available, especially after the capture of numerous vast Luftwaffe bases in France during August, but this was hardly the answer to the requirement in terms of volume. The USAAF had hundreds of Douglas C-47 Skytrains in the European theater, but their maximum payload capacity was about 13,000 pounds, and this included the aviation fuel in their tanks. Of course, on each flight, the Skytrains had to carry not only enough fuel to get them to France, but enough to get them back to England.

There was also the problem with unpredictable flying

weather, and with the physical limitations of the internal shape of the Skytrains' cargo holds. They could carry jeeps, but no larger vehicles. Nevertheless, the C-47s proved vital for carrying such precious small-volume materiel as blood plasma and radio gear.

By the end of August, it was estimated that as much as 95 percent of the unconsumed supplies that had been delivered into France still lay in the sprawling supply dumps in Normandy. General Omar Bradley of 12th Army Group commented August 27 that his troops would go "as far as practicable and then wait until the supply system in rear will permit further advance."

Despite everything that *was* being done, the supply situation had gotten way out of hand. Something had to be done and done quickly.

The agency officially responsible for supplying US Army troops in France was known as the Communications Zone, European Theater of Operations (COMZ-ETO). Formed in England under SHAEF command, COMZ had moved its headquarters into the Cotentin Peninsula in late July. On August 25, COMZ had relocated to Paris, because the recently liberated capital was more centrally located—and because who *wouldn't* want to be in Paris rather than Normandy?

Also on August 25, COMZ initiated one of the most brilliant—albeit obvious—supply schemes of World War II. To do so, the agency would lean heavily on one of the must unassuming secret weapons of World War II—the 2.5-ton army transport truck. General Eisenhower would credit this vehicle, known universally to GIs as the "Deuce-and-a-half," with being one of the most important American weapons of World War II. By August 25, it had already proven invaluable on the Western Front when COMZ initiated the idea for an amazing logistical operation that would be known as the "Red Ball Express."

An emergency measure that became an institution, the Red Ball Express would be a twenty-four-hour-a-day, seven-day-a-week, nonstop, long-haul trucking system that started on the beaches of Normandy and ran directly to the front lines. The name derived from the symbol used by the railroads within the United States to designate fast, priority freight trains.

COMZ selected its routes and arranged for the exclusive use of two separate, parallel highways across France on which the Red Ball Express trucks, and *only* the Red Ball Express trucks, would travel day and night. Because of Allied air superiority, there was no longer any serious Luftwaffe activity over France, so the drivers could ignore blackout rules and drive at night with their headlights on and keep up daytime speeds.

On August 25, the day that the Red Ball Express was officially initiated, 67 truck companies were operating between St. Lô and Chartres. Four days later, 6,000 Deuce-and-a-half trucks, tanker trucks, and tractor-trailer rigs, belonging to 132 truck companies, moved *24 million* pounds of supplies in a single day. This was three times the volume that had been brought in by air in the preceding two months. As the daily fuel needs of the two field armies topped the million-gallon point in September, the Red Ball Express kept pace.

COMZ quickly installed signage to keep truck drivers from wandering off the route, and created mobile repair teams to cruise the Red Ball Express route looking to aid broken-down trucks. Rest stops were established so that truckers would have places to stop for a hot meal or to take a nap. Of course, the bane of all truck drivers, the highway patrol, was also present. The MP "Smokies" would patrol for speeders, but also for hijackers. The hijacking problem involved not Germans, but American units. Sometimes seeing a truck loaded with supplies destined for another unit was a temptation that was too much to bear.

Originally, COMZ and SHAEF had envisioned the Red Ball Express as a temporary emergency measure to run only through September 5. However, its initial success led to a series of extensions. The Red Ball Express would continue to operate until November 16, 1944. By that time, the Allies had resumed the offensive that had slowed to a crawl at the end of September, and were so far from Normandy that it took about 300,000 gallons of fuel daily just to keep the Red Ball Express itself going. In its eighty-four days, the Red Ball Express had transported more than a billion pounds of materiel.

Thursday, August 31

On the Third Army front, Combat Command A of Tiger Jack Wood's 4th Armored Division reached the Meuse River at the city of Commercy on the last day of August and literally overpowered Germans who were set to detonate explosive charges placed on the bridges. It was the stuff of which they write books. By the end of August, the 4th Armored Division alone had captured 11,000 prisoners, while taking only 1,100 casualties.

As General Sir Miles Dempsey's British Second Army and the United States Third Army were crossing paths with the ghosts of World War I on the final day of August, General Omar Bradley was formulating a plan of attack for his United States First Army. On Thursday afternoon, he sent his 12th Army Group Operations officer, Brigadier General Truman Thorson, to call on General Charles Corlett at the XIX Corps field headquarters northeast of Paris. Thorson outlined a bold new plan for XIX Corps. In essence, Bradley wanted to set up a repeat of what had—sort of—been accomplished at Falaise.

The Bradley plan, as presented to Corlett that afternoon in a Picardy farm field, was to create another "pocket," such as had existed at Falaise, and use it to trap what was left of the German forces west of the Siegfried Line.

It was evident that major flow of the German withdrawal was through the big French industrial city of Lille, across the border and up through the Belgian capital of Brussels. The key to cutting off the main highway between Lille and Brussels was the Belgian crossroads city of Tournai. Thorson explained that Bradley wanted Corlett to move out immediately and move quickly. He wanted XIX Corps in Tournai by Saturday.

Ahead of XIX Corps lay the cities of Montdidier and Peronne, the latter astride the Somme River, upstream from Amiens, where the British were, at that moment, securing a bridgehead. If XIX Corps continued to move as previously planned, each of those cities would be entered and occupied. If German defenders were present, a battle would ensue. There was little doubt that the Yanks would be able to defeat any opposition, but Bradley knew that each such action would take, at the least, the better part of a day. Even if no Germans were present, it would take time for the Americans to secure each of these cities, and all of the smaller villages along the way.

What Bradley wanted Corlett's command to do was to bypass Mondidier and Peronne, and to drive with all deliberate speed to Tournai, which was located just across the *British* zone of jurisdiction. Planning an encroachment into Montgomery's bailiwick apparently didn't trouble Bradley.

Bradley would also order General Leonard Gerow's V

Corps to undertake a drive of its own toward Tournai, but Corlett's XIX Corps was closer, and hence it would be the primary unit in the operation. In this process, both V Corps and XIX Corps would be crossing prearranged corps boundaries. As XIX Corps moved left into British Second Army territory, V Corps moved left into XIX Corps country.

Bradley also had Belgium in mind for Lightning Joe Collins's VII Corps. On Thursday, orders reached Collins that he, like the two adjacent corps to his left, was to drive north, crossing into V Corps territory to capture the old Belgian fortress city of Mons. From there, he would cross back into the sector designated for VIII Corps and move toward Namur and Liege. The latter city was practically on the Belgian border with the Netherlands.

At the same moment that Collins was being ordered to make haste toward Mons, a sizable German force was also being ordered into the city. Neither side would know that the other was going to Mons. General Erich Straube, commanding the LXXIV Korps, had been ordered to take over two additional units, the II SS Panzer Korps and the LVIII Panzer Korps and organize the three into a provisional army. Mons had been picked as the assembly point because on the last day of August, it appeared that it was safely back from the front lines. This was changing—and faster than either Collins or Straube would have predicted.

Friday, September 1

To accomplish a forty-eight-hour dash for a hundred miles to the Belgian border, XIX Corps's General Corlett realized that he needed to get all of his foot soldiers off their feet. He took all the trucks that he had, and divided his infantry into those trucks. The sum of this arithmetic equaled just three regiments. He chose one regiment from the 30th "Rock of Mortain" Infantry Division, and two from the 79th Infantry Division. The tanks of the 2nd "Hell on Wheels" Armored Division would form the spearhead for this task force.

Having configured the force, Corlett ordered the men to get a good night's sleep on Thursday night, because they'd be on the road all of Friday night in order to get to Tournai by Saturday. The troops headed out at the crack of dawn on Friday, with Combat Command A of the 2nd Armored Division leading the way. Bypassing Montdidier, they reached and crossed the Somme River by noon and pressed northward.

Meanwhile, General Gerow ordered Combat Command A of his 5th Armored Division to spearhead the V Corps drive into Belgium. As with Corlett, Gerow would use all the trucks that he could scrounge to send several regiments of the 4th Infantry Division and 28th Infantry Division on the adventure. Gerow's operation jumped off on Thursday night, ahead of the XIX Corps start, and continued through Friday.

At the same time, Lightning Joe Collins had formed up a VII Corps task force for the adventure involving Mons. The 3rd "Spearhead" Armored Division, now under the command of Major General Maurice Rose, would be the centerpiece of the action. On the flanks would be the 1st Infantry Division—the Big Red One—on the left, and the 9th Infantry Division on the right.

Saturday, September 2

Saturday morning found elements of both Charles Corlett's XIX Corps and Leonard Gerow's V Corps moving northward toward Belgium at top speed. German troops had been left in the various cities of northeastern France and given orders to fight any Allied troops who came knocking. The Yanks, however, bypassed the towns, leaving them to be captured by nonmotorized elements of the two corps that would be moving through early in the coming week.

Before noon, the advance units of V Corps had reached Landrecies, barely twenty miles from Belgium, where they literally ran out of gas.

At 10:00 P.M., Combat Command A of the 2nd Armored Division, under the command of Colonel John Collier, reached the city of Tournai, followed soon after by advance units of the motorized 30th Infantry Division. The 1,300 German troops at Tournai were stunned by the sudden arrival of Allied troops. They had predicted that the city would be safe from their enemy until early in the coming week. Had it not been for Bradley's sudden thrust, they would have been right.

On the 21st Army Group segment of the front, General Crerar's Canadian First Army had moved out from their bridgehead at Rouen on Thursday, and were heading up the coastline of the English Channel. The two corps under Crerar's command moved in different directions. While General John Crocker's I British Corps undertook the siege of the big seaport of Le Havre at the mouth of the Seine, the II Canadian Corps under the command of General Guy Simonds began inching eastward toward the English Channel ferry ports.

On Saturday, Simonds captured Dieppe. If names such as "Verdun" and "the Somme" conjured up ghosts from World War I, then the drive that Simonds's corps was making brought back bitter memories from the first phase of World War II.

Dieppe was the coastal city that had been targeted in the famous commando raid on August 19, 1942, that had cost so many Allied—especially Canadian—lives before the attackers retreated into the sea. Dieppe had remained one of those dark clouds under which the Allies had labored for two years, but which were now being cleared. Today, with minimal German resistance, Dieppe was added to that list of French towns and cities to which the Allies had returned—not just in a desperate hit-and-run commando attack—but to stay.

From Dieppe, Simonds would move up the coast to the city whose very name was synonymous with British disaster in the first year of World War II. Dunkirk had been the place to which the British Expeditionary Force had retreated in June 1940 as France fell to the German armies. Finding themselves on the shoreline at Dunkirk, with their backs to the sea, were 338,000 Allied troops—mostly British. Had it not been for the bravery of the crews manning more than 800 small vessels, they would certainly have been captured by the Germans.

Though the men had escaped from disaster at Dunkirk, the British army had lost virtually all of its tanks and heavy equipment. Dunkirk represented the first minutes of what Prime Minister Churchill would characterize as Britain's "darkest hour."

Finally, it was the turn of the British and Canadian troops of Simonds's corps to return the favor. On the first weekend of September 1944, it was the Germans who were surrounded at Dunkirk, with their backs to the sea. Unlike the scene in 1940, there were no boats bobbing on the horizon to come to their aid.

Sunday, September 3

John Collier's 2nd Armored Division Combat Command A had arrived at Tournai before midnight Saturday, and by the early hours of Sunday, the task forces that had been sent to Tournai by both V Corps and XIX Corps had converged on the city. Elements of both the 30th Infantry Division and the 79th Infantry Division of XIX Corps were on hand around midnight. Combat Command B of the V Corps 5th Armored Division arrived shortly thereafter. By first light, the German garrison had given up.

Meanwhile, British forces had started arriving in Tournai, surprised to find that the Americans had crossed the jurisdictional boundary and were already in town. They complained to Montgomery, who in turn complained to Bradley, who had authorized the infringement.

The British bypassed Tournai and pressed forward. By late morning they were in the vicinity of Waterloo, where they duly noted a previous success of the British Army on this ground. It had been here at Waterloo, in June of 1815, that the British general Arthur Wellesley—the Duke of Wellington—had led the force that dealt the final and decisive blow to the armies of Napoleon Bonaparte. Having cast a glance to the enormous monument to that bygone British victory, they raced ahead, capturing Brussels—virtually abandoned by the retreating Germans—by nightfall.

The anticlimactic liberation of Brussels had not been unexpected. Indeed, a German broadcast over Radio Brussels on Friday night had been unambiguous. In fact, it almost bordered on apologetic.

"The enemy is approaching at a rapid pace," the German announcer had told the citizens of Brussels. "You who stay here, remain calm. We Germans will always remain correct. We shall never rob you, and we shall never pillage you. We shall do no harm to anybody. Do not show hatred against us or those in your country who have worked for us."

More ominous than the announcer's guarded insistence that Germans would be "correct" was the bitter statement broadcast by SS General Hans Friedreich.

"I know you are friends of the British, that you are eagerly awaiting the British and American forces." The SS gauleiter sniffed, speaking in French. "Within a short while, you will fill the streets of Brussels and shout, 'At long last they are here, the liberators.' You will acclaim the Allied troops as they march through your streets. You will do so because you know that Britain has never lost the last battle. But one day we shall come back. Until then, *à bientôt*."

Forty-eight hours after Friedreich spoke, the British tanks were in the second European capital to be liberated by the Allies who came ashore in Normandy. There was not even a pretense of the German resistance that had occurred in Paris. A few snipers were reported, but the cheering crowds were not disturbed.

The people of the city filled the streets and shouted, "At long last they are here, the liberators." The people of the city acclaimed the Allied troops as they marched through the streets. At some places, the British columns ground to a halt, but only when the crowds of well-wishers grew too large for them to pass.

By Friday, the bureaucrats and elected politicians of the prewar Belgian government—including Prime Minister Hubert Pierlot—who'd been biding their time for four years in London were back at their desks in Brussels. They were the first normally constituted government of a German-occupied nation to resume business as usual. Given the situation that would soon be evolving in the areas of Eastern Europe that would be "liberated" by the Soviet armies, this idea of resuming business as usual would be a rarity in postwar Europe.

As for the SS man's final prediction, Germans have returned to Belgium as tourists and bureaucrats, but not as rulers. The march of history and the evolution of the European Community have probably rendered it impossible that the German occupation of 1914–1918 that Friedreich remembered, and of 1940–1944, which he administered, will ever be repeated. Ironically, Brussels would become the capital of the European Community, of which Germany is a member.

About thirty miles southeast of Tournai, American troops had reached Mons, even as the British were being feted in Brussels. However, Bradley had, by now, changed his mind about Mons. On Saturday, he had asked the First Army commander, General Courtney Hodges, to contact Collins and ask him to halt his advance short of the city to avoid outrunning the ability of the quartermasters to keep up with a supply of fuel. Hodges had tried all day, but the fast-moving VII Corps had apparently outrun the ability of the Signal Corps to string telephone wire.

The 3rd Armored Division was in the Mons vicinity by late Saturday night, and by midday on Sunday, the city center was in American hands. By the time that word had come for VIII Corps to *not* capture Mons; it had already been captured. Through the day, the units from the Big Red One and the 9th Infantry Division fought their way into Mons and the surrounding area.

As the British and Americans seemed to slide fairly easily into Brussels and Mons on Sunday, events were shaping up to present the Americans with some of the most difficult fighting that they had seen since the Seine.

At the end of the preceding week, neither General Collins of VII Corps nor General Erich Straube of the German LXXIV Korps—and the newly attached provisional army— had been aware that the other was moving into the Mons area.

The Americans had the city as their objective, while Straube's army was headed to an assembly point outside of town, so the main center of the two forces did not actually cross paths. When units from the opposing sides made contact over the weekend, neither side was fully aware of the size and scale of the opposition.

By Sunday, the sheer number of firefights being reported to the respective headquarters brought the situation into focus, and the shootout intensified. At one point a German column was targeted by 3rd Armored Division tanks and shot to bits in its tracks. Monday morning would dawn on a burned-out line of German vehicles that was a mile long.

The worst of the fighting seemed to have peaked on Sunday, but it would continue into Monday and Monday night.

A "Ghost" Story

Among the 9th Infantry Division units in southern Belgium that Sunday was the 2nd Battalion of the 60th Infantry Regiment, commanded by Captain Matt Urban. He was the former company commander who had been severely wounded while personally leading two infantry attacks in Normandy on June 14—and who'd checked himself out of a hospital in order to hitchhike back to Normandy in time to lead troops into battle on the opening day of Operation Cobra.

Matt Urban, now commanding his battalion, had been in action all across France. Wounded on both August 2 and August 15, he had repeatedly refused evacuation, even when strongly urged by the battalion surgeon. Each time he was hit, Urban seemed to get back in action almost immediately. He even had a cult following among the Germans who called him *der Geist*—"the ghost."

On September 3, as the 9th Infantry Division moved into Belgium, the 2nd Battalion was given the mission of establishing a point at which troops could ford the Meuse River near the village of Heer. Moving toward the river, the battalion came under ferocious enemy artillery, small arms, and mortar fire.

True to form, Urban quickly left his command post to lead the battalion from the front. Reorganizing the attacking elements, he led the charge toward the enemy's strongpoint himself. As the troops moved across the open ground, Urban was shot through his neck, leaving him bleeding profusely and in obvious danger of losing his life. Although he could barely speak because of his wound, he refused to be medevacked until the Germans had been routed and the 2nd Battalion had secured the crossing point over the Meuse River.

"Wars may be fought with weapons," George Patton had observed, commenting on heroes such as Matt Urban. "But they are won by men. It is the spirit of the men who follow and the man who leads that gains the victory."

Urban would recover from what had been diagnosed as a "mortal" wound, although his vocal cords were damaged permanently. He would retire from the service as a lieutenant colonel.

Later in the war, the 2nd Battalion was badly depleted, and many of its troops wound up as prisoners of war. One of them was Staff Sergeant Earl Evans, who had served with Urban in both Europe and North Africa, and who was present on September 3. Evans would be released after the end of World War II, and would return to the United States in July 1945, where he promptly prepared a letter recommending Urban for the Congressional Medal of Honor. The letter would languish in the morass of postwar paperwork, and would not surface until June 1978. The Army Military Awards Branch would attempt to reconstruct the evidence of events that had occurred thirty-four years earlier. As this process unfolded, eyewitness statements emerged, which would reveal an amazing picture of exceptional heroism.

On July 19, 1980, in a ceremony at the Shoreham Hotel in Washington, D.C., President Jimmy Carter referred to Matt Urban as "the greatest soldier in American History," as he finally awarded him the Congressional Medal of Honor—for his heroism over those eleven weeks between June 14 and September 3, 1944. With this decoration, Urban would eclipse the great Audie Murphy as the most decorated American soldier ever.

Matt Urban would die in March 1995—from the collapse of a lung that had been injured during one of his numerous combat actions in 1944.

Monday, September 4

Matt Urban's would not be the only Congressional Medal of Honor to be awarded for actions during the battle around the Mons Pocket during the first week of September.

On Monday, the 18th Infantry Regiment of the 1st Infantry Division were dug in outside the village of Sars-la-Bruyere, near Mons, when they were attacked by a larger German force. They were quickly overrun and driven back by withering German firepower. Private First Class Gino Merli, a machine gunner from Peckville, Pennsylvania, found himself surrounded. Nevertheless, he maintained his position, covering the withdrawal of American troops and breaking the desperate thrust by Erich Straube's provisional army.

Eventually, Merli's assistant machine gunner was killed

and their position was captured. Eight GIs were forced to surrender, but Merli slumped down beside the dead assistant gunner and feigned death. No sooner had the enemy group withdrawn than Merli was up and firing at the German lines. Once more his position was taken, and the Germans found two apparently lifeless bodies—one of which was the not-so-lifeless Merli. The Germans stepped away and Merli was back at it. He would stay at his weapon throughout the night, inflicting heavy enemy losses.

As the 1st Infantry Division troops counterattacked at dawn, they found Germans ready to surrender. They also found Merli, still at his gun, surrounded by fifty-two enemy dead. Gino Merli would be awarded the Congressional Medal of Honor.

Exhausted by the fighting, and by the months that had led them to Mons, the Germans gave up. VII Corps would take at least 10,000 prisoners in the "Mons Pocket," including nearly everyone in Straube's provisional army except the II SS Panzer Korps and LVIII Korps senior staff, who escaped eastward in disarray. Only about fifty armored vehicles were captured, and not all of them tanks. That was all that the three German korps had left.

The pocket of German troops that Omar Bradley had hoped to snare at Tournai had indeed been snared—but *not*, as he had planned, at Tournai.

By Monday night, three armored divisions of the British Second Army had moved on from Brussels and had captured the great Belgian port of Antwerp. For *months*, SHAEF had anguished over the French ports of the Brittany Peninsula and their vital importance in supplying the Allied troops on the continent—especially with winter coming.

Indeed, VIII Corps—formerly of the Third Army but

now reassigned to the newly activated United States Ninth Army—was still besieging Brest in early September. Now, suddenly, the Brittany ports faded from significance.

Here was Antwerp. With four times the prewar tonnage as Cherbourg, it was the greatest port in continental Europe—and the third largest in the world after New York and London. Antwerp, with its twenty-five miles of docks, its twenty-nine miles of quays, and its huge railway yards was a prize of unmentionable magnitude.

The retreating Germans had done considerable damage at Antwerp and had sabotaged many facilities, but had then relinquished the great seaport without a siege. Though it would not be fully restored until November, parts of the port facilities would be functioning within weeks.

The capture of Antwerp would be a gift that would be of immense benefit to the Allies until the end of World War II.

Tuesday, September 5

Before the weekend, as his troops were streaming out of France like ants, General Field Marshal Walther Model had considered where next to make his stand. Model had assumed—more accurately, he had *hoped*—that the Allies would run out of steam, or fuel, and he could pause in Belgium to regroup and to hold them, as von Kluge had done with the British and Canadians at Caen in June and July. If he could accomplish such a feat with the British and Canadians now, it would be winter and the forward momentum would go dormant.

Then came the weekend. Erich Straube's provisional army had gone into the woods near Mons to regroup—and had wound up being effectively chopped up and spit out by Americans that weren't supposed to be anywhere near Belgium. Then the British, who had been held at bay for months in Normandy were cutting through Belgium like a hot knife through butter.

On Sunday, Model had gotten the bad news: Brussels had fallen to Dempsey's British Second Army.

On Monday, Model had gotten more bad news: Antwerp had fallen to Dempsey's British Second Army.

On Tuesday, Model had gotten yet more bad news: Ghent—the second largest city in Belgian Flanders after Antwerp—had fallen to Dempsey's British Second Army.

Instead of the Allies running out of steam, Model realized that *he* was running out of Belgium—both in the sense that he was losing ground in the small kingdom, and that he was on the run, *and* on the way out.

If Model was despondent on Tuesday afternoon, his boss was apoplectic. Adolf Hitler, who had ordered von Kluge to hold Normandy at all costs and von Choltitz to hold Paris at all costs, was at wit's end by the weekend. By Tuesday, he was berserk. Normandy had been lost; then Paris was lost. Now, as he saw all of France falling next with the German armies in full retreat, the Führer was livid. He needed help, he needed his superstar.

Out of retirement, Hitler called the legendary Field Marshal Karl Rudolf Gerd von Rundstedt, the mastermind of the Blitzkriegs that swallowed Poland, France, and the Ukraine in 1939, 1940, and 1941. Hitler had "nudged" him into retirement from the Oberbefehlshaber West job earlier in the summer, but now he was being asked once again to answer his master's call. Hitler named von Rundstedt to once again take the helm of Oberbefehlshaber West, while Model was allowed to retain the subservient position as commander of Army Group B.

The sour-faced Prussian field marshal looked at what had curled Model's hair that week and cringed. Von Rundstedt saw the German troops—he couldn't call them German armies because that would imply more organization than there was—and he recoiled. He saw the once proud Wehrmacht running out of Belgium, and knew that this was the only way to run.

As he took command of a retreat on the scale of Napoleon's from Moscow in 1812, the old Prussian observed that from France to the German frontier, his troops were outnumbered two to one. His Oberbefehlshaber West command was outnumbered twenty-five to one in artillery, and twenty to one in tanks—an advantage that clearly favored the agile M3A4 Shermans over the technically superior Tigers and Panthers. Despite this, the Wehrmacht was far from beaten. In the autumn of 1944, von Rundstedt had a larger force than any county on Earth would have at the dawn of the twenty-first century—and the old man still had some tricks up his gold-braided sleeve.

The first of these surprises would be the Meuse-Escaut Canal on the border between Belgium and the Netherlands, and the Albert Canal west of it. Together, they formed a better barrier than anything that had been available to the retreating Germans since the Seine River. Beyond these canals lay the mass of rivers and canals across the southern Netherlands that made up the Rhine delta. The obstacles that would be thrown down for the Allies here would give von Rundstedt the time he needed to prepare and reinforce the *next* major line of defense on the Western Front—the Siegfried Line.

The British had confidently reported on Tuesday that they had taken Breda, the first city in the Netherlands reported to have been reached by Allied forces. However, the communiqué carrying this pronouncement was later qualified as "premature."

Model may have been run out of Belgium, but von Rundstedt had just run the British out of Breda, and he still had *plenty* of Netherlands left in which to play his tricks.

Wednesday, September 6

On the far left flank of the Allied advance, General Guy Simonds's II Canadian Corps Army had captured Dieppe and surrounded Boulogne and Dunkirk. His troops were attacking overland into the region where Adolf Hitler and the Oberkommando der Wehrmacht bigwigs had been expecting the Allied cross-channel amphibious invasion for four years. They had prepared for such an event since 1940, and had constructed the thickest part of their Atlantic Wall fortifications here to thwart it. Now these great forts sat idle, their guns pointed to an empty sea as Canadian Grizzlies chewed at their rear. Even two months after the Allies came ashore in Normandy, the German defenders seemed as though they had still been expecting the Pas-de-Calais invasion that would never come.

A more important objective than the big guns pointed forlornly in the wrong direction lay here in the Pas-de-Calais region. There was another very serious problem lurking in bunkers in the region that had caused a great deal of worry and consternation for the Allied leaders for nearly three months.

It had been on the night of June 13–14, 1944, that the citizens of London had awakened to strange warbling sounds in the sky that were followed by explosions. The city was coming under a massive air attack, the likes of which its citizens had not experienced since the Blitz of the autumn of 1940.

Only a week after the Operation Overlord invasion of

Normandy on D-Day, just as the people of London had started to smile again, the capital of the United Kingdom had the dubious distinction of being the first city in history to be attacked by cruise missiles.

Adolf Hitler had been promising his people that "wonder weapons" would be coming and that they would change the course of the war. Now, they were here. The missiles were pilotless pulsejet-powered Fiesler Fi.103 airplanes, better known "V-1s." The V-1s would be the first of three secret weapons to officially receive the Führer's personal approval to be designated with a "V" for *Vergeltungswaffe,* meaning "vengeance weapon."

Each of the V-1s carried nearly a ton of high explosives, and had a range of about 150 miles. By launching them from northern France—in the Pas-de-Calais region—the Germans could hit London. Their guidance system was not very accurate, but they could be targeted to within a ten-mile radius, and London was a big target. They were not meant to hit specific targets, but to terrorize people. In this, they were extremely successful.

Though Londoners adopted silly popular nicknames for the V-1—such as "Doodlebug," "Robot," and "Buzz Bomb"—it quickly became one of the most-feared terror weapons of the war.

The V-1s were launched from horizontal launch ramps constructed at an inclined angle. Beginning in September 1943, nearly one hundred such ramps were constructed throughout northern France, especially near Calais. These sites, which had an appearance that reminded photo-reconnaissance analysts of ski jumps, were detected by the Allies, who figured out what they were. Allied bombing raids against the ski jumps began in December 1943 under the code name Operation Crossbow. These attacks caused serious delays, but did not deter the Germans. The V-1 attacks could have begun as early as February or March 1944, but were delayed until just after the Allies had arrived in Normandy.

Because they were so fast, the Robot Bombs were harder to stop than conventional bombers, although the Royal Air Force Fighter Command had gradually developed techniques for shooting them down or stopping them.

The V-1s presented the Allies with a major crisis. Prime Minister Winston Churchill requested that Allied commanders "take all possible measures to neutralize the supply and launching sites subject to no interference with the essential requirements of the Battle of France."

At one point, Churchill even suggested that the Allies break their self-imposed ban on the use of poison gas in order to attack the V-1 sites. Stopping short of such an extreme, it was decided on June 18, 1944, that Crossbow targets should have a higher priority for Allied bombers than anything "except the urgent requirements of the battle [in Normandy]."

General Eisenhower would later admit how truly seriously SHAEF took the Robot Bomb menace. As he wrote in his memoirs: "I feel sure that if [the Germans] had succeeded in using these weapons over a six-month period, and particularly if they had made the Portsmouth-Southampton area one of the principal targets, Overlord might have been written off."

When the ski jumps came under repeated intensive attacks in June, the Germans had simply resorted to simpler prefabricated launchers. These were initially spared when photo interpreters mistook them for decoys. After a short lull in V-1 activity in July while the switch to simpler sites was made, the Luftwaffe was able to resume full-scale attacks in August.

Despite nearly 125,000 tons of bombs having been

dropped on northern France, the V-1s—more than 3,500 in total—continued to rain down on the United Kingdom. *Aiming* them may have been hit or miss, but the Germans had the process of *launching* the V-1s down to a carefully crafted art. The nightmare would end only when the Robot Bombs were stopped at their source.

Stopping them at the source became a priority mission for Crerar's Canadians as soon as they crossed the Seine River. By September 1, they reported having captured approximately 120 of the infernal launch sites in the thousand-square-mile rectangle between Rouen, Amiens, Abbeville, and LeHavre. However, it was being reported that there were hundreds of these sites, with one discovered about every three miles along the highway between Rouen and LeHavre alone.

It was not until Wednesday, September 6, that Londoners could sleep peacefully once again. The Grizzlies of III Canadian Corps had finally taken control of the Pas-de-Calais region and physically captured the last of the V-1 launch sites.

Thursday, September 7

The first week of September had begun with the fifth anniversary of the start of World War II. In Berlin, the man who had given that fateful order to start the great conflagration was not a happy Führer.

The week had been marked by astounding advances for the Allied armies on the Western Front. The week had opened with German armies controlling about as much of France as they had at the apex of their successes in the First World War. It ended with Belgium almost entirely under Allied control. Sir Miles Dempsey's Second British Army had taken both the capital of Belgium and the largest port in what had been

Hitler's Fortress Europe. VII Corps had surprised both itself and the Germans by capturing more than 10,000 Wehrmacht troops in the Mons Pocket.

Farther south, the United States Seventh Army under General Sandy Patch had taken Lyon on Sunday, the same day Brussels had been captured by the British. On the Eastern Front, Germany's fortunes were collapsing just as fast. On Sunday, what was left of the German forces surrounded in the Kishinev Pocket had surrendered to the Soviet armies. On Tuesday, Soviet forces invaded Bulgaria, and extended their gains in Romania.

After Mons, Lightning Joe Collins's VII Corps had continued to move through Belgium on a line south of that which had taken the British Second Army into Brussels and Antwerp during the week. The organization was the same as it had been going up to Mons from France. The 3rd "Spearhead" Armored Division took the spearhead, flanked by the 9th Infantry Division and the Big Red One, although the flanks were some distance from the armor, so that they were moving, essentially, in three separate columns.

They secured Namur, but found that the bridges between there and Dinant had been destroyed by the retreating Germans. By Wednesday morning, the engineers were, to paraphrase one observer on the ground in Belgium that week, spinning new bridges like spiders.

On Wednesday evening, the 9th Infantry Division, commanded by Major General Louis Craig, ran into a roadblock at Dinant, as elements of the 2nd SS Panzer Division and the 12th SS Panzer Division chose to dig in and offer stubborn resistance. The firefights that would ensue overnight were some of the stiffest opposition that the division had seen since the Mons Pocket.

On Thursday morning, General Rose's Sherman tanks arrived on the scene at Dinant. Collins had sent Rose and the 3rd Armored Division north of Dinant, where they had seized a bridgehead over the Meuse River at Namur and had taken an estimated 2,500 German prisoners. From Namur, they had circled south, where they had helped the 30th Infantry Division defeat the SS Panzer roadblock and secure Dinant for the Allied column. By Thursday evening, the 3rd Armored Division moved into position outside Liege, Belgium's fourth largest city.

Friday, September 8

On Friday, the British Second Army crossed the Albert Canal at Beeringen and moved on Boug-Leopold. The Canadians, meanwhile, secured Ypres, a Belgian city that had been mauled by a series of bloody battles in 1914, 1915, and 1917. The latter, which was centered at nearby Passchendaele, had lasted more than five months and cost the Allies 310,000 casualties.

However, September 8, 1944, is remembered for other incidents of World War II in northeastern Europe than what occurred on the Western Front. Specifically, there was one turn of events that occurred directly over the heads of the apparently victorious Allied armies, but over which they had no control. Just two days after the last of the launch sites for the dreaded V-1s had been put out of commission, the Germans cut loose with the second version of Hitler's "vengeance weapon."

Allied intelligence had known for some time that the Germans were developing a *second* vengeance weapon, the V-2. The Royal Air Force had even bombed the German Army's rocket research station at Peenemünde on the Baltic Sea coast where the flight testing had taken place, and Allied bombers had targeted V-2 as well as V-1 launch sites in France under Operation Crossbow. The Allies had known that the V-2s were coming, but until September 8, they hadn't known *when*.

The V-2 had been created for the German army by rocket genius Werner von Braun, who claimed that it was part of his interest in "space travel." On the night of September 8, his rocket traveled not to space, but to London. Once again, the citizens of Britain's capital endured a reign of terror raining from the sky.

This time, there was no distant thunder of piston-engine bombers, nor the hideous warble of the V-1's pulse-jet engine. The V-2 was supersonic, so it arrived before any sound that it made. There was only silence, then the explosion of a ton of TNT. The terror induced by the earlier attacks only paled by comparison.

Technically designated as A-4—until Hitler took over the naming process—the V-2 was an immensely sophisticated weapon. As well as being faster, the V-2 had a much longer range than the V-1, and could be launched from inside of Germany. Its supersonic flight path took the unstoppable V-2 literally over the heads of the Allied troops in France. After World War II, it would form the technological basis of all the Intermediate Range and Intercontinental Ballistic Missiles produced in the Soviet Union and the United States during the four decades of the Cold War. The infamous "Scud" missile that became a household word during the 1991 Gulf War was only a slightly more sophisticated variation on the V-2.

Nor were Londoners alone in the terror. The Germans also began using V-2s against Paris the same night. Within a week, V-2s would begin falling on the great port of Antwerp.

The former jewels of Hitler's empire were now the targets of his cruel secret weapons. Like the V-1, the V-2 had a poor guidance system and precise targeting was impossible, so little predetermined damage was done. Like the V-1, it was deployed to terrorize.

Unlike the V-1, however, the V-2 would be launched by a mobile launching system, so the Allied armies were never able to capture all of the launch sites. With the V-1, there *had* been elaborate fixed launch sites constructed in France, coincidently in the Cotentin Peninsula, the first area seized by the Allies. In fact, American reporters had been taken to see these sites in July. Unlike the V-1 system, however, the notion of using fixed sites had been quickly abandoned and superseded by a serious effort to develop a practical mobile system. This effort had worked out, and had worked very well for the Germans. The V-2 blitz would subside only when the Germans began running out of parts for the missiles and their launchers.

Saturday, September 9

For those who watched the progress of World War II from the comfort of their homes in the summer of 1944, war news was of constant interest. This led to the pastime of marking progress with a list of countries liberated by the Allies. Newspapers published little colored facsimiles of flags that people could snip out and paste to the war maps that everyone seemed to have on their walls. The United States Post Office Department went so far as to issue a series of postage stamps depicting the flags of particular countries, each with the picture of a person with broken chains hanging from the wrists.

The first week of September had seen people tentatively snipping out the flags of France and Belgium. On Saturday, they would have been reaching for their scissors for a third flag as General Leonard Gerow's V Corps crossed into the Grand Duchy of Luxembourg.

As it had been for other Allied corps commanders, it was a busy week for Gerow. After V Corps's 5th Armored Division had participated in the capture of Tournai on Sunday, First Army Commander Courtney Hodges had ordered V Corps to withdraw *through* the VII Corps sector and preposition itself on the First Army's right flank, adjacent to Patton's Third Army left flank. With his move against Mons, Lawton Collins's VII Corps had encroached on what would have been V Corps country.

Indeed, for all practical purposes, VII Corps had emerged from the events of the weekend adjacent to Charles Corlett's XIX Corps on the First Army's far left flank. With these two corps adequate for what he had in mind inside Belgium, Hodges ordered V Corps to move south and east, through the highest and most rugged part of the Ardennes highlands of southern Belgium, and into Luxembourg.

Gerow's command crossed the Meuse River on Monday and began climbing through the Ardennes. With the 5th Armored Division and the 102nd Cavalry Group leading the way, and the 4th and 28th Infantry Divisions following, V Corps travelled in about twelve columns on the narrow roads that snake through southern Belgium. They encountered pockets of German resistance, but no sizable enemy force. Just as France had neglected to defend against an invasion through the Ardennes in 1940, the Germans offered no determined resistance in 1944.

By midweek, V Corps had reached and liberated Bastogne, a small, sleepy crossroads city that was hardly noticed as Gerow's jeep cruised through its modest little central square.

Of minor importance during the early days of September, Bastogne would soon take on much more profound importance to the Allied armies. Three months later, it would be the turn of the Germans to come in force to Bastogne. Before the Battle of the Bulge ended in the cold, deep winter snow of January 1945, this little crossroads would have become one of the dozen or so most important place-names in the history of the United States Army in World War II.

On Saturday, Gerow's troops entered Luxembourg. Riding with them would be Prince Felix of Bourbon-Parma, the husband of Grand Duchess Charlotte, the Grand Duchy's reigning monarch, and their twenty-three-year-old son, Crown Prince Jean. Carrying a rank of brigadier general in the British Army, Felix had commanded a small group of Luxembourg expatriate troops that had been fighting with the Allies since Normandy. The Grand Duchess herself, who was presiding over a government in exile formed in Canada in 1940, would not return to Luxembourg until April 1945, but the presence of the Prince was a tremendous boost to the morale of the Luxembourgers.

Having captured Tournai on Sunday, General Corlett's XIX Corps was ordered to hold the town as the British Second Army moved through. General Ira Wyche's 79th Infantry Division—which had been on loan to Corlett since late August at the time it captured the bridgehead at Mantes-Gassicourt north of Paris—was reassigned from XIX Corps back to Patton's Third Army.

With Tournai secure, XIX Corps had moved out midweek, with the 30th Infantry Division foot soldiers making their way on foot because fuel shortages compelled most of the vehicles to remain behind in Tournai for the time being. What fuel that was available was allocated to the 113th Cavalry

Group—which led the corps across Belgium—and to the 2nd Armored Division. The 113th reached the Albert Canal on Thursday, and by Saturday night, both the 2nd Armored Division and the Rock of Mortain had caught up and were facing the Germans across the canal.

Sunday, September 10

Sunday was the day that the Allies finally brought the ground war to the German Fatherland.

VII Corps was advancing from the Belgian city of Liege on a direct line toward the German city of Aachen, which lay in the afternoon shadow of the Siegfried Line, less than twenty miles away. On Saturday, VII Corps had taken Verviers, halfway from Liege to Aachen, and on Sunday, Lightning Joe Collins was studying the Siegfried Line through his field glasses.

Aachen, alternatively known by the French name Aix-la-Chapelle, was a city with a prewar population of more than 150,000 and the first major city that the Anglo-American Allies would target for capture within the Reich. Patton had proposed that this dishonor should be bestowed upon Trier, located in *his* Third Army sector, but to the SHAEF map readers, the roads from Aachen led into the Ruhr, and that was where they wanted to be.

More than merely a symbolic gateway, Aachen was also an important industrial center and railway hub. Historically, Aachen had been frequented by the Romans, who came for its hot springs and then constructed fortifications. Charlemagne, the great emperor of the Franks, had probably been born here, and he certainly used the city as the northern capital of his vast and powerful Frankish empire at the turn of the ninth century.

For centuries before and after Charlemagne, invading armies had crossed these rolling hills, coming to Aachen to conquer or die trying. Now it was the turn of VII Corps of the United States First Army to come to town.

Late Sunday afternoon, Private First Class Joseph Muckton from Carteret, New Jersey, fired what was believed to be the first American artillery shell to strike the Siegfried Line. The 155mm shell would be the first of a barrage that would continue until Tuesday, when VII Corps would launch its armor and infantry assault against the Siegfried Line.

From the gates of Aachen, the VII Corps line extended south into the Ardennes from Liege through Malmedy, nearly to Bastogne. Like Bastogne, Malmedy was one of those place-names that meant nothing to the GIs in September 1944, but which would emerge from December's Battle of the Bulge with an ominous connotation. On December 17, in the early hours of the massive German counteroffensive that would create the "Bulge" in the American lines, a 1st SS Panzer Division task force under the command of SS Obersturmbannführer Joachim Peiper would break through American lines near Malmedy. They would capture a number of American soldiers and turn them over to SS guard units, who would march them into a field and gun them down. The Malmedy Massacre would be just the first of several such atrocities committed by SS troops that would leave 350 American POWs and 100 unarmed Belgian civilians dead. According to the subsequent investigation, Hitler had ordered that the lead units in the attack should create a "wave of terror and fright and . . . no human inhibitions should be shown."

In September, however, the Germans were still hoping for "human inhibitions" to be shown toward them. Far to the west, on this second Sunday of the month, kinder, gentler

Germans were playing to the kindness of American troops near the Loire River.

It was on September 10 that American Major General Robert Macon accepted the unexpected surrender of all the German forces south of the Loire. Cut off from the German armies on the Western Front, and from a planned escape through Dijon, German Major General Botho Elster had decided that it was time to give up. Elster, who had earlier served as the German commandant at Biarritz, now had de facto command of all the German forces in an area larger than Belgium, Luxembourg, and the Netherlands combined—although they were mainly a disorganized amalgamation of noncombat occupation troops.

Two days earlier, Elster had made contact with 1st Lieutenant Sam Magill, a reconnaissance and intelligence platoon leader with the 329th Infantry Regiment of the 83rd Infantry Division. He had offered to surrender, and Magill had arranged for him to come behind the American lines to meet General Macon. The surrender included nearly a thousand motor vehicles as well as 19,604 men—including 754 officers—and 10 women.

Virtually all of France had now been liberated.

The same media commentators who had, just two months earlier, suggested that a stalemate in Normandy could last a year or more were now suggesting that the war would be over by Christmas.

Across the globe in North America, President Franklin Roosevelt, British Prime Minister Winston Churchill, and their respective gold-braided entourages were arriving at the Hotel Frontenac in the city of Quebec on Sunday. The Allied leaders were coming together for the conference code-named Octagon, at which they would be discussing the global scope of the war in general, and specifically, the plan drafted by United States Secretary of the Treasury Henry Morganthau for dealing with a defeated Germany. Joe Muckton had only just dropped the first shell on the Siegfried Line, and already Roosevelt and Churchill were deciding on postwar occupation zones for a defeated Third Reich. As Muckton was firing his gun, the Allied brass were jumping theirs.

Monday, September 11

By September 11, the Allies had liberated virtually all of Belgium, and the British 49th Infantry Division had finally succeeded in taking the French seaport of Le Havre at the mouth of the Seine River. General Gerow's V Corps was securing its hold on the Grand Duchy of Luxembourg. Prince Felix, husband of the reigning monarch, was back in town to serve as head of state, while Gerow appointed Lieutenant Colonel Edgar Jett to take charge of the nuts and bolts of maintaining order and restoring public services.

British forces were on the Meuse-Escaut Canal, and at the border of the Netherlands. On Monday, at Sombernon, twelve miles west of Dijon, Patton's Third Army formally linked up with Sandy Patch's Seventh Army, which had been moving north from its invasion of the French Riviera on August 15.

As the week began, XII Corps of the Third Army was tasked with securing a crossing of the Moselle River, and with capturing the city of Nancy, then firmly in the control of the German First Army. Located about forty miles south of Metz, Nancy was the largest city in Lorraine with 120,000 people compared to 78,000 in Metz.

The 80th Infantry Division had made an initial attempt near Pont-à-Mousson on the previous Tuesday, but this had failed due to a variety of factors, including inadequate artillery preparation. The 3rd Panzer Grenadier Division, recently relocated from the Italian Front, held the high ground and had managed to beat back the Americans.

Another factor, not surprisingly, was gasoline. The Achilles heel of the Third Army was that its tanks continued to outrun their fuel supplies. During the previous week, the 4th Armored Division in the VII Corps spearhead had run out of gas on the road to Nancy. General Wood had been forced to resort to siphoning gasoline from his tanks in order to give his division cavalry squadron enough to simply conduct a reconnaissance of the approaches to Nancy.

Fuel shortages would bedevil XII Corps and the Third Army throughout the Lorraine campaign. As General Wood observed, "The volume of supplies reaching the 4th Armored Division was not sufficient to sustain full-scale armored exploitation."

Because they were at the end of the pipeline insofar as fuel and ammunition allocations were concerned, the Third Army had to become extremely resourceful and to develop an ability to "live off the land." Some sizable German fuel dumps had been captured as the army dashed toward Lorraine. Other materiel, especially artillery ammunition, was also scrounged from captured German stocks. The Third Army even used captured German guns so that they could make use of 88mm ammunition. On several occasions, more than half the guns being used by the Third Army artillerymen were not American made.

Supported by the largesse of the French people, the Third Army would also take over the French railroad network in Lorraine, as well as factories that turned out everything from tank hatches to tires, all made expressly for the Third Army.

By September 11, XII Corps had finally gotten the necessary gasoline, and General Eddy was ready for Nancy. With the 80th Infantry Division attacking from the north, Eddy sent the 4th Armored Division and the 35th Infantry Division to outflank the German strong points and to circle west and south of the city. The Moselle was shallower here, where a number of smaller tributaries had not yet joined the main branch of the river.

The flanking maneuver had succeeded. Combat Command B of the 4th Armored Division forded a series of streams with their Sherman tanks and backed the 35th Infantry Division in beating back the German 15th Panzer Grenadier Division. They soon had organized a bridgehead across the Moselle on the south side of the city.

As the engineers arrived to install the treadway bridges, a battalion of the 15th Panzer Grenadier Division counterattacked. Combat Command B rapidly surrounded the battalion and put them out of commission.

Tuesday, September 12

By Tuesday, both VII Corps and V Corps of the United States First Army were inside Germany. Having taken the Belgian city of Eupen, near Viviers on Monday, VII Corps launched an attack on Tuesday aimed at flanking the city of Aachen. Lightning Joe Collins's corps attacked along a wide front. Aided by a withering artillery barrage, the 1st Infantry Division and 3rd Armored Division punched through the barbed wire and concrete barricades of the Siegfried Line near the German town of Roetgen, about ten miles south and a bit east of Aachen. In addition to the artillery preparation, the breakthrough was also aided by combat engineers wielding flamethrowers and explosive charges placed with long poles.

While Collins was slamming through the front door, along a route that had seen countless invasions throughout history, Leonard Gerow's V Corps was sixty-five miles to the south, passing through the hills and valleys east of Luxembourg on that segment of the Western Front that was *not* a "traditional invasion route."

By Monday night, V Corps' 28th Infantry Division, under the command of General Norman Cota, had reached Kalborn, Luxembourg, which is located on the Our River, which forms the Grand Duchy's border with Germany. At dawn on Tuesday, the division's 109th Infantry Regiment began fording the Our in order to take the high ground on the opposite, German, bank.

Covered by early morning fog, the 3rd Platoon of Company K waded across, followed by the 2nd Platoon. As the latter group reached the far shore, German machine gunners and riflemen who had observed the crossing opened fire. The platoon leader and his top sergeant were killed almost immediately and the troops found themselves hugging the ground in a very exposed position.

Tech Sergeant Francis Clark of Whitehall, New York, a squad leader in the 3rd Platoon, crawled out of his relatively safe location and crossed the field through a hail of bullets. After he had managed to lead the men to safety, he crawled back out into the killing field to rescue a wounded man.

Having gotten everyone out of the line of fire, Clark organized the two platoons and led an assault on the enemy positions. He attacked the machine gun with hand grenades, killed two Germans and kept going. Clark managed to kill a number of the enemy personally, and the attack that he led forced the survivors to retreat into the dense woods beyond

the Our River. The 28th Infantry Division spearhead was now
in Germany. For Tuesday's actions, and for another on the
coming Sunday, Clark would receive the Congressional Medal
of Honor.

Having liberated Luxembourg's capital over the weekend,
the 5th Armored Division had continued to advance toward
the Reich on Monday. The division's primary mission was to
clean up enemy pockets of resistance in Luxembourg, but having encountered virtually no enemy troops there, the first patrol crossed the German border near the German town of
Wallendorf in the afternoon.

At 7:00 P.M. Brigadier General Eugene Regnier, commanding the division's Combat Command A, was ordered to
send a light, fast force across the border to seize the radio station at Junglinster. By 8:50 Tuesday morning, Combat Command A reported that the radio station had been seized intact,
and the 112th Infantry Regiment was ordered to relieve the
detachment of Combat Command A and to protect the station.

During the day, Combat Command A's contact with
German troops was described as mainly consisting of roadblocks and delaying actions. The first day of operations within
this sector of the Third Reich had been generally uneventful.

Wednesday, September 13

By Wednesday night, the United States First Army press office
was able to announce that the town of Roetgen was the first
German hamlet ever to fall to troops of an American army.
Located less than four miles inside the border, the town had
been targeted by the VII Corps spearhead that had pierced the
Siegfried Line on Tuesday. The V Corps force had penetrated

somewhat farther into Germany opposite Luxembourg, but they had not yet actually taken a German town.

General Rose's 3rd Armored Division exploited the VII Corps breakthrough, driving north of Roetgen through Hergenrath toward the high ground south of Aachen. The Yanks were amused to discover that the road leading north out of Roetgen was the *Rommelweg*, named for Field Marshal Erwin Rommel, Germany's late, great master of mobile tank warfare. Meanwhile, engineers had begun widening the breach in the Siegfried line by demolishing the dragon's teeth tank traps and other obstacles.

The 5th Armored Division of V Corps would have two combat commands operating within Germany all day Wednesday in the sector defended by LXXX Korps of the German Army Group G. Combat Command A was operating in the vicinity of Grevenmacher. Meanwhile, the division's Combat Command R shelled the Siegfried Line pillboxes between Ammeldingen and Gentingen with tank and artillery fire, but found these enemy positions to be strangely quiet. Colonel Glen Anderson, commanding Combat Command R, reported that "no enemy fire was returned."

At 7:25 Wednesday evening, General Oliver, the 5th Armored Division commander, received orders from V Corps headquarters to proceed with previously discussed plans to capture the high ground near Mettendorf. From here, he was to attack the German city of Bitburg, about ten miles due east of the Luxembourg border and eighteen miles northwest of Trier. Combat Command A—with one battalion of infantry attached—was to continue to protect the city of Luxembourg. Combat Command B, commanded by Colonel John Cole, was ordered to continue into Germany.

In contrast to what Colonel Anderson had observed during the day, the Germans seemed now to be coming alive. During the night, patrols would find themselves encountering enemy troops along the entire line. By morning, the 112th Infantry Regiment reported that the road between Minden and Edingen was mined.

Farther south, on the Third Army's front in Lorraine, XII Corps' 35th Infantry Division and Combat Command B of the 4th Armored Division had succeeded in securing a bridgehead across the Moselle River on Monday. The following day, the 80th Infantry Division had matched the effort by capturing a bridge north of Nancy, at Dieulouard.

Late on Tuesday, Colonel Bruce Clarke, leading the 4th Armored Division's Combat Command A, brought his tanks up to the eastern side of the Dieulouard bridgehead late on Tuesday. His plan was to cross the bridge early Wednesday, moving quickly to make an armored thrust toward Château-Salins, a town twenty miles closer to Germany.

Just after midnight, in the small hours of Wednesday, the German First Army's 3rd Panzer Grenadier Division attacked the bridgehead in force, nearly compelling XII Corps to abandon the crossing point. It was now doubtful whether Combat Command A could succeed in making it across. Even if the bridge survived the shelling, crossing the river under fire would be a difficult task, and General Eddy was reluctant to order such a move.

Lieutenant Colonel Creighton Abrams, commanding the 37th Tank Battalion, suggested that his battalion would lead Combat Command A across. As the story goes, he pointed across the river and told the general that *this* way was the "shortest way home."

At about 8:00 A.M., Abrams began leading the Combat Command A Sherman tanks across the Dieulouard bridgehead, with their guns blazing. They managed to overpower the 3rd Panzer Grenadiers, who, just a few hours earlier had threatened to drive XII Corps out of the bridgehead. Without pausing, Abrams led Combat Command A as they proceeded to execute their attack, planning to reach Château-Salins by Wednesday evening.

With Bruce Clarke overhead in a Piper Grasshopper observing their progress, Combat Command A raced down the highway toward their objective. They would encounter a number of roadblocks and a sizable number of German troops, but Abrams slammed through each obstacle, blasting away with the 76mm guns on the lead tanks and taking out anything that got in the way of the column. In the process, Combat Command A destroyed a dozen German tanks, five artillery pieces, and eighty-five vehicles. They took 354 prisoners, while losing just 12 of their own men.

Abrams's boss, Third Army commander General George Patton, would have been pleased with his performance that day. Patton liked to see his tanks firing on the run. He had once said that "a tank which stops to fire gets hit." This wasn't always true, but tanks that fired on the run almost never got hit.

By 5:00 P.M., Combat Command A had arrived on the high ground west of Château-Salins, and promptly surrounded the town. Creighton Abrams was the hero of the day. He would survive the war and rise through the ranks, capping his military career as a four-star general, and Chief of Staff of the US Army between 1972 and 1974. In the meantime, Abrams would put in a tour of duty as commander of all United States forces in Vietnam. Serving under Abrams in Southeast Asia would be Brigadier General George Patton, the son of Abrams's World War II commander.

Thursday, September 14

As the battle for the Moselle bridgeheads and the terrain beyond reached its crescendo on Thursday, the units of XII Corps faced some of the toughest fighting that they had encountered for weeks. The intensity of the combat would bring to the fore, an unrivaled level of heroism that would result in not one, but *two*, Congressional Medals of Honor being awarded to corps personnel for actions this day.

Though Horace McBride's 80th Infantry Division had initially captured the Dieulouard bridgehead on Tuesday, this site was by no means secure and uncontested on Wednesday and Thursday. Abrams had pushed his tanks over the bridge on Tuesday, but he'd done so while taking fire. After he'd gotten across, the Germans had by no means given up.

There was still a heavily fortified enemy position overlooking the Dieulouard bridgehead that was manned by roughly two hundred Germans with automatic weapons. Company E of the division's 319th Infantry Regiment was assigned the mission of taking down this German strongpoint. Spearheading the company's effort was a rifle platoon led by 1st Lieutenant Edgar Lloyd of Blytheville, Arkansas. When Lloyd's platoon had worked its way to a point about fifty yards off the enemy strongpoint, they came under heavy machine gun and rifle fire, which quickly resulted in a large number of casualties. The men immediately took cover and it seemed as though the assault had ground to a halt. Catching his breath, Lloyd jumped up, told his men to follow him, and rushed the Germans.

Lloyd and his team dodged withering enemy fire, managing to reach the German strongpoint after what probably seemed like an eternity. The lieutenant himself jumped into the first machine gun nest, slugged the gunner with his fist, dropped a grenade, and jumped out before it exploded.

Still urging the platoon along, Lloyd dashed from one machine gun nest to the next. He would pin down the German gunners with his submachine gun fire until he was within grenade-throwing distance. He personally destroyed five machine guns as he led the platoon in overrunning the German position. For what his award citation described as "audacious determination and courageous devotion to duty," Lloyd would be awarded the Congressional Medal of Honor.

On Wednesday, Combat Command A of the 4th Armored Division, spearheaded by the 37th Tank Battalion under Creighton Abrams, had crossed the Moselle River under fire at Dieulouard, north of Nancy.

Having smashed through the German First Army's 3rd Panzer Grenadier Division, Combat Command A sprinted twenty miles eastward to the crossroads at Château-Salins. General Wood, the division commander, meanwhile, had ordered his Combat Command B to exploit its own crossing of the Moselle south of Nancy. This command had crossed the Meurthe River and was advancing on the Marne-Rhine Canal, where a sizable German contingent was known to be present.

Wood then ordered Combat Command A commander Bruce Clarke to detour around Château-Salins instead of becoming embroiled in a fight to take it. He sensed that it was more important to keep up the momentum of the Combat Command A drive on Wednesday. To the east lay the Rhine, Germany, and final victory. To paraphrase Abrams's comment the previous day, *this* was the way home.

Clarke's Combat Command A was ordered to continue toward the city of Arracourt, and then to link up with Combat Command B in the vicinity of its crossing of the Marne-Rhine Canal.

Meanwhile, the German 15th Panzer Grenadier Division had moved to cut off Combat Command B. However, Clarke's command stumbled across them first, surprised them, and attacked. Combat Command A knocked out two dozen armored vehicles and ten artillery pieces, while taking four hundred prisoners. The Germans managed to knock out two of the American Shermans, while inflicting just thirty-three casualties.

As Combat Command A reached the town of Valhey in the afternoon, Abrams's 37th Tank Battalion was still in the vanguard, and Sergeant Joseph Sadowski of Perth Amboy, New Jersey, was commanding the lead tank. The battalion ran into a sudden and powerful barrage of enemy fire as it made its way through the town.

It is axiomatic that defeating a column of tanks working its way through narrow streets begins with targeting the lead tank, thus bottling up the column. The German gunners had read the manual. A shell from a German "eighty-eight," fired from a range of about twenty yards, knocked out Sadowski's tank. The sergeant immediately ordered his crew out of the burning tank, but discovered the gunner was unable to get out. Although the tank continued to be under German automatic weapons fire, Sadowski returned to the tank to try to save the man.

Though Sergeant Sadowski was shot to pieces by German machine gun fire before he could pry open the gunner's hatch, his bravery inspired the other tank crews to move forward and completely destroy the enemy forces in Valhey without American casualties. The action also earned the man from New Jersey a posthumous award of the Congressional Medal of Honor.

Late in the day, patrols from the two 4th Armored Division combat commands made contact with one another, and Clarke dispatched units toward the Marne-Rhine Canal. By 7:00 P.M. Thursday night, Combat Command A was in a position to surround Arracourt, as they had Château-Salins the night before. Artillery units attached to Clarke's command were ordered to undertake an all-night bombardment of the city's defenders.

Since crossing the Moselle River at Dieulouard on Wednesday morning, Clarke's Combat Command A had traveled forty-five miles in just thirty-seven hours. They had surrounded Arracourt and Château-Salins, but more important, by circling east across the river, they had also cut Nancy off from the rest of German-held Europe, preventing any German escape from the beleaguered city. In the process, they had also destroyed the German headquarters in charge of the entire sector that included Nancy.

Farther north, opposite Luxembourg, units of the 5th Armored Division continued to operate across the border and within Germany itself. More such units would be moving across on Thursday. The 1st Battalion of the 112th Infantry Regiment joined Colonel Anderson's Combat Command R at noon, and they promptly attacked, crossing the border across the Sauer River near Wallendorf.

An hour later, they were attacking the Siegfried Line with tanks and artillery and encountering automatic weapons fire from the fortifications on the forward slope of a hill. The German pillboxes that had been eerily quiet on Wednesday were no longer silent. White phosphorus rounds fired by the 5th Armored Division artillery brought the enemy soldiers out into the open and under American machine-gun fire.

Meanwhile, Combat Command R's 47th Armored Infantry Battalion entered Wallendorf with a platoon of tanks and captured the high ground beyond. The 112th Infantry Regiment reached Wallendorf later in the afternoon and finished the job of securing the town.

Pierre Huss of the International News Service, who accompanied the 47th Armored Infantry Battalion into Wallendorf on Thursday, reported the village to be a virtual ghost town. Only a few hundred children and elderly people out of a prewar population of 5,000 remained. The older people were sullen, while the curious children automatically greeted the Yanks with the straight-armed Nazi salute. It had been nearly a dozen years since Hitler had come to power, and they knew no different.

By early evening, Colonel Anderson had the majority of his personnel and equipment through the town, across the river and on the high ground to the east. Here, however, the command was meeting some complications in moving toward the city of Beisdorf. In contrast to the town itself, the valley beyond Wallendorf was strongly held by German troops. The 112th Infantry Regiment was working its way north through the valley against steady enemy fire from antitank guns.

Across the river in Luxembourg, General Regnier's Combat Command A was reporting heavy highway traffic, mainly consisting of German civilians, trying to get into Germany from Luxembourg. When these reports reached headquarters, General Oliver ordered Regnier to prevent all civilian traffic from moving to or from Germany, and to increase security throughout the entire Grand Duchy.

Friday, September 15

After a week of punching at Lorraine's largest city, Manton Eddy's XII Corps would finally capture Nancy on Friday. The honors would fall to General Paul Baade's 35th Infantry Division. In the division lineup for the assault would be the division's 320th Infantry Regiment, whose 1st Battalion was commanded by Major Bill Gillis, the captain of the 1940 West Point football team, who had also distinguished himself at the Battle of Mortain by leading the force that recaptured Hill 217 and saved the Americans trapped there.

Now, in the final push to win Nancy away from her German captors, Gillis's battalion was tasked with knocking out the German defenses on the Rhine-Marne Canal at Dombasie, just below Nancy. Gillis accomplished the mission by leading a direct assault over unimproved bridging while under intense direct enemy machine gun fire. In the process of knocking the German defenses, Gillis waded and swam across the canal several times under heavy enemy fire—earning a Distinguished Service Cross to go with the Silver Star he'd earned at Mortain. Two weeks later, he would earn a Bronze Star for leading a charge against a German artillery position in the Foret de Gremecy. In this action, he would be mortally wounded. He would die of his wounds on October 1.

About 150 miles north of Nancy, Friday morning found Combat Command R of the 5th Armored Division occupying the hill east of the German "ghost town" of Wallendorf. A heavy fog lay across the Ardennes and visibility was virtually nonexistent. As Anderson's Combat Command R moved out around 11:00 A.M., they discovered that, overnight, the Germans had gotten organized for a counterattack, having moved tanks and artillery into the area. A number of tank battles would ensue as Combat Command R made its way slowly through Hommerdingen toward Beisdorf. By 1:00 P.M., the 112th Infantry Regiment, attached to Combat Command R, had finally reached the city, and by 3:00, the command was clearing enemy positions between the nearby villages of Hommerdingen and Cruchten.

By 6:00 P.M. the forward elements of Anderson's command reached Enzen, where they spotted enemy troops withdrawing to the north. An hour later, the advance units had reached Bettingen, the halfway point between the Luxembourg border and Bitburg. By the time that the remainder of the command rolled into Bettingen, it was too dark to continue.

It was not to be a restful night. All night long, German patrols infiltrated the area along the Sauer River near Wallendorf, where the Yanks had crossed the river, and caused a great deal of trouble. American patrols worked through the night to keep the German patrols from slipping behind the American lines.

Saturday, September 16

By Saturday, the American XIX Corps could confirm the liberation of the first major city in the Netherlands to be taken by the Allies. The report eleven days earlier that the British had captured Breda had been overruled as "premature," but by Saturday night, a "confirmed" report could be issued regarding a city at the opposite end of the country. At the southern tip of the Netherlands, the city of Maastricht was firmly in the hands of the 30th Infantry Division. The division's 113th "Red Horse" Cavalry Group—flanked by the 125th Cavalry Reconnaissance Squadron and accompanied by a small contingent of Dutch troops—had spearheaded the division's drive into the southern Netherlands that morning. They would discover that the Germans had withdrawn for what a report on German radio would characterize as "tactical reasons." This was not a place that Gerd von Rundstedt would fight for.

On the Siegfried Line thirty miles south of Maastricht it

was a somewhat different story. Having captured Roetgen—the first German town taken by American forces—on Wednesday, VII Corps was widening its hold on a tiny sliver of Germany nearby. By Friday, the neighboring villages of Forstbach, Gemmenich, Hergenrath, Kopsechen, and Wurmhof were tentatively penciled in on the list of captured towns.

Driving north from Roetgen toward Aachen, the corps was meeting increasing German resistance from the German Seventh Army defensive positions near the city. With this in mind, the 1st Infantry Division swung wide to the east in order to flank the city. By midday Saturday, the 1st Infantry Division had reached Stolberg, six miles east of Aachen, and less than thirty miles from the Rhine River at Cologne.

German determination was also stiffening in the heavily forested hills and valleys east of the Luxembourg border. General Regnier's Combat Command A of the 5th Armored Division—tasked by V Corps with securing all of Luxembourg—had discovered that the Combat Command A entire front was heavily defended by entrenched German infantry. They were well armed with antitank weapons and machine guns, and they were on full alert for an attack by American forces. In the early hours of Saturday, the enemy went on the offensive. Combat Command A came under fire from the German guns, and three Shermans were soon knocked out. V Corps ordered Regnier to move his command post south into vicinity of Beidweiler and to maintain a mobile force to be ready to attack any threat to the corps south flank, or the city of Luxembourg.

After an uneasy night at Bettingen, Colonel Glen Anderson's Combat Command R continued its advance into Germany. As had been the case on Friday morning, a heavy ground fog clung ominously to the heavily wooded terrain. Indeed, the visibility was down to about fifty yards.

At around 10:00, Anderson reported that he had run into a concentration of German armor in the area southeast of Niedersgegen. Anderson requested that Colonel Cole's Combat Command B—then on the move north of Beisdorf—send a force to relieve the Combat Command R rear elements. Even with help from Cole's outfit, Anderson made no progress during Saturday in his efforts to move out of Niedersgegen toward Bitburg. Deep mud and the nagging low visibility presented by the ground fog were also contributing to the mobility problems.

Shortly before midnight, V Corps headquarters ordered the 5th Armored Division contingents within Germany to send reinforced reconnaissance patrols toward the Bitburg area. However, the orders cautioned the division not to attack Bitburg itself—except and until explicit orders were issued from V Corps.

To the south in Lorraine, the Third Army's XII Corps had captured Nancy, although there was still some mopping up to be done before Nancy could be considered secure. Third Army troops now occupied the city, but German artillery was still able to lob shells on them. The enemy continued to occupy the heights east of the city and across the Meurthe River, allowing artillery observers located here to call in coordinates to gunners hidden in distant woods. The next step in the task of truly securing the city was for 35th Infantry Division troops to capture the Plateau de Malzeville, a flat-topped hill that rose more than six hundred feet above the river.

The job of taking the hill was assigned to the 134th Infantry Regiment of the 35th Infantry Division. Commanded by Colonel Butler Miltonberger, the 134th Infantry Regiment was the nucleus of the division's Task Force S, which was, in turn, commanded by Brigadier General Edmund Sebree, the assistant commander of the 35th Infantry Division.

Under the temporary structure of this task force, also known as "Task Force Sebree," the 134th Infantry Regiment was augmented by groups drawn from other units. These included the 161st Field Artillery and a company of the 737th Tank Battalion, as well as a company of the 654th Tank Destroyer Battalion and the 155mm howitzers of the 127th Field Artillery Battalion.

The first regimental reconnaissance units went out very early Saturday morning, and the regimental attack would jump off from a point near the town of Maxeville at noon. The plan of attack was for the 3rd Battalion to be first across the Meurthe, spearheaded by Captain Francis Greenlief's Company L. The 3rd would be followed, in turn, by the regiment's 1st Battalion, under Major Warren Wood. The primary crossing point, referred to in the order of the day as "Site A," was a place immediately downstream from a dam where the river was reportedly fordable.

Able Company of the 1st Battalion, under the command of Lieutenant Constant Kjems, would go upstream from the dam for about a mile and cross the river at "Site B" using assault boats. This effort would ideally give the regiment two separate bridgeheads, and it would put GIs in a position to take the village of Tomblaine, which was near the upstream site. This latter location was also seen as ideal for the installation of a treadway bridge.

When Able Company was in position, Captain Greenlief began the main assault at Site A. The troops received sporadic fire as they moved out, but for the most part, they were out of the view of the German artillery spotters. The Yanks found the fast-moving river to be relatively shallow—waist deep at the most—and the whole company was across in about fifteen minutes. Greenlief's spearhead was quickly followed by Company I and vehicles towing the battalion artillery, with Company K bringing up the rear.

Amazingly, the crossing drew little response from the Germans, who had been expecting a crossing farther downriver near Malzeville, where there was still an intact bridge. The Site B crossing also went off without opposition. Had the Germans taken notice, however, the assault boats would have been particularly vulnerable. Able Company's crossing went so well, in fact, that Wood decided to send the whole 1st Battalion across at Site B. Unfortunately, Wood's luck was about to run out.

Having not noticed Able Company until they were across the river, the Germans concentrated fire on the units that followed. Because the battalion had a foothold on the eastern shore, the Germans were not able to do as much damage as they might have, but the going was still quite rough.

The two battalions of the 134th Infantry Regiment had their work cut out for them Saturday afternoon. The 1st Battalion pursued the task of capturing Tomblaine and securing a perimeter, while the 3rd Battalion moved on the primary objective. Company L moved on the town of Malzeville, while Company I and Company K fought their way up the heavily wooded slopes of the Plateau de Malzeville.

By sundown Saturday night, the ridgetop was under American control, and the GIs could look out across the valley below. They could see Nancy from the same vantage point that had been used twelve hours before by German artillery spotters, and they could see Tomblaine, where the 1135th Combat Engineer Group was putting the finishing touches on the treadway bridge.

Elsewhere in the Third Army sector in Lorraine, the Americans were preparing for their assault on the great fortress city of Metz. General LeRoy Irwin's 5th Infantry Division began the attack on Saturday. However, just as there were signs that General Oliver's 5th Armored Division was reaching its limits opposite Luxembourg, so too would General Irwin soon realize that the blistering speed of the Blitzkrieg across France over the past month would soon have run its course.

Nancy, a larger city than Metz, had fallen after four days of concerted effort. Irwin's division went to work on Saturday with similar expectations, but they were in for a rude surprise.

A month later, on October 16, they would wind down the attack, having failed to capture Metz. It would take a brutal ten-day battle in mid-November to finally subdue the German garrison within the fortress.

Instead of dropping off the vine as easily as Amiens, Antwerp, Brussels, or even Nancy, Metz would require a vicious round of siege fighting such as that which was, even now, still taking place in mid-September on that distant and nearly forgotten front called Brittany.

✪ TEN ✪

THE FORGOTTEN FRONT
IN BRITTANY

By the middle of September, a hundred years seemed to have passed since the first week of August. The campaign in Brittany, which had consumed the primary attention of the Third Army that week, seemed long ago and far away. It had been on August 1, Third Army's first day in the field, that General George Patton had given his first order to Major General Robert Grow, commanding the 6th Armored Division: "Take Brest."

Grow had set out on a spectacular drive through Brittany that morning. In terms of distance covered, Grow had accomplished more than nearly any Allied division in France since D-Day. Within four days, his tanks had been within sight of the city and there were rumors that he'd already taken Brest. The rumors were premature.

At first light on August 8, Grow had sent the 6th Armored Division intelligence officer, Major Ernest Arnold, into the city along with German-speaking Sergeant Alex Castle. They had driven into Brest under a white flag and had offered the Germans an opportunity to surrender. The fortress commander, a tough paratrooper named Lieutenant General Hermann Ramcke, refused. He had been given orders to defend, not give up, and orders were to be obeyed.

At the end of the first week of August, the Allies had just a tenuous foothold in Europe, so an ultimate German victory in France was not entirely out of the question. At the end of the first week in August, thumbing his nose at an opportunity to surrender had been an easy decision to make.

Grow's lightning dash through Brittany had abruptly become a stalemate, the duration of which, no one could know. As the weeks had dragged on, and as the Allies broke through and began racing across France in the opposite direction, the defenders of Brest, and the Yanks who besieged them, became more and more isolated from World War II. Gradually, Brittany became the "forgotten front."

Meanwhile, the Allies had met a similar stalemate at the port of St. Malo, located on the neck of the Brittany Peninsula. The German garrison had stubbornly resisted, compelling the artillery of the 83rd Infantry Division and the big guns of Allied warships to pound St. Malo into oblivion.

St. Malo's commander, Colonel Andreas von Aulock, was a veteran of Stalingrad, and he was reported to have said that he intended to turn St. Malo into "another Stalingrad"— meaning a bloodbath that would see the destruction of the city and every human being who came near it. The man whom the Allies would soon dub "the Madman of St. Malo" was planning to go down with the ship and to take everyone else with him.

On August 18, however, after a long and ferocious siege involving US Army artillery and naval gunfire, St. Malo had surrendered, and the "Madman" was just another prisoner of war. Von Aulock had made good on part of his threat. St.

Malo, like Cherbourg on the Cotentin Peninsula, would be useless as a port for many months.

German garrisons still held out at Brest, Lorient, and St. Nazaire, however. Estimates suggested that the Brest garrison numbered about 16,000 personnel, with 9,500 each in the other two ports. Despite other events redirecting the attention of planners toward the east, SHAEF continued to consider the capture of one of the major Brittany ports to be not just important, but vital to the war effort in northern Europe.

Brest presented a formidable obstacle. Ramcke was ready for a long siege. The Germans had transformed the old central part of the city into a fortress, with elaborate bulwarks, tying together a number of old French forts that dated back to the nineteenth century and before. German engineers had installed thousands of cubic meters of new reinforced concrete. In addition, the defenders were well armed and well protected beneath these tons of concrete. The number of these defenders would turn out to be more than double the American estimates.

General Troy Middleton's VIII Corps was tasked by the Third Army to complete the mission to "take Brest." The timetable called for the Brest to be taken by September 1.

At the time that the siege began in the second week of August, Middleton's command contained the 83rd Infantry Division under Major General Robert Macon, Major General Harry Maloney's 94th Infantry Division, and Grow's 6th Armored Division. The 8th Infantry Division began to arrive near Brest on August 18. The 4th Armored Division, which had been attached temporarily, reverted back to XII Corps, as would Combat Command B of the 6th Armored Division. Patton had decided that armor was more useful in exploiting the offensive from LeMans to Orleans than in the static siege of Brest. For this siege, General Bradley, commanding 12th Army Group, would transfer the 2nd Infantry Division and the 29th Infantry Division from the First Army to VIII Corps.

Middleton's first objective would be to begin breaking through the ring of German strongpoints that existed at a radius of about five miles outside Brest itself. This effort would begin on August 21, with an attack against the town of Plougastel-Daoulas, located on the south bank of the Elorn River across the bay from the city. The mission would involve Task Force B of the 2nd Infantry Division, which would be under the command of Brigadier General James Van Fleet, the division assistant commander.

Task Force B was stopped in its tracks soon after it got underway by German gunfire emanating from pillboxes on Hill 154, which guarded the approaches to Plougastel-Daoulas. The Americans were pinned down for two days, with artillery fire proving ineffective in taking out the pillbox.

On August 23, Staff Sergeant Alvin Carey of the 38th Infantry Regiment agreed to lead a machine gun team up the right flank of the hill. Having placed his machine guns in as advanced a position as possible, Carey armed himself with as many hand grenades as he could carry and crawled up the hill toward the pillbox alone. Keeping barely inches beneath a stream of German machine gun fire, he had inched about 150 yards when a German rifleman attempted to intercept him. Carey returned fire with his M1 carbine, killing the German.

Continuing his steady forward movement until he reached grenade-throwing distance, Carey jumped up under intense enemy fire and tossed a couple of grenades, which missed. Though he'd been wounded, Carey continued his grenade attack until one of the grenades finally exploded inside the pillbox, killing the gunners and putting their guns out of action. Carey died of his numerous gunshot wounds and was posthumously awarded the Congressional Medal of Honor.

In the overall action, the Americans suffered 7 men—including Sergeant Carey—killed in action. The Germans lost approximately 100 killed and 143 captured.

By the end of the month Task Force A had secured Plougastel-Daoulas and the peninsula south of the bay, taking about 2,700 prisoners. From here, VIII Corps artillery could bombard Brest from across the water.

Middleton would spend two weeks stockpiling artillery ammunition, literally having to scrounge for it. Middleton had estimated that he needed 20,000 tons of munitions, but both Bradley and Patton felt that this estimate was four times what would actually be required for the attack. However, on August 23, two days before the siege was formally scheduled to begin, they agreed to bump Middleton's allotment up from 5,000 tons to 8,000 tons.

Both Hermann Ramcke and Troy Middleton realized that they were going to fight to the last German soldier, and both knew that this was not going to be easy for the Americans.

Friday, August 25, through Tuesday, September 12

On August 25, the same day that Paris was liberated, the VIII Corps artillery opened fire on the heavily fortified old city center of Brest with the corps artillery. Meanwhile, the USAAF Eighth Air Force contributed 150 B-17 heavy bombers, and the British Royal Navy dispatched the battleship HMS *Warspite*, to bombard Brest from the bay. That night, the Royal Air Force also sent heavy bombers over the city. They were guided in by a huge fire that the B-17s had started in the Recouverance suburb of Brest.

The artillery, air, and naval gunfire barrage was accompanied by an infantry assault by three infantry divisions moving abreast, attempting to squeeze the German outer perimeter. The 8th Infantry Division moved in the center with the 29th Infantry Division on its right flank and the 2nd on its left.

As had been the case across the bay at Plougastel-Daoulas, the interlocking fields of fire from the German pillboxes tore into the infantrymen, giving them little opportunity to fight back—or even to raise their heads.

Shortly after dusk on Tuesday, August 29, the 2nd Infantry Division's 23rd Infantry Regiment was in the process of digging into defensive positions along a hedgerow just beyond the outer perimeter of the German defensive line. One platoon of the battalion's Company G had not yet dug into its foxholes, when a German platoon, covered by fire from machine guns and antiaircraft guns, launched a counterattack. The enemy moved so quickly that they overwhelmed the Americans and were almost on top of the platoon's machine gun position.

Seeing this, Sergeant John McVeigh, a young Philadelphian assigned to the battalion's H Company, intervened. Dodging an immense stream of automatic weapons fire, he stood up and directed his squad to fire on the attackers. When the Germans almost overran the H Company position, McVeigh drew his trench knife and charged several of the enemy single-handedly. In a savage hand-to-hand struggle, McVeigh killed one German with the knife—his only weapon—and had attacked three more when he was shot down and killed with small-arms fire at point-blank range.

Two other GIs in McVeigh's squad concentrated

machine-gun fire on the attacking enemy and then turned their weapons on the three Germans that had killed McVeigh. The action led by McVeigh was credited with being almost entirely responsible for stopping the enemy assault and saving G Company. He was posthumously awarded the Congressional Medal of Honor.

As the week wore on, a storm blew in from the North Atlantic, lashing the Americans in their makeshift slit trenches and eliminating their tactical air cover. Tactical air was only marginally effective in the action, anyway, because the Germans were not in the open, but rather in very well made concrete structures.

By the first day of September, the date that had earlier been expected for the completion of the operation, it was by no means anywhere near complete. The corps artillery was running out of 105mm and 155mm shells. Middleton went begging, telling Omar Bradley that there was no sign of a lessening of resolve on the part of the Germans. Bradley agreed to reconsider the ammunition allotment, and to supply more mortars and artillery. The flow of supplies increased, and by September 7, Middleton was able to resume a continuous barrage.

On September 8, Middleton resumed the infantry assault as well. Each of the three divisions managed to extend their reach a bit farther, taking hills and strongpoints that had been out of their grasp during the previous assault. In the center, the 13th Infantry Regiment spearheaded the 8th Infantry Division action. When the two battalions on the 13th Infantry Regiment flank were brought to a halt by intense German mortar and machine gun fire, snipers went to work and started picking off the hapless GIs who were trapped in the open.

Finally, Ernest Prussman, a young Private First Class from Brighton, Massachusetts, had enough. He jumped up and led his squad on a counterattack. Jumping across a hedgerow, he disarmed two German riflemen and led the squad across an open field to the next hedgerow. He then personally attacked a machine gun nest, destroyed the gun, and captured several Germans.

From there, Prussman led his squad deeper into German lines until he was shot by an enemy rifleman. As he went down, however, he threw a hand grenade at the German, blowing him to bits. Prussman's superb leadership and action were credited with so demoralizing the Germans that resistance at this point collapsed, permitting the two battalions to proceed. Private First Class Prussman was posthumously awarded the Congressional Medal of Honor.

By the end of the day, all three divisions had reached the edge of the city, and the 8th Infantry Division had two regiments inside, fighting on city streets. The bloody street fighting would continue until September 12, with the Germans contesting nearly every building and street corner with well-prepared machine gun positions.

Those bloody days merely brought the Yanks to the walls of the fortified old city center, an even more formidable obstacle. Here, they faced walls as high as thirty-five feet that lay across a moat that was nearly as deep and covered by gun emplacements with interlocking fields of fire.

Meanwhile, on September 10, as the attack at Brest continued, VIII had been realigned under the command structure. With Patton's Third Army headquarters now more than three hundred miles east of Brittany, VIII Corps was reassigned, being placed under Lieutenant General William Simpson's Ninth Army. Simpson had just arrived in France on

September 5, and had established his headquarters nearby at Rennes.

Wednesday through Tuesday, September 13 through 19

By the morning of September 13, the German perimeter had been reduced to just the fortified city center and its nearby forts, with the Americans mopping up outlying pockets. A substantial number of Germans had surrendered, and a great deal of blood had been spilled on both sides. Middleton figured that it was about time to ask General Ramcke to reconsider surrendering. The German commander again refused, and Middleton again ordered his men to attack.

The 29th Infantry Division was tasked with attacking Fort Keranroux, which flanked the Brest fortifications on the west. Fort Keranroux was heavily defended, with concentric rings of strongpoints and machine gun positions.

On the afternoon of September 13, the 2nd Battalion of the 175th Infantry Regiment worked its way close to the outer ring of enemy defenses. The battalion's Company F had advanced to within several hundred yards of Fort Keranroux, when it was halted by intense fire from inside. Realizing that this gun position had to be neutralized without delay, Staff Sergeant Sherwood Hallman of Spring City, Pennsylvania, ordered his squad to cover him while he advanced alone.

Hallman crawled to a point from which he could make his solo assault. He leaped over a hedgerow into a sunken road that was known to be covered by a German machine gun nest, as well as by at least thirty enemy riflemen. Firing his M1 carbine and tossing grenades, Hallman managed to kill or wound four Germans, while capturing a dozen others. Company F then moved in to secure the position. Hallman's action had a domino effect. When they watched what had happened, another seventy-five Germans hiding in nearby positions also gave up. At that point, the overall German defensive network collapsed, and by the end of the day, Fort Keranroux was in American hands. For his part in making this happen, Hallman was awarded the Congressional Medal of Honor.

With Fort Keranroux in hand, the Yanks moved on to nearby Fort Montbarey, where British tanks equipped with flamethrowers were used to get the 121st Engineer Combat Battalion close enough to the walls to set 2,500 pounds of explosive charges. With a hole knocked through the wall, the infantry was able to break into Fort Montbarey on September 16 and capture it.

Also on September 16, troops of both the 2nd Infantry Division and the 29th Infantry Division managed to penetrate the fortified center of Brest. By September 18, 10,000 members of the garrison had formally surrendered. Hermann Ramcke and his entourage managed to escape to the Crozon Peninsula, an islandlike promontory in the bay. He finally surrendered to Brigadier General Charles Canham of the 8th Infantry Division the following evening.

The siege of Brest had been a sobering lesson in urban warfare. The United States forces took 38,000 prisoners—from a garrison that they had earlier estimated to be manned by only 16,000—but suffered more than 9,800 casualties.

With Brest in American hands at last, VIII Corps and its new Ninth Army parent, relocated to the distant Western Front. Both the 2nd Infantry Division and the 8th Infantry Division went with VIII Corps, while the 29th Infantry Division was returned to First Army control.

Brest may have been taken, but the Germans at Lorient

and St. Nazaire would continue to hold out until the end of the war. No effort to capture the cities would be made. The two isolated garrisons would not surrender to the United States 66th Infantry Division until May 10, 1945—three days *after* V-E Day.

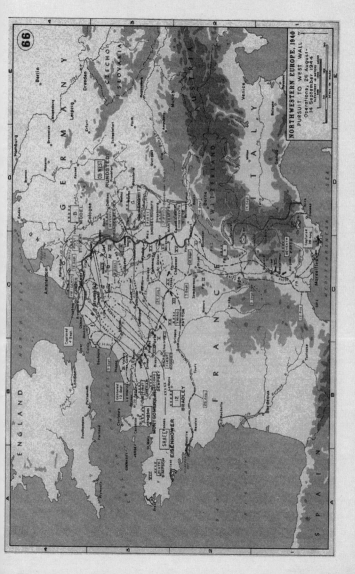

NORTHWESTERN EUROPE, 1940
PURSUIT TO WEST WALL
Operations, 26 August–
14 September 1944

ELEVEN

THE END WAS NEAR

The end was near—or so it seemed. By September 16, just three weeks after the liberation of Paris, the Allies had liberated nearly all of France, Belgium, and Luxembourg. In some cases the Allied armies had discovered the Germans running away so fast that they had trouble keeping up with them. Isolated German garrisons such as those at Brest and Metz were still holding out, but arguably more important cities, such as Brussels, Antwerp, and Maastricht, had been taken with hardly a shot being fired.

Just two weeks earlier, a smiling General Dwight Eisenhower had implied at his press conference that he still stood by his prediction that the war against Germany would be over by December.

In Washington, an even more optimistic timetable was being bandied about. Without naming his source, the chairman of the House of Representatives Post-War Military Policy Committee had told reporters that the US Army's "tentative date for finishing its job against Germany" was *October first!*

Conferring at the Octagon Conference in Quebec in mid-September, President Roosevelt and Prime Minister Churchill were already discussing and planning the minute details of the postwar occupation of Germany.

On the battlefronts of northern Europe, the Allied armies were still operating under the momentum that had carried them from the beachheads of Normandy in one hundred days. By the time that this milestone was reached in mid-September, the first German town had been captured by Collins's VII Corps, and the patrols of Gerow's V Corps were operating inside the Reich.

Meanwhile, Patton's Third Army occupied positions in Lorraine that Allied planners had predicted would not be reached until May 1945. The *New York Times* editorial page made the comment that those hundred days had "clinched the Allied victory and have sealed the fate of Hitler," but hastened to add that "it will take bitter fighting before the lights go on everywhere in Europe."

Indeed it would.

The Plan for Market Garden

After their sweep through Brussels, General Sir Miles Dempsey's Second British Army had hit the wall of the impossible defenses east of the Albert Canal at the Meuse-Escaut Canal on the border between Belgium and the Netherlands. They thought they'd taken Breda, but found themselves thrown out on their tail. This was problematic, because the main thrust of the Allied advance into Germany was targeting the Ruhr, and getting there required that Allied forces should dash across the Netherlands as briskly as they'd dashed across

Belgium. Once into Germany, they'd be operating across open, flat country that would be ideal for fast, mobile warfare that had become the Allied stock in trade since Operation Cobra—but first, they had to get there.

As discussed previously, to move across the Netherlands required the Allies to cross the myriad of rivers and canals that made up the delta of the mighty Rhine. By mid-September, the bridges in the area were still intact. They were too far from the front for the Germans to have executed plans for their demolition. Getting to these bridges by traveling overland might take weeks. It was time for that bold strategic thinking that had made such actions as Operation Cobra possible.

At SHAEF, the "bold" solution to the Rhine delta bridge problem was to simply leap over the German defenses at the Meuse-Escaut Canal with the First Allied Airborne Army. This "bold" solution was bold indeed. The plan was to involve the largest airborne operation in military history.

Championed by Field Marshall Montgomery, in whose 21st Army sector it would take place, the operation was actually to be *two* operations. The airborne operation, called Market, would be tasked with seizing the bridges. It would be closely coordinated with a ground operation, called Garden, that was designed to support the paratroopers shortly after they seized their objectives. Because the two operations became so inextricably entwined, they are now typically referred to as one—Operation Market Garden.

Operation Market would drop three airborne divisions into three locations behind German lines in the southern part of the Netherlands. The westernmost of these sites, near Eindhoven, would be the drop zone of the United States 101st Airborne Division, tasked with capturing the Wilhelmina Canal and the city of Eindhoven itself. Next would be the United States 82nd Airborne Division drop zone near Nijmegen, between the Maas River and the Waal River. Finally, the British 1st Airborne Division—incorporating the Polish 1st Parachute Brigade—would land at Arnhem on the Neder Rijn (Lower Rhine). The latter was, in the minds of the operational planners, the most important objective. It was also the deepest into enemy territory.

Operation Garden would involve four divisions of the British XXX Corps under Lieutenant General Brian Horrocks, who would be advancing overland from the Meuse-Escaut Canal on the Belgian border to relieve the "sky troops." The plan was for Horrocks to reach Eindhoven and link up with the 101st Airborne Division on the first day, and get all the way to Arnhem the next.

Operation Market would be under the command of British General Frederick Arthur Montague "Boy" Browning, deputy commander of the First Allied Airborne Army. In the planning process, Field Marshal Montgomery had asked Browning how long he would estimate that the paratroopers would be able to hold their respective drop zones while waiting for the ground forces to arrive to reinforce them. He told Montgomery that they could hold for two days—four days at the maximum.

In looking at the map, Browning noted the respective distances of the three targets from Allied lines. According to the popular legend, Browning told Montgomery that Arnhem, the most distant drop zone from the XXX Corps point of origin, might be "a bridge too far."

Sunday, September 17
(With the First Allied Airborne Army)

Operation Market Garden jumped off in the predawn darkness as hundreds of C-47 and C-53 troop transports—some pulling gliders and all carrying paratroopers—headed into enemy air space over the Netherlands. Major General Maxwell Taylor's 101st "Screaming Eagles" Airborne Division landed near the towns of St. Oedenrode and Veghel north of Eindhoven and the Wilhelmina Canal. Here they found themselves under counterattack by the German 59th Division commanded by Major General Walther Poppe. Against heavy German fire, the 502nd and 506th Parachute Infantry Regiments moved to take the bridges across the canal at the towns of Best and Son. They discovered that the latter's bridge was destroyed by the Germans.

Major General James "Jumping Jim" Gavin's 82nd Airborne Division enjoyed somewhat greater success. Although they failed to take the city of Nijmegen, their 504th Parachute Infantry Regiment had moved out from its drop zone at Overasselt and had managed to take and hold a bridge across the Maas River at Grave. They had also worked with the 505th Parachute Infantry Regiment to take several bridges on the canal connecting the Maas to the Waal River, but the division did not reach the Waal itself.

Boy Browning landed with the 82nd Airborne Division at Nijmegen in order to establish the Operation Market Garden operational headquarters at the middle of the three landing sites, which were being referred to as "air heads," a paraphrase of the term "beachhead," which entered the popular lexicon after D-Day in June.

Major General Robert "Roy" Urquhart's 1st British Airborne Division executed a successful landing west of Arnhem. Unfortunately for Urquhart, the city's German garrison was at the time reinforced by the II SS Panzer Korps. Both sides were taken off guard.

The German Korps commander, SS General Wilhelm Bittrich, immediately ordered his troops into action against the paratroopers. He ordered the 9th "Hohenstaufen" SS Panzer Division, under Lieutenant Colonel Walter Harzer, to seal off the roads leading in and out of Arnhem. The 10th "Frundsberg" SS Panzer Division under Brigadier General Heinz Harmel was directed to hurry toward Nijmegen to deal with the 82nd Airborne Division that was landing there.

General Brian Horrocks's XXX Corps got under way as scheduled, but did not reach Eindhoven as planned. Because of unexpected counterattacks by German antitank guns, they managed to get only as far as Valkenswaard. In securing the town, one group of British troops occupied the mayor's office within the city hall. Suddenly, the telephone rang. As a British officer picked up the receiver, the voice on the other end of the line, speaking in German, demanded that the Valkenswaard be held against the British advance at all costs. The British officer, replying in German, assured the Wehrmacht officer on the other end of the line that Valkenswaard *would* be held at all costs. He didn't add against whom it would be held.

Operation Market Garden had gotten off to an extremely inauspicious beginning. Meanwhile, even as the British XXX Corps was heading beyond the Meuse-Escaut Canal for operations behind enemy lines, the Allied bridgeheads across the canal were coming under increasing counterattack.

Monday, September 18
(With the First Allied Airborne Army)

The citizens of Valkenswaard were celebrating, bringing out
and displaying their Netherlands flags for the first time in four
years. However, their little city was merely a waypoint in the
strategic scheme of things this week.

At Arnhem, Nijmegen, and Eindhoven, the three Allied
airborne divisions that had dropped into the Netherlands with
Operation Market Garden on Sunday were surrounded and
under heavy German counterattack. Attempts to reinforce
them by air were only marginally successful because bad
weather had moved over the First Allied Airborne Army's air
bases in England. Aerial resupply efforts, including the use of
Eighth Air Force bombers as supply aircraft, were also just
partially successful because most of the supplies fell outside
the perimeters that were held by Allied troops.

At Arnhem, General Urquhart established a 1st British
Airborne Division command post west of the central part of
the city, while one battalion had managed to penetrate the city
during the night and to capture the north end of the principal
bridge across the Neder Rijn. On Monday, they beat back several attempts by the Germans to retake the bridge, but the artillery of Harmel's 10th SS Panzer Division took a terrible toll
against the defenders.

The 82nd Airborne Division south of Nijmegen was also
under German fire for most of the day. The 508th Parachute
Infantry Regiment, which had landed practically on the German border, attempted, without success, to reach Nijmegen or
the Waal River bridge. The 504th, 505th, and 508th Parachute Infantry Regiments, which had succeeded in capturing
all of the remaining division objectives including bridgeheads

on the Maas and the Mass-Waal Canal—just dug in to consolidate their positions.

On Sunday, most of the 101st Airborne Division had remained under fire and pinned down near the principal division drop zone at St. Oedenrode. None of its units had come near reaching the city of Eindhoven.

Monday morning, the division's 502nd Parachute Infantry Regiment moved to capture and hold the Wilhelmina Canal bridge at Best, while General Taylor ordered the 506th Parachute Infantry Regiment to move south toward Eindhoven. Meanwhile, the 501st Parachute Infantry Regiment was in a position at Veghel north of the principal division drop zone at St. Oedenrode.

Throughout the morning, Walther Poppe's German 59th Division made repeated attempts to wrestle control of the Best bridge from the 502nd Parachute Infantry Regiment. The regiment was soon surrounded by the German force, which was superior in both personnel and firepower. As the Germans closed in on the regimental perimeter, Private First Class Joe Mann of Seattle, a lead scout with Company H, crept to within bazooka range of an enemy artillery position. Braving heavy machine gun fire, he destroyed an 88mm gun and an ammunition dump. Despite continuing automatic weapons fire, from which he was hit four times, he remained in his exposed position, and killed a sizable number of enemy troops with his M1.

Perhaps because of Joe Mann's heroic stand, Walther Poppe decided that his troops could neither capture nor hold the Best bridge, and shortly before noon, he ordered it blown up.

Meanwhile, the Screaming Eagles had succeeded in taking several bridges across the Dommel River, and the 506th Parachute Infantry Regiment had reached Eindhoven. No sooner had they reached the city than they met the advance guard of Brian Horrocks's XXX Corps, who had just fought their way up from Valkenswaard through a major shootout with Germans defending the city of Aalst.

Monday, September 18
(With V Corps across the German Border)

On Sunday morning, as Operation Market Garden was getting under way in the Netherlands, several V Corps units were still operating inside Germany opposite Luxembourg. Combat Commands B and R of the 5th Armored Division were east of Wallendorf and the 109th Infantry Regiment of the 28th Infantry Division was near Sevenig. As would be the case at Arnhem, the going would not be as easy as first anticipated.

The terrain and weather were clearly not in the favor of V Corps as it probed carefully into Germany. Located in the German Army Group G sector, just south of the boundary with Army Group B, the area was on the mountainous backside of the Ardennes highlands. It was heavily wooded and hilly, with narrow winding roads and numerous streams. The weather, as it had been throughout the region, was rainy and overcast, with dense morning ground fog that reduced visibility to the "hand-in-front-of-your-face" variety.

At Sevenig, the 109th Infantry Regiment of the 28th Infantry Division was the target of a determined German counterattack on Sunday morning. The regiment's Company K was especially hard hit. The 2nd and 3rd Platoons had lost most of their commanders, and were being led by Tech Sergeant Francis Clark of the 3rd Platoon. He had been wounded during the attack on Sunday, but insisted that he remain with his troops and he refused to be medevaced. Clark was the same man who had distinguished himself by saving one platoon and then leading the two platoons in a rout of a full German company that had ambushed them on the Our River on September 12.

At dawn on Monday, Clark spotted Germans moving about in the near darkness, obviously intending to surprise and overwhelm Company K. Clark quietly slipped out of the captured pillbox in which he'd spent the night and silently killed a German who was setting up a machine gun not more than five yards away. He discovered another enemy gun, moved in unobserved, and killed two Germans with his M1 carbine. During the ensuing fire fight, the injured Clark continued to help the company beat off attacks, and to lead counterattacks against the heavily armed Germans. For his actions on Monday, and for those the previous Tuesday, Sergeant Clark would be awarded the Congressional Medal of Honor.

By early Sunday, the 5th Armored Division's Combat Command R, under Colonel Glen Anderson, had penetrated as far as Bettingen, about half way to the German city of Bitburg from the frontier with Luxembourg. The 5th Armored Division had been assigned Bitburg as its first major objective within the Reich, but on Saturday, as German resistance began to increase, V Corps headquarters had ordered Anderson to consolidate his position. He was to take the town of Mettendorf, north of Bettingen, but to await explicit orders from V Corps before going into the city of Bitburg—where enemy defenses were expected to be quite strong. By Monday, the command had gotten only as far as Bettingen.

Over the weekend, the German resistance had seemed to materialize out of nowhere. On the previous Wednesday, when Combat Command R had spearheaded the V Corps movement across the border, they'd found many Siegfried

Line pillboxes unmanned. Despite the rugged terrain, the Americans had made good progress against sporadic German resistance, and had reached Bettingen on Friday. By the next day, the Germans seemed to be suddenly waking up to defend their Fatherland.

Still in the vicinity of Bettingen after two days of fighting, Anderson had observed that German artillery fire was coming from the north, northeast, and east and German tanks were to the northeast and east. This was the general direction of Bitburg, where the major German troop concentration was located. If this heavy fire was coming from an identifiable direction, machine gun and mortar fire seemed to be emanating from everywhere.

At 8:30 A.M. on Sunday, Combat Command R was beating back its fifth German counterattack, with a total of eight German tanks destroyed. By early afternoon a German attack from northeast had been deflected with fourteen German tanks knocked out. The Yanks too were taking losses and casualties, and the decision was made to pull back from Bettingen to a point on the Sauer River about half way between the two border towns of Wallendorf and Bollendorf.

Combat Command B, commanded by Colonel John Cole, had come across the border to cover the Combat Command R "tail" and was in the area close to the border near Wallendorf. Combat Command B was also under fire from German artillery. Because the command was in the low ground near the Sauer River, they were mired in the mud and found it difficult to move their tanks. During the day, the command would lose three Shermans to German rocket-launcher fire.

By mid-afternoon, both commands had come under full-scale counterattack. Nevertheless, Combat Command R had managed to reach Mettendorf by dark. They attacked, but soon discovered that the town—supposedly lightly defended—was heavily defended. By midnight on Sunday, the German machine gun fire died out, although all units of the command were still under German artillery fire.

Monday, September 18
(With the Third Army in Lorraine)

In the Lorraine campaign, the Third Army had moved across the Moselle, with the 4th Armored Division in the vanguard. Meanwhile, the 6th Armored Division was beginning to arrive in Lorraine after making a marathon march all the way across France from Brittany. The 35th Infantry Division, which had occupied the city of Nancy, at week's end had seen little rest.

Among the hardest-working personnel in the 35th Infantry Division had been the men of the 134th Infantry Regiment. On Saturday, they had captured the Plateau de Malzeville, the high ground across the river from the city that continued to be used by German artillery spotters. In the process, they had secured two bridgeheads across the Meurthe River. On Sunday, they had continued to press the enemy at the towns of Essey-les-Nancy and Pulnoy, taking heavy fire from German machine guns and artillery all the way.

The 3rd Battalion's Company K had captured Butte Ste. Genevieve—a shoulder of the Plateau de Malzeville—after heavy fighting late Sunday. This was a key tactical move because German artillery spotters active on this hill were able to call in strikes against Americans moving around and past the Plateau de Malzeville.

Monday morning, the 134th Infantry Regiment met stiff

resistance as they continued to probe German positions on the far slope of the plateau. The GIs were discovering that the Germans had both heavily and carefully fortified the area with well-hidden machine-gun nests that were positioned for optimum fields of fire. It was deadly going, and the companies assigned to the 3rd Battalion, especially Company I, were taking the brunt of German resistance.

From Pulnoy, the 1st Battalion moved north, past the Plateau de Malzeville, on the 3rd Battalion's right flank. Their way was made easier by the fact that the 3rd Battalion had taken control of the Butte Ste. Genevieve, thus blinding the German artillery observation post. However, as they continued, they came into binocular view of German observation posts farther along. One was located in the village of Amance, which was on a ridge line northeast of the town of Selchamps. Of more immediate concern was one that was located on a lone, steep hill that rose nearly 650 feet. This hill was known to the French as Pain de Sucre, meaning "Sugar Loaf."

The Pain de Sucre dominated the valley, offering an excellent view for a radius of nearly a mile. Anything within this radius was at the mercy of German guns. As with the Plateau de Malzeville on Saturday, this was a textbook illustration of the importance of controlling high ground. In order for the 134th Infantry Regiment to continue, the Pain de Sucre had to be outflanked and captured.

The job of leading the assault against the Pain de Sucre fell to Dog Company of the 1st Battalion, backed by the Sherman tanks of the 737th Tank Battalion's Able Company. The spearhead of the attack would be Dog Company's machine-gun squad, led by Sergeant Ralph Greely.

It was a day for heroes. The GIs came under withering German automatic-weapons fire as they moved up the wooded slopes. They were pinned down and simply could not move—except for Ralph Greely. Deciding that he'd had enough of hugging the ground, Greely got up and dragged a mounted heavy machine gun into a position where he could pour a stream of effective return fire into the German heavy-weapons location.

The fire from the stunned Germans slackened and the GIs moved out. Sergeant Greely continued firing as the Yanks rushed the Germans, but soon his luck ran out. He had eluded the hail of German bullets swirling around him for many minutes, but finally he was caught in the fusillade and his lifeless body collapsed across the pile of spent shell casings.

Meanwhile, the troops of the 1st Battalion's Able and Baker Companies, flanking the Pain de Sucre to the northwest, also ran into a leaden roadblock. A hail of automatic weapons fire stopped the infantry, and a German tank gunner scored a direct hit on an M4 tank, which burst into flames. A young artillery observer from Wyoming, Lieutenant Gerald Hassel, got into a position where he could see the German line and began to call in artillery fire. Unfortunately, he survived only momentarily before he was fatally shot.

Baker Company's commander, Lieutenant Francis Mason, took the initiative and began leading his men slowly forward against the enemy, backed by the 737th Tank Battalion Shermans. It was hard going, but the GIs managed to push the Germans back. As the battle tumbled backward into a cluster of buildings, the fight became virtually hand-to-hand. The Sherman tanks, meanwhile, managed to outmaneuver their German counterparts in the close quarters among the buildings, and one Panther detonated under a direct hit.

The fighting dragged on as the afternoon waned into evening. As darkness began to fall, the confused battlefield morphed into chaos. A group of about eighty Able Company GIs, mainly from a platoon commanded by a young Nebraska sergeant named Thaine Hale, discovered that they were separated from the rest of the battalion. They took cover inside a large barn to catch their breath and to figure out what to do. As they assessed their predicament, they took stock of the fact that their situation was further complicated by the nearly two dozen German prisoners that they had in tow.

Sergeant Hale, who had just returned to the company after recovering from wounds that he'd suffered in Normandy, moved to resolve the predicament. By now, it was pitch-dark, but Hale was able to use the flames from the burning German tank as a guide as he left the barn and went in search of help. Working his way through the darkness and the sporadic German gunfire, he finally spotted an American tank and flagged it down. With Hale perched atop it, the tank maneuvered to the barn where the eighty GIs were stranded. Supported by the tank, the men would be able to work their way back to American lines.

The tank was minus a machine gunner, so Sergeant Albert Rogers, a machine-gun squad leader from the infantry platoon, climbed aboard to take over. Hale also remained atop the tank to direct the action as the men moved out. Just as they had almost made it to relative safety, a lone German bullet struck Sergeant Hale, mortally wounding him. For his action, he would be posthumously awarded the Silver Star.

It had been a costly day of fighting for the 134th Infantry Regiment, but the objective, the Pain de Sucre, was successfully taken by nightfall, even as the fighting still raged on the northeast flank of the hill.

Even before dark on Monday night, General Edmund Sebree and Colonel Butler Miltonberger had begun working out the details for Tuesday's operations for Task Force S. The ambitious plan called for the regiment to move approximately five miles, simultaneously to the north and northeast. The 2nd Battalion was to drive north at 7:00 A.M. to take down the village of Chamois. The 1st Battalion would move out three hours later toward the town of Bouxieres-aux-Chenes, which was to the northwest of the Pain de Sucre, past Amance, the location that the Germans were using as an observation post. The 3rd Battalion would be held in reserve to be used to support whichever battalion needed help.

It had been a costly day of fighting for the 134th Infantry Regiment, but it was not yet over. At about 3:00 A.M. Tuesday morning, the Germans suddenly launched a determined counterattack with mortars and machine guns. The 1st Battalion's Able and Charlie Companies took the brunt of the attack, suffering severe casualties before the men were able to wake up and return fire. Sergeant Philip Blair, a veteran who'd been with the regiment continuously since Normandy, and Lieutenant Constant Kjems, Able Company's commander, were among those who lost their lives in the ensuing firefight.

With Lieutenant Kjems dead, Able Company's executive officer, Lieutenant Edward Hum, assumed command straightaway and rallied the troops as best he could under the conditions. He directed a fierce counter to the German counterattack. Hum led his men as they blasted away in the darkness at close range, and even as they found themselves brawling with the Wehrmacht in belt-buckle-to-belt-buckle combat.

Meanwhile, four GIs found themselves cut off from the rest of the battalion—Staff Sergeant George Daugherty, Sergeant Penn Soland, Sergeant Harold Schultz, and Private First Class Hobert Hunt. Schultz volunteered to provide cov-

ering fire while the others crawled to safety. Operating as a
sniper and targeting individual Germans, Schultz kept the enemy off balance while his comrades crept through the enemy
lines.

By dawn, the ground fog, which typically clings to the
hills of Lorraine on early autumn mornings, allowed Schultz
to slip through to the rest of the battalion. Lieutenant Hum,
meanwhile, had also used the fog as cover for leading his men
back to the main American force.

Monday and the wee hours of Tuesday had, indeed, been
a time for heroes.

Tuesday, September 19
(With the First Allied Airborne Army)

Operation Market Garden, the bold plan that SHAEF had de-
vised to leapfrog over the German Army Group B and seize
the Rhine delta bridges, was still mired in difficulty. The
British XXX Corps ground force had succeeded in linking up
with the paratroopers of the United States 101st Airborne Division at Eindhoven on Monday, but the Yanks at Nijmegen
and the British at Arnhem were still surrounded and fighting
for their lives.

During Tuesday morning, there was a series of German
counterattacks north of Eindhoven against the 101st Airborne
Division's 501st Parachute Infantry Regiment at Veghel and
the 502nd Parachute Infantry Regiment on the Wilhelmina
Canal. Meanwhile, Joe Mann, the regiment's hero of Monday's fighting, had insisted on remaining with Company H
despite his serious wounds. One of the enemy assaults struck
near his position. The Germans moved in, tossing hand
grenades as they approached. One of these landed within a

few feet of Mann. Unable to raise his arms, which were bandaged to his body, he yelled "grenade" and threw his body over the explosive device. He was blown to bits, but those around him were saved, and the counterattack was repulsed. For his gallantry on those two consecutive days in the Netherlands, Joe Mann was awarded the Congressional Medal of Honor.

The first XXX Corps scout cars moved out from Eindhoven at dawn. They would be able to reach Nijmegen using back roads, but the British tanks would not be able to move east until there was an adequate bridge across the Wilhelmina Canal. The British XXX Corps Engineers had worked through the night to construct a Bailey bridge across the canal to replace the two that Poppe's 59th Division had popped on Monday. Despite the German counterattack, which almost undid their work, the Engineers completed the bridge and the armored columns of Horrocks's Corps moved east toward where the 82nd Airborne Division was surrounded at Nijmegen. The corps had now penetrated forty miles through German lines from their jumping-off point on Sunday morning.

The XXX Corps advance units managed to reach the Nijmegen area by around 9:00 A.M., where they linked up with the 504th Parachute Infantry Regiment near Grave. Jim Gavin and Boy Browning mapped strategy for a major assault on the Waal bridge at Nijmegen, but decided to wait for the full weight of XXX to arrive on Wednesday.

While the Allies were gaining the upper hand at two of the Operation Market Garden "air heads," the situation at Arnhem was deteriorating rapidly. The 2nd Battalion of Roy Urquhart's 1st British Airborne Division still held the north end of the Neder Rijn bridge, but it was cut off from the other units and under heavy attack from Wilhelm Bittrich's II SS Panzer Korps. During an attempt by the Allies to bring supplies to the beleaguered paratroopers by glider, the Luftwaffe made one of its rare appearances over the battlefield. Many of the Allied transports were shot down, and only 10 percent of the supplies meant for the British troops managed to actually reach them.

Tuesday, September 19
(With the Third Army in Lorraine)

Down in Lorraine, the Third Army had seized bridgeheads across the Moselle and were pressing eastward toward the Reich. Paul Baade's 35th Infantry Division had captured Nancy—Lorraine's largest city—over the weekend, while Tiger Jack Wood's 4th Armored Division was still very active in the rolling countryside beyond the Moselle. However, the going was much slower across this river than it had been when Patton's army had vaulted the Seine, the Marne, and the Meuse a few weeks earlier. The 4th Armored Division was about to encounter the full weight of a rejuvenated Fifth Panzer Army, while the 35th Infantry Division was taking heavy losses in bitter counterattacks as they moved east.

The 35th Infantry Division's 134th Infantry Regiment had spent all of Monday battling to take the high ground at the hill known as Pain de Sucre—"Sugar Loaf"—only to have an overnight counterattack reverse most of the day's gains. As this came to light with the first rays of the Tuesday morning sun, XII Corps was anxious that the 134th Infantry Regiment reassert its control over the Pain de Sucre. General Edmund Sebree of the 35th Division's Task Force S and Colonel Butler Miltonberger of the 134th Infantry Regiment would have to develop a new battle plan.

The regiment's 1st Battalion had been badly mauled in

the nocturnal fighting, and those who had not gotten a bit of rest since the Germans had attacked at 3:00 A.M. were exhausted. They would now have to be rested and redirected back into the Pain de Sucre operation rather than being used to push forward.

On the other hand, both the 2nd Battalion and 3rd Battalion were rested and ready. The 2nd Battalion would be able to jump off as previously planned at 7:00 A.M. morning, while the 3rd Battalion would be available to join the 1st Battalion in the Pain de Sucre action.

At first light, General Sebree met with Major Warren Wood of the 3rd Battalion, Colonel Alford Boatsman of the 1st Battalion, and Major Dan Craig, the acting executive officer of the 1st Battalion, to draft the Pain de Sucre plan. They discussed moving the 3rd Battalion through the 1st Battalion position, but Major Wood suggested—and the others agreed—that it would be more straightforward for his battalion to attack directly to the east from their position atop the Plateau de Malzeville. The 1st Battalion would provide backup for the 3rd Battalion from the position that it now held.

The Pain de Sucre operation got underway at 1:30 Tuesday afternoon with an artillery barrage. The assault involved 3rd Battalion moving in two columns, each spearheaded by infantrymen riding tanks and followed by more infantry on foot. As they reached the woods around the base of the Pain de Sucre, the two columns spread out to form a line. They advanced up the hill in this manner, supported by artillery and machine-gun fire. The 3rd Battalion assault moved quickly, with the tanks and infantry reaching the peak of the Pain de Sucre shortly after 2:00 P.M.

The 1st Battalion contributed diversionary fire, while

Company I, commanded by Lieutenant James Cecka, moved around the Pain de Sucre and into the scene of the bitter fighting overnight where Sergeant Hale had been killed. It was a replay of Monday's action, complete with a tenacious German tank defending the position. As on Monday, the tank was taken out and this proved to be the last obstacle to the Yanks' retaking the positions that they had occupied twenty-four hours earlier.

The déjà vu would, however, continue to include yet another vicious German counterattack against the GIs on the Pain de Sucre. As on Monday, the attack would come under cover of darkness, and once more the firefight would devolve into hand-to-hand fighting.

As had been the case on Monday, Tuesday would be another day for heroes within the 134th Infantry Regiment. When one group of GIs found themselves surrounded in a building, squad leader Sergeant Huston Temple ordered the men to slip away singly while he provided covering fire. The Germans continued to attack the building as Temple moved and fired from many of the structure's windows to establish the misconception that there was still a whole squad inside. He managed to kill a sizable number of Germans, while most of the GIs escaped. In the ensuing confusion, Temple also got away, and he was later awarded a Silver Star for his actions.

Another Silver Star went to Technical Sergeant Charles Ostrom, an Oregonian platoon sergeant in K Company. He observed a pair of enemy machine gunners that were surreptitiously making their way toward an American antitank gun position. Ostrom managed to sneak up on the two Germans and kill them with hand grenades before they were able to attack the American position. Unfortunately, Ostrom was gunned down by German fire as he attempted to return to his platoon, and his Silver Star would be posthumous. Only moments after he was killed, the American gun that Ostrom had saved managed to stop a German tank in its tracks.

The Germans' Tuesday counterattack essentially failed, and the Yanks managed to retain control over the bloody Pain de Sucre.

While the 134th Infantry Regiment's 1st and 3rd Battalions remained engaged at the Pain de Sucre, however, Lieutenant Colonel James Walker's 2nd Battalion had proceeded with the earlier plan to continue the regimental drive north toward the village of Chamois. They jumped off early Tuesday morning, supported by a tank destroyer platoon and spearheaded by George Company.

The going would not be easy for Walker's battalion. The terrain was rugged and it was soon bitterly evident that the Germans had prepared a terrible briar patch of ambushes. Near the tiny hamlet of Lay St. Christopher, German machine guns located all across a ridge overlooking the road raked the right flank of the advancing column.

However, Tuesday was another day for heroes within the 134th Infantry Regiment, and Tuesday would be the day that Hitler's armies would get to know the scrappy country boy from Russell County, Kentucky, that would come to be known as the "One-Man Army."

As the GIs hit the dirt or crouched behind the armored tank destroyers, Staff Sergeant Junior James Spurrier climbed up onto one of the tank destroyers and grabbed the .50-caliber machine gun atop the vehicle. Pointing up the hill, he ordered its crew to attack immediately in the direction of the enemy fire.

Spurrier himself raked the Germans with machine-gun fire as the big machine trundled forward, killing many and compelling others to run away as fast as they could. He then jumped off the tank destroyer, dashed straight for a German dugout, and tossed in several hand grenades. Next, he climbed back aboard the moving tank destroyer, which he directed to attack toward another German dugout. Using his own weapon, Spurrier destroyed the enemy gun and all troops in the dugout.

Junior Spurrier stayed with the tank destroyer until it reached the crest of the hill, then jumped down and rushed the enemy. As the rest of George Company swept up the hill behind him, he accepted the surrender of twenty-two German soldiers.

Junior Spurrier may have been on his way to his reputation as the "One-Man Army," but he was not George Company's only hero that day. Young Private First Class Thomas Holt from Misssissippi also leaped aboard a tank destroyer to effectively man a .50-caliber machine gun. Despite the fact that he was blown off the vehicle by the concussion of an exploding artillery shell, Holt climbed back up to the machine gun and continued to rake the enemy with a stream of large-caliber automatic-weapons fire.

Holt earned a Silver Star that day, and for his actions, Junior Spurrier would be awarded the Distinguished Service Cross.

However, the war was not over for the "One-Man Army." Eight weeks later, on November 13, as the 134th Infantry Regiment was in action near the French village of Achain, Junior Spurrier would attack literally as an army of one. When George Company encountered German fire at the approaches to Achain, he entered the town alone, armed with a Browning automatic rifle and with an M1 carbine slung over his back.

From midafternoon until darkness fell, Spurrier worked solo. He took out three Germans immediately with the BAR and then simply walked through Achain, alternating between the automatic weapon and his carbine. Despite intense German fire, he moved casually, but brutally. He held his fire from time to time, but only to toss a hand grenade into a building. At one point, he picked up a German Panzerfaust rocket launcher from an enemy soldier that he'd shot and used it to take out several more enemy. He picked up a Luger automatic pistol from yet another dead German, and used that as well.

When Junior Spurrier's afternoon in Achain was finally over, the town was in American hands. The death toll suffered by the Germans at his hands that day was at least twenty-four, but possibly as many as forty. He also captured a pair of officers and two enlisted men. For his valor on that November day, Junior Spurrier would receive the Congressional Medal of Honor and the French Croix de Guerre. He returned home alive, settled in Bluefield, West Virginia, and survived until 1984. However, his life after World War II would be sad and troubled by failure and alcoholism. Like so many veterans, he would never make the mental transition to civilian life.

As the regiments of the 35th Infantry Division were slogging through the thickets of German opposition around the Pain de Sucre, Third Army's 4th Armored Division was moving ahead with a great deal more speed.

Combat Command A of the 4th Armored Division had reached the city of Arracourt on Thursday night and began early Friday to mop up German forces in the area. They destroyed eight German tanks and twice that number of large artillery pieces. They also had destroyed or captured more than two hundred other vehicles while taking an estimated 1,000 prisoners.

On Saturday, both Combat Command A and Combat Command B had crossed the Marne-Rhine Canal, leaving the division's Combat Command R to guard the crossing point. Having accomplished this, the 4th Armored Division—as a spearhead for Manton Eddy's XIII Corps—had broken through the German defensive line in Lorraine. The remaining Germans in the area were essentially on the run. There was nothing between the 4th Armored Division and the German border but retreating enemy soldiers.

Colonel Bruce Clarke of Combat Command A had proposed an immediate drive toward the Lorraine town of Sarrebourg, then wearing the German appellation "Saarburg," which was within a few miles of the border and a couple of days' drive—at the speed the Sherman tanks had been traveling—from the German industrial city of Karlsruhe.

General Eddy nixed the idea on Saturday. It was the old "broken neck" theory. He didn't want to see the 4th Armored Division so deeply committed in the east that it would get cut off.

Eddy reminded the armored division men that the XII Corps foot soldiers were yet to catch up and that the corps's two infantry divisions were still engaged. The 80th Infantry Division was still fighting the 3rd Panzer Grenadier Division in the vicinity of the Dieulouard bridgehead, and the 35th Infantry Division was chasing the 553rd Volksgrenadier Division, which had escaped from Nancy just before it was captured.

Eddy had hoped that these loose ends could be tied up over the weekend, and that he would be able to get XII Corps under way again by Monday. However, when bad weather moved in, he decided to postpone until the following day.

By Tuesday, though, it would be too late. While Eddy had managed to solidify the XIII Corps position, so too had the Germans. General Hasso von Manteuffel, who had assumed command of the Fifth Panzer Army from Sepp Dietrich a week earlier, had used that time to assemble a sizable force with which to launch a serious counterattack.

On September 19, the Fifth Panzer Army was assigned the 11th Panzer Division, as well as both the 111th and 113th Panzer Brigades. These brigades were newly formed and possessed a rarity on the Western Front in September 1944—new equipment.

Manteuffel had attacked in the rainy weather on Monday, knowing that Allied airpower would be grounded and unable to help. His first counterblow came at Luneville against Combat Command R of the 4th Armored Division. Other 4th Armored Division units came to the rescue, and the Third Army also sent tanks from the 6th Armored Division into the fray.

On Tuesday morning, again under cover of thick ground fog, Manteuffel ordered the 113th Panzer Brigade to continue the attack, hitting Combat Command A at Arracourt. They struck through the fog at 8:00 A.M.

The ensuing battle pitted the Shermans against Panthers and Tigers at close range. Of course, the 88mm guns on the Tigers had a superiority over the 76mm weapons of the Shermans in terms of both range and hitting power. However, the fog negated the range superiority because in order for a tank to fire on another tank, the other tank has to be *visible*.

Bruce Clarke ordered his mobile artillery vehicles, with their 105mm guns, to fire directly at the German tanks. While the Tigers could withstand a blow from the front by a 76mm, their armor was no match for a 105mm round at close range. Around midday, the attack by the 113th Panzer Brigade had run out of steam and Clarke ordered his Shermans to outflank the panzers. By nightfall, Manteuffel's army had gained little ground, but had disrupted the American offensive. The most serious outcome was that the Germans had lost fifty of their new tanks.

Wednesday, September 20
(With the First Allied Airborne Army)

By Wednesday, the focal point of Operation Market Garden was clearly at Nijmegen. Eindhoven had slipped to the Allies on Tuesday, but General Model of the German Army Group B was determined not to let this happen again at Nijmegen. All day long, there would be fierce battles all around the city, with some positions being taken and retaken several times. The Allied airborne divisions continued to suffer a high number of casualties. However, the prearranged plan to bring in reinforcements from England had to be canceled for the second day running because of terrible weather in England. The troops of the 325th Glider Infantry Regiment had been scheduled to arrive at Nijmegen on Tuesday, but had not. The 504th Parachute Infantry Regiment was still holding the landing zone at Overassalt, watching and waiting hopefully.

The weather across the Netherlands had been clear, however, and Allied tactical aircraft had been out in force, attacking German positions on the ground that were tormenting the paratroopers. The Luftwaffe was also out in force, although the Allied fighters had a clear edge. According to the official SHAEF communique on Wednesday, the Allies had lost nine aircraft in the area, while claiming twenty-six enemy fighters.

The primary goal for the Allies at Nijmegen was to use Horrocks's XXX Corps tanks to back up Gavin's 82nd Airborne Division in a final decisive effort to take the huge, 6,000-foot Waal River bridge north of the city.

Assault boats had been brought in for the 504th Parachute Infantry Regiment to use to get across the Waal to try to outflank the bridge. They managed to get across and to capture the town of Lent across the river from Nijmegen. From this point, events moved quickly. Too quickly, in fact, for the German sappers who should have been working to demolish the bridge the moment that it looked as though it might be captured. They had, in fact, mined the bridge and had it ready to blow. They just hadn't been able to push the detonator in time.

As it was, the Irish Guards of the XXX Corps managed to take the bridge from the south side and they quickly linked up with the 504th Parachute Infantry Regiment, who had already hung an American flag over the opposite end of the span. British engineers now moved to defuse the demolition devices that the Germans had planted.

Though they failed to prevent capture of the big prize on the Waal on Wednesday, the Germans did make life difficult for Allied troops south of the city. When the bridge at Grave proved unsuitable for heavy equipment, the 505th Parachute Infantry Regiment was tasked with taking yet another one at Heumen, and it was not easy going.

At Arnhem, the situation for General Roy Urquhart's 1st British Airborne Division was desperate. Late in the day, the 2nd Battalion holding the Neder Rijn bridge was forced to withdraw, relinquishing control of the bridge to the Germans. They retreated to join the rest of the 1st British Airborne Division, which was surrounded and holed up in the suburb of Oosterbeek west of central Arnhem.

Wednesday, September 20
(With V Corps Across the German Border)

At that same moment, 150 miles south of Arnhem, the American V Corps spearhead had also been forced over to a defensive posture. Operating for a week inside Germany near the Luxembourg border, Combat Command R and Combat

Command B of the 5th Armored Division had encountered little enemy resistance when they'd first crossed the frontier, but had been experiencing waves of heavy German counterattacks since the weekend. While Colonel Cole's Combat Command B guarded the Sauer River bridgehead near Wallendorf that served as the border crossing, Colonel Anderson's Combat Command R had penetrated about twenty miles into Germany. They'd captured Bettingen, and had reached the well-defended city of Mettendorf on Monday night.

Early Tuesday, the Combat Command R units at Mettendorf came under heavy German artillery fire. Meanwhile, American patrols observed that the German panzer activity in the fog-shrouded hills and valleys around Mettendorf had increased dramatically. Screened by heavy artillery fire, the Germans seemed to be moving into place for a repeat of the heavy tank action that Combat Command R had experienced in the Bettingen sector on Sunday.

At around 8:00 A.M., the German LXXX Korps launched a two-pronged attack from Mettendorf against Combat Command R with Mark IV tanks—rather than Panthers or Tigers—backed by infantry. The Yanks beat back this assault, managing to take out at least eighteen of the tanks. Despite the losses, the Germans would continue to harass the Americans with automatic weapons fire, and both sides would trade artillery fire throughout the day.

A simultaneous, albeit lighter, German attack was launched against Combat Command B, which was guarding the Sauer River crossing. Shortly before noon, German infantry—supported by tanks—managed to capture the bridge at Wallendorf, but the Yanks managed to take it back by midafternoon.

At V Corps headquarters, General Gerow was starting to perceive that General Oliver's division was getting itself overextended across the river in Germany. The LXXX Korps activity was worrying him. Late Tuesday afternoon, he finally ordered all of the 5th Armored Division artillery to be withdrawn back across the river into Luxembourg. His orders contained the phrase "without delay." On Saturday, Gerow had canceled orders for the division to penetrate all the way to Bitburg, and now he was thinking that it would be prudent to pull back and to consolidate the bridgehead positions and make the mission of protecting Luxembourg the corps's only priority.

Gerow next ordered Anderson to withdraw Combat Command R from Germany entirely and relocate to Diekirch in Luxembourg, about five miles west of Wallendorf. The 112th Infantry Regiment, meanwhile, which had been taking a beating from German artillery for the past several days, was detached from Combat Command R and given the task of protecting the bridgehead at Wallendorf through Tuesday night. Colonel Cole was ordered to consolidate the Combat Command B position, and prepare to follow Anderson out of Germany on Wednesday.

During the night, Combat Command R began its withdrawal toward the Our River, which forms the border between Germany and Luxembourg north of Wallendorf. By daybreak on Wednesday, the continuing German LXXX Korps assault was focused the Wallendorf bridgehead. Heavy artillery fire rained down on the town as the 112th Infantry Regiment beat back a series of German tank and infantry attacks.

Thursday, September 21
(With the First Allied Airborne Army)

As it entered its fourth day, the best that could said of Operation Market Garden was that it was a partial success. Eindhoven had been captured, but the 101st Airborne Division was still encountering resistance as it tried to expand its tenuous perimeter around the city. Nijmegen was more or less under Allied control, although the German counterattacks remained furious. The situation for the British and Polish paratroopers at Arnhem seemed hopeless, and most of the additional airborne troops that were desperately needed in the Netherlands were still grounded by bad weather in England.

A portion of Major General Stanislaw Sosobowski's 1st Polish Parachute Brigade did arrive in Arnhem on Thursday, but their transports were badly mauled by German antiaircraft fire. Many Polish paratroopers were lost, and those who did jump, landed south of the Neder Rijn, across the river from Urquhart's positions in Oosterbeek.

When they had finished securing the big Waal River bridge on Wednesday, the men of the 82nd Airborne Division had expected that Brian Horrocks would have had the armored columns of his XXX Corps racing to save the men at Arnhem, but this had not happened. Horrocks was nervous. He was still waiting for the XXX infantry units to catch up to his tanks, and he felt vulnerable without them. He would wait.

Certainly, there was some justification for caution. The American paratroopers and Anglo-Irish tankers certainly had their necks extended here at Nijmegen. Even though Allied armor had bulldozed its way this far all the way from Belgium, the ground they gained was a thin and tenuous corridor held by small clusters of airborne troops. This corridor, which the Allied troops had dubbed "Hell's Highway," was under constant attack by the enemy. The Germans were clearly capable of cutting the corridor and of surrounding Nijmegen and Eindhoven again. They were certainly making that effort.

One of the many counterattacks endured by the American paratroopers was launched against the 504th Parachute Infantry Regiment near Oosterhout west of the recently established Nijmegen bridgehead. The regiment's position was hit by a strong German force of about one hundred infantry troops supported by two tanks and armored vehicles. Private John Towle, a bazooka man from Cleveland, Ohio, jumped out of his foxhole and ran about 200 yards in the face of a hail of small-arms fire to a position on an exposed dike roadbed. From this precarious position, Towle fired his bazooka, hitting and damaging both tanks.

Still under enemy fire, Towle then attacked a nearby house that nine of the Germans were using as a strongpoint. With one bazooka round, he killed all the occupants.

Hurriedly replenishing his supply of ammunition, Towle dashed another 125 yards through enemy fire to attack a German half-track. Before he could fire, he was hit by a mortar shell and mortally wounded. For trading his life to break up the enemy counterattack, John Towle was posthumously awarded the Congressional Medal of Honor.

Thursday, September 21
(With V Corps across the German Border)

On Thursday morning, the bridges in the Netherlands were not the only ones over which the Allies and the Germans were battling for control. The 5th Armored Division bridgehead across the Sauer River between Germany and Luxembourg continued to come under relentless attack. During the night, German artillery had wrecked both the treadway bridge and the timber bridge at Wallendorf, and had mined the approaches to the bridges on the German side. Meanwhile, German infantry used the heavy morning ground fog to mask an attack against Colonel Cole's Combat Command B, which held the ford across the Sauer River south of Wallendorf. Colonel Cole estimated that his command had taken casualties of 30 to 50 percent, and his sector still remained under heavy fire from the German artillery.

American tactical air power was able to help somewhat in the afternoons, but could do nothing early in the day when the heavy fog blanketed the terrain. The Germans had also gone to ingenious lengths to conceal their artillery. At one point, a pilot noticed a muzzle flash emanating from a house. On closer inspection, it turned out to be a carefully concealed "eighty-eight." The gun was promptly put out of business.

Tactical air also proved useful against afternoon tank attacks. At one point late on Thursday, Cole called in the fighter-bombers when about twenty German tanks were spotted attempting to ford the river near the village of Niedersgegen. Most of the panzers didn't make it.

By the end of the day, however, General Gerow had decided to accept what the Germans were making obvious. Continued operations inside Germany were no longer possible. Gerow ordered Colonel Cole to pull back into Luxembourg, and to regroup near the town of Bettendorf (not to be confused with Bettingen, across the river in Germany, from which the Yanks had just withdrawn).

Friday, September 22
(With the First Allied Airborne Army)

Referred to by General Brian Horrocks of the British XXX Corps as "Black Friday," this would be the day that Operation Market Garden would sputter to a disappointing halt.

Nowhere was Friday blacker than in Arnhem, where the men of Roy Urquhart's 1st British Airborne Division and Stanislaw Sosobowski's 1st Polish Parachute Brigade were surrounded on opposite sides of the Neder Rijn and were being mercilessly pummeled to death by German artillery and automatic weapons fire.

Horrocks's tanks had been in Nijmegen and ready for action since Wednesday, but he wanted to wait for the XXX Corps infantry before pressing on toward Arnhem—a dozen miles away—to relieve the British and Polish paratroopers fighting for their lives there. Of course, the scene was not peaceful in Nijmegen on Black Friday either. Though they were in a far stronger position, the Allied troops here were under constant German fire as they continued to hold the big Waal River bridge, and the Overassalt "air head," where they'd been awaiting reinforcements since midweek.

The Germans, meanwhile, were determined to cut the lines of communication running from Nijmegen back to Eindhoven. At Veghel, between Eindhoven and Nijmegen, the 501st Parachute Infantry Regiment of the United States 101st Airborne Division had been holding the bridgehead since the first of the week. It was just one of the many vital bridgeheads on Hell's Highway that had to be held if the rest of XXX Corps was to get through to Nijmegen.

On Friday morning, the German 107th Panzer Brigade moved in with three dozen panzers and three battalions of infantry to capture or destroy the Veghel bridge. Backed by artillery and additional troops from Walther Poppe's 59th Division, they slammed the paratroopers hard.

The 501st Parachute Infantry Regiment at the bridgehead was soon reinforced by the 506th Parachute Infantry Regiment and elements of the British 44th Tank Regiment.

Together the Allies managed to hold the bridgehead, but the Germans were able to block the highway to the north. This effectively stopped the XXX Corps advance and isolated all of the Allied troops at Nijmegen.

Friday, September 22
(With V Corps Across the German Border)

It was a Black Friday on the V Corps front as well. Spirits were turning dark as the advance units of the 5th Armored Division, which had entered Germany the previous week, were withdrawing under fire. Colonel Anderson's Combat Command R, which had gone as deep into Germany as Bettingen and Mettendorf, had pulled back to the frontier along the Our River. Colonel Cole's Combat Command B, which had been guarding the Sauer River crossing at Wallendorf, had withdrawn into Luxembourg. Brigadier General Eugene Regnier's Combat Command A, which had remained in Luxembourg, continued to patrol the border, executing the primary V Corps mission to protect the Grand Duchy from a German counterattack.

For the week from September 14 to September 22, the first week of Allied action within this part of Germany, the 5th Armored Division had killed an estimated 2,353 enemy troops, destroyed nearly fifty tanks, and taken 3,571 prisoners—but now it was withdrawing from its foothold inside the Reich.

Saturday, September 23
(With the First Allied Airborne Army)

By the weekend, Operation Market Garden had evolved from a bold offensive maneuver into a series of desperate defensive actions. If the day before had been "Black" Friday, there were few adjectives to describe the situation in Arnhem on Saturday except "even worse."

The 1st Polish Parachute Brigade and the British 1st Airborne Division were still surrounded, although a handful of XXX Corps tanks had broken through to help them. The "even worse" aspect described a force that had been battered for yet another day, and for which casualties were mounting. In the face of the increasing number of wounded, medical supplies, as well as rations, were dwindling precariously. The media was already referring to Roy Urquhart's division as "the lost division."

Airborne troops, by definition, travel light as they parachute into their objectives, and are heavily dependent on prompt resupply from the air. Yet attempts by the First Allied Airborne Army to accomplish the resupply mission had been failing all week. There were a number of factors. First, there had been the weather in England, and second, there was the mass of German antiaircraft artillery at Arnhem. This fed into the third factor, which was the narrow perimeters of the zones held by the paratroopers. In order to drop supplies into these small areas, the C-47s had to fly a very tightly defined flight plan. The German antiaircraft gunners knew exactly where this was, so targeting the cargo aircraft was incredibly easy. Most of the C-47s were being shot down, and most of the supplies that actually *were* dropped, continued to fall outside the Allied perimeter.

At Nijmegen, where the capture of the big Waal River bridge on Wednesday had seemed like a major success for Operation Market Garden, the tactical situation was starting to resemble that being experienced at Arnhem. The Germans were applying constant pressure on the Allied perimeter. The good news was that the weather had improved, and more than 3,000 men of the 325th Glider Infantry Regiment finally were able to reach the long-held landing zone at Overasselt on Saturday. With them, they brought desperately needed supplies, as well as light artillery.

Of course, Nijmegen, like Arnhem, was surrounded on Saturday morning, with the Hell's Highway to Eindhoven still blocked by the German 107th Panzer Brigade north of Veghel.

At Veghel, the 501st Parachute Infantry Regiment and troops of the 506th Parachute Infantry Regiment and the British 44th Tank Regiment fought to keep the bridge under Allied control. On Saturday, they were reinforced by the 327th Glider Infantry Regiment, which had arrived at Eindhoven. Together, these forces counterattacked against the panzer brigade. Meanwhile, Horrocks had sent part of his tank force back down the highway to hit the Germans from the other side. Working from both sides, the Allies were finally able to force the highway open again. The remainder of Horrocks's XXX Corps could now resume its move up the highway from Eindhoven to Nijmegen.

Saturday, September 23
(With V Corps, No Longer Across the German Border)

Saturday was marked by less than perfect news on the V Corps front in Luxembourg as well. Having operated within Germany for a week, the 5th Armored Division had now completed its pull-back into Luxembourg. As had been the case in the Netherlands, the bridgeheads across the Our River and Sauer River had been bridges too far.

Colonel Anderson's Combat Command R had withdrawn

across the Our River and was regrouping in the area around Diekirch. Colonel Cole's Combat Command B had pulled back from the Wallendorf bridgehead and were encamped at Bettendorf, a few miles down the road from Diekirch. The 112th Infantry Regiment, which had been attached briefly to the armored commands, was ordered to rejoin the 28th Infantry Division, from which it had been "borrowed."

Though Combat Command A would be ordered to continue small patrols across the border, the 5th Armored Division and V Corps was now essentially in a defensive posture for the first time since they'd come out of Normandy in August.

Saturday, September 23
(With the Third Army in Lorraine)

On Saturday in Lorraine, a week of bitter fighting for the 134th Infantry Regiment of General Paul Baade's 35th Infantry Division would finally reach its climax. On Friday, the XII Corps Commander, General Manton Eddy, had met with General Edmund Sebree at Colonel Butler Miltonberger's 134th Infantry Regiment command post. General Eddy had decided to disband Task Force S—which had been operating as a temporary command with 134th Infantry Regiment as its centerpiece—and return the regiment to the direct control of the 35th Infantry Division.

By now, General Robert Grow's 6th Armored Division had been integrated into the Lorraine operations and Eddy waned to use it, along with Baade's division in a final effort to link up with General Horace McBride's 80th "Blue Ridge" Infantry Division and clean out the last vestiges of German opposition in the hills across the Moselle River from Nancy.

This German opposition, meanwhile, consisted of elements of the 92nd Luftwaffe Regiment and the 593rd Flak Battalion, as well as three Grenadier Regiments, the 1119th, the 1120th, and the 1121st. They were reported to be dug in around Bois de Faulx. On paper, it seemed a sizable force, but all of the units were badly depleted by now.

The 6th Armored Division led the assault, jumping off at 7:00 A.M. Saturday morning, while the 134th Infantry Regiment spearheaded to 35th Infantry Division attack five hours later. The 1st Battalion was tasked with moving on Lay St. Christopher and Eulmont, while the 2nd Battalion drove toward Bouxieres-aux-Hames.

The hard-won heights of the Pain de Sucre, long used as a German artillery observation post, now served the Yanks. From here, observers could see in the distance that the German front was starting to break up. Lines of German motor and horse-drawn vehicles could be seen escaping north from Eulmont toward Bouxieres as the 1st Battalion moved toward them. At about 2:45, Major Warren Wood of the 1st Battalion called Colonel Miltonberger's headquarters to request an air strike on these columns, but the XIX Tactical Air Command P-47s were already on their way. By 3:00, the Thunderbolts were creating havoc for the retreating Germans with both high explosives and napalm, and Major Wood was reporting a "complete rout."

Within an hour, the battalion had reached the scene. Damaged vehicles lay burning and draft horses that had broken loose were grazing on the hillsides.

It was to be a relatively easy day for the regiment—compared, that is, to the week just past. It would be the 2nd Battalion that would encounter the hardest going that the regiment would experience on Saturday. This would involve crossing a narrow canyon through which ran a small stream paralleled by a rail line. The Germans had correctly identified this location as an ideal choke point and had installed a number of machine-gun nests with interlocking fields of fire.

Able Company and Baker Company managed to get across the rail line and stream by around 2:30 P.M., but it was after 8:00 P.M. when the two companies managed to fight their way to the top of the ridgeline opposite the canyon. A tank destroyer force was deployed to outflank the German positions. They struck at around 10:30 in the evening with cannon and machine-gun fire, finally providing the breakthrough that the battalion needed.

On Sunday, the 134th Infantry Regiment would reach Bois de Faulx without confronting any German opposition and the 2nd Battalion made contact with the 80th Infantry Division at Custines. The 3rd Battalion moved easily through Eulmont and Bouxieres-aux-Chenes, reaching the main highway leading to Leyr, which was, by now, controlled by Combat Command B of the 6th Armored Division.

As the 3rd Battalion made its way toward Leyr, contact with the enemy was fierce, but sporadic. Ironically, the 134th Infantry Regiment was gaining momentum even as the Third Army's great offensive was about to be halted in its tracks.

A Bridge Too Short, A Cup Half Full

For a full week, Operation Market Garden had held the attention of both the SHAEF high command and the world press, even as the paratroopers on the ground perilously held their drop zones. Though two of the three bridgeheads had been taken and kept, it had been at far greater cost than Allied planners had anticipated.

Arnhem had been a costly disaster. By Monday morning, those British and Polish paratroopers who were unable to escape the tightening German net were prisoners of war. Arnhem was once more a German strongpoint. The Germans proudly announced that the Allied force that had held a portion of the city for a week had been "liquidated."

General F. A. M. Browning had been hauntingly prophetic when he had described Arnhem as "a bridge too far."

Buoyed by how easily Belgium had slipped into their pocket, the Allies had reached too far and had come up a bridge too short. They extended themselves too deeply into German territory, and across too many waterways. In the Netherlands, they dropped paratroopers beyond a place where armor could reach and support them in a timely fashion.

The operation had also occurred too close to the German border. Whereas it might have been easier for the Oberkommando der Wehrmacht to let France and Belgium slip away, the Fatherland was sacred. Fighting a defensive war on or near their home turf was a different matter for the Germans. What the First Allied Airborne Army had now discovered in September would become painfully clear to the other Allied armies by October.

Writing in his memoirs, General Eisenhower would insist that Operation Market Garden "unquestionably would have been successful except for the intervention of bad weather. This prevented the adequate reinforcement of the northern spearhead, and resulted finally in the decimation of the British airborne division and only a partial success in the entire operation. We did not get our bridgehead [across the Neder Rijn at Arnhem], but our lines had been carried well out to defend the Antwerp base."

For Ike, the glass was half full. The Allied front line across the Netherlands *had*, in fact, been extended, but by a bridge less far than he and his SHAEF staff had hoped.

Sunday, September 24 (With VII Corps near Aachen)

As the First Allied Airborne Army and the First Army's V Corps both withdrew from having reached their respective bridges too far, the First Army's VII Corps had remained entrenched inside the Reich, in the German Seventh Army sector of the Rhineland. After the initial crack in the Siegfried Line at Roetgen, the Americans had penetrated the barrier ten miles south at Hoefen, near Monschau.

The 1st Infantry Division had flanked the great city of Aachen to the east on Saturday, September 16, while other units confronted the city from the south. By Thursday, with the Big Red One involved in heavy fighting in the industrial suburb of Stolberg, about six miles east of Aachen, other units were moving east toward the smaller city of Duren, which was on the road to Cologne. In the latter city, now less than twenty miles from American artillery, the natives were becoming jittery. A radio newscast from Berne, Switzerland, on Thursday had carried a report that Josef Grohe, the gauleiter in charge of Cologne, had ordered a limited evacuation of civilians from the city.

At first light on Sunday morning, the 18th Infantry Regiment of the 1st Infantry Division was holding the line when two German companies supported by machine guns launched an attack to seize control of the crossroads at Stolberg then being held by the 2nd Platoon of the 18th Infantry Regiment's Company I. One of the 2nd Platoon's squads was captured in the initial German attack, and the other was seriously mauled.

Staff Sergeant Joseph Schaefer now found himself leading the only American squad still in a position to hold the crossroads. Operating under heavy machine gun fire, the young New Yorker quickly moved his men into a masonry structure that would afford better protection. No sooner were the men in relative safety from the small caliber weapons, than the Germans called in an artillery bombardment aimed at softening up the Yanks for an infantry assault.

After they had survived the artillery pounding, Schaefer and his men braced themselves for the infantry attack that they knew would follow. Schaefer placed the men where they each would have a good field of fire, taking a dangerously exposed location near a doorway for himself. Schaefer and his squad managed to drive off the first assault, but the Germans came back with hand grenades and flamethrowers. Amazingly, the Yanks were able to break up this second attack as well.

After a time, the Germans returned, this time with another frontal assault, while a second group of men sneaked toward the building under cover of a hedgerow. Schaefer spotted the ones behind the hedgerow, but opened fire on those coming from the front. After wiping out the entire first group, Schaefer hurried over to the hedgerow and, again, opened fire. This time, he killed five, wounded two, and forced the rest to run for their lives. Schaefer then went hunting, rounding up ten prisoners.

For personally wiping out as many as twenty Germans with just his M1, capturing the ten, beating back the German attack, and holding the crossroads, Joe Schaefer would be awarded the Congressional Medal of Honor.

As General Patton had said, "War is a killing business. You must spill the enemy's blood or they will spill yours."

Sunday, September 24 (With the Third Army in Lorraine)

In Lorraine, the assault against the United States 4th Armored Division that had been initiated by General Hasso von Manteuffel's Fifth Panzer Army on Tuesday, September 19, had continued through the end of the week and into the weekend. Having been assigned the 11th Panzer Division and both the 111th and 113th Panzer Brigades, von Manteuffel had launched what was to be the biggest tank battle that the Third Army had yet fought.

All week, the Germans had attacked under cover of the morning ground fog, and each day, a running tank-on-tank gunfight ensued in the rolling hills and valleys of eastern Lorraine. Late each day, as the fog burned off, General Weyland's XIX Tactical Air Command was able to enter the fray and achieve some spectacular hits. Nevertheless, the initiative remained with von Manteuffel. The 4th Armored Division was definitely on the defensive much of the time.

Through the end of the week, the battle centered at Arracourt, but on the weekend, Manteuffel shifted his focus to Château-Salins where he organized his effort with the German First Army's 559th Volksgrenadier Division against Combat Command B of the 4th Armored Division.

It took a coordinated effort by Tiger Jack Wood's Shermans and Weyland's Thunderbolts, but, at last, by the end of the day on Sunday, von Manteuffel's nearly weeklong counterattack was beaten.

There would not, however, be a Monday morning resumption of the 4th Armored Division's march toward Germany. Orders were already on their way to George Patton for the Third Army to halt its great offensive.

The show was, for the moment, over.

TWELVE

EPILOGUE

Of the battles that General Eisenhower faced in the last week of September 1944, none loomed larger than the battle of supply. The supply problems about which he was constantly nagged by Patton were now growing acute for all the Allied armies. The troops were now beyond the practical limitations of the Red Ball Express, and the ports of Brest, Le Havre, and Antwerp would not be fully up and running before the first snows fell. On the opposing side, the German supply lines had grown shorter. They were much shorter, and they were within the Reich, where sabotage was virtually impossible. There would be no Forces Françaises de l'Intérieur to harass the German rear.

The tactical obstacles that Eisenhower now faced, especially the Siegfried Line, loomed larger than anything that the Allies had faced since the breakout from Normandy. It was easy for SHAEF to extrapolate that the two-month siege of the completely surrounded German garrison at Brest was merely a microcosm of the upcoming siege of the Reich itself.

The tiny breaches made in the Siegfried Line during mid-

September were mere pinpricks compared to what would be necessary to thrust the Allied armies inside Germany.

For the Allies, the tactical situation had now become like breaking through the looking glass and discovering that things were not exactly as they had seemed when viewed from the other side.

The German armies, especially those fighting on the soil of the Fatherland, were now exhibiting a renewed determination. Field Marshal Karl Rudolf Gerd von Rundstedt at Oberbefehlshaber West and General Walther Model of Army Group B had drawn a new line in the damp black earth of central Europe, and one by one, the mighty Allied armies were reaching it.

Monday, September 25
(With the Third Army in Lorraine)

Even as SHAEF was pondering the catastrophe at Arnhem, an order was being prepared for Patton's Third Army. The memo told Patton to halt his advance through Lorraine toward the Saar. With Allied forces suffering the dramatic, blood-letting failure in the north, the momentum achieved by the Third Army in the south must now be discontinued.

A great deal has been said of the fact that the Third Army's rapid blitzkrieg was a victim of its own momentum. The easy catch phrase is that they stopped because they had simply "run out of gas." Certainly this was a key factor, but it was obviously just one part of what the Army likes to characterize as "the Big Picture."

Balance of forces, and the desire to have the main thrust of the war against the Reich to be centered in the north was a key strategic reason, but there were tactical reasons other than running out of gas. Fuel shortages were critical, but another arguably more significant, shortage was that of experienced front-line troops. More to the point were the problems inherent in the system that the US Army used for maintaining head count within its front-line units. The controversy surrounding the "Replacement System" was a prominent issue both within the Army and in the media as summer gave way to autumn that year, although it has been little considered by military historians in the years since.

By early September, American troops had been fighting in Europe for more than three months. Except for the swift gains of August, they had been experiencing some of the toughest fighting of the war, and it was certainly on a much larger scale than on most other fronts. By September, the individual infantry companies that were directly involved in front-line combat were composed primarily of replacements.

In previous major conflicts, specifically in World War I, the US Army had allowed divisions to remain in the line as attrition gradually reduced the unit's personnel strength. The Army would then withdraw the division as a unit and rebuild it as a unit in the rear. In World War II, the Replacement System was introduced. The idea here was that the division would remain in the line, with individual losses replaced man for man with no interruption in division momentum. This looked good on paper.

The problem with the Replacement System was that it looked good *only* on paper. It created the illusion that a unit was continuously effective, even when the majority of its personnel were inexperienced recruits rather than battle-toughened veterans. Within the units themselves, there was, of course, a natural psychological divide between the recruits and the veterans. There was natural friction between the insiders and the "new guys," and units ceased to be well-oiled, well-integrated fighting forces. In units that had shared experiences, there was a great deal of esprit de corps and willingness to support the unit. When surrounded by a bunch of strangers in his first firefight, a replacement would be more likely to put his head down, while a veteran would have more of a sense that he was fighting for the good of his entire unit.

From this standpoint, the halt ordered on September 25 would allow the units that had seen the most action in the preceding sixty days—especially those of Third Army—to rebuild themselves as cohesive organizations.

Patton grudgingly accepted his orders to sit tight. He told his men to go on the defensive, but not to dig in. He halted the troops, not in terrain that would benefit a long-term defense, but in terrain that one would select if one were to be launching a major offensive the next day.

He would order all the Third Army armor to be ready to move out at any time, and to have their routes of advance prepared and planned. All the Third Army artillery was to be prepared to go into action to support the advance. He would tell his men to be ready for the signal to resume what he called "our career of conquest."

On Monday, Patton reluctantly issued the following memorandum:

HEADQUARTERS
THIRD UNITED STATES ARMY
APO 403
25 September 1944
SUBJECT: Letter of instruction No. 4
TO: Corps Commanders and the Commanding General XIX Tactical Air Command

1. The acute supply situation confronting us has caused the Supreme Commander to direct that until further orders, the Third Army, with its supporting troops, and those elements of the Ninth Army placed in the line, will assume the defensive.

2. It is evident that the successful accomplishment of this mission will require particular concentration upon two points;
   a. First, this change in attitude on our part must be completely concealed from the enemy, who, should he learn of it, would certainly move troops from our front to oppose other Allied Armies.
   b. Second, we must be in possession of a suitable line of departure so that we can move rapidly when the Supreme Commander directs us to resume the offensive.

3. In order to carry out the requirements of Paragraph 2a, above, we will not dig in, wire, or mine; but will utilize a thin outpost zone backed at suitable places by powerful mobile reserves. We will further insure that all possible avenues of tank attack are registered in by all our batteries—Division, Corps, and Army—whose guns can bear. Under the supervision of the Army Artillery Officer these zones of concentration will be numbered from north to south and recorded on a uniform map to be distributed to the units concerned, so that fire may instantly be opened in any zone.

Further, a copy of this map will be placed in the possession of the Commanding General XIX Tactical Air Command so that he may coordinate the concentration of planes upon any critical area in the most expeditious manner. Counterattacks by our mobile reserves should be planned and executed to secure a double envelopment of the hostile effort with the purpose of not only defeating it, but destroying it.

4. To insure our possessing a suitable line of departure for the future offensive, we shall secure the dotted line shown on the attached overlay by means of limited operations in consonance with our reduced scale of supply. To provide the necessary means for such limited operations, the utmost parsimony will be used in the expenditure of gasoline and ammunition consistent with the economy of the lives of our troops.

5. Whenever circumstances admit, troops not in the immediate presence of the enemy will be billeted. As soon as the troops so billeted have rested and have been equipped, they will be given constant practice in offensive tactics.

6. The defensive instructions contained in this letter will not be circulated below the grade of General Officer.

7. In closing, I desire to again compliment all of you on the magnificent dash and skill which you have shown in the operation to date. We only await the signal to resume our career of conquest.

G.S. Patton, Jr.
Lt Gen, US Army, Commanding

Distribution:
CG Twelfth Army Group
CG XII Corps
CG XV Corps
CG XX Corps

The Third Army would, by October, resume its "career of conquest." Patton's legions would reach the Reich, cross the Rhine, and occupy all of southern Germany and most of Austria, ending the war at the gates of Prague. The Third Army would, to paraphrase Patton, advance farther and faster in nine months than any comparable army in the history of warfare. The Third Army would go on to capture or liberate nearly 82,000 square miles, including twenty-seven cities of 50,000 or more. By V-E Day, they would take more than 1.2 million prisoners, including a half million in the last week of the war.

Patton had said that, given enough gasoline, "I could go all the way to Berlin!" By the spring of 1945, adequate fuel supplies were flowing, but Patton's army would never go all the way to Berlin. Nor would any of Eisenhower's armies. It was not for want of ability, but because of political decisions in which Patton played no part. But that, as they say, is another story.

The success of the Third Army in battle was remarkable. Patton had defined the doctrine and refined the textbook for fast, mobile, war-winning armored warfare. However, Patton's greatest achievement had not been that which was measurable by square miles. He had been personally responsible for an esprit de corps within the Third Army that was unmatched elsewhere within the U.S. Army during World War II.

As Patton had once said, "The important thing in any organization is the creation of a soul, which is based on pride, in the unit."

This objective had been achieved.

Ironically, it was also on September 25 that Adolf Hitler, sitting in his Wolf's Lair headquarters at Rastenberg in East Prussia, gave an order to Generaloberst Alfred Jodl, head of operations for the Oberkommando der Wehrmacht, who was now serving as essentially the Führer's military aide. Hitler ordered Jodl to begin a detailed analysis of the concept for a great winter offensive through the Ardennes that would surprise and annihilate the Allies. The operation would carry the German code name Wacht am Rhein (Watch on the Rhine), but to the Allies, it would be known as the Battle of the Bulge.

September 25 had been a true turning point in World War II.

After sixty days of unprecedented success and dramatic forward momentum, the Anglo-American Allies had now slowed to a crawl, if not to a complete stop.

Ahead of them, they now faced six months of the bloodiest fighting of the war. On the heels of Arnhem would come Aachen. Lawton Collins's V Corps had no inkling of what was in store in the first battle in and for a major city within Germany. The coming Battle of Aachen would last more than a month and would be bloodier that anything yet experienced by the Americans in Europe. Then, there would be the hellhole of the Hurtgen Forest.

In December, the Battle of the Bulge would stun the Allies and put the gains of August and September in jeopardy. In early 1945, there would be the bloody battles in the

Rhineland and beyond, before the German will to resist in the West finally collapsed.

On September 25, an exceptional chapter had come to a close. Sixty days after the start of Operation Cobra, the greatest campaign in American military history was over.

APPENDIX 1:

The Allied High Command in the European Theater of Operations (July 25, 1944 through September 25, 1944)

Note: The United States Seventh Army and Allied 6th Army Group in Southern France are excluded because they were not part of Eisenhower's command until later, and because their actions are beyond the scope of this book.

Supreme Commander of Allied Forces in Europe:
General Dwight David Eisenhower

12th Army Group:
General Omar Nelson Bradley

    United States First Army:
    General Omar Nelson Bradley
        (until the activation of 12th Army Group)
    Lieutenant General Courtney H. Hodges

    United States Third Army:
    Lieutenant General George Smith Patton, Jr.

    United States Ninth Army:
    Lieutenant General William H. Simpson

21st Army Group:
General (later Field Marshal) Sir Bernard Law Montgomery

    Canadian First Army:
    Lieutenant General Henry D.G. Crerar

    British Second Army:
    Lieutenant General Sir Miles Dempsey

    First Allied Airborne Army:
    Lieutenant General Lewis Brereton

All Free French Forces:*
General Charles de Gaulle
          * While de Gaulle was technically the leader of all Free
          French troops, they were operationally under the com-
          mand of the Allied army group commanders.

APPENDIX 2:

US Army Divisions in the European Theater of Operations (July 25, 1944 through September 25, 1944)

Note: The Organic Units include those assigned on a permanent basis and do not include temporary assignments, attachments, and detachments. Each division also had a headquarters company, a military police platoon, and other such housekeeping organizations.

1st Infantry Division
"Big Red One"

Commanding General:
Major General Clarence R. Huebner

Assistant Division Commander:
Brigadier General Willard G. Wyman

Organic Units Integral to the Division:

16th Infantry Regiment
18th Infantry Regiment
26th Infantry Regiment
1st Reconnaissance Troop (Mechanized)
1st Engineer Combat Battalion
1st Medical Battalion
1st Division Artillery
    7th Field Artillery Battalion (105mm Howitzer)
    32nd Field Artillery Battalion (105mm Howitzer)
    33rd Field Artillery Battalion (105mm Howitzer)
    5th Field Artillery Battalion (155mm Howitzer)

Special Troops
      701st Ordnance Light Maintenance Company
      1st Quartermaster Company
      1st Signal Company

Assignments and Attachments to Higher Units:

February 2, 1944: V Corps (First Army)
July 14, 1944: (First Army)
July 15, 1944: VII Corps (First Army)
August 1, 1944: VII Corps (First Army)

2nd Armored Division
"Hell on Wheels"

Commanding General:
March 18, 1944: Major General Edward H. Brooks
September 12, 1944: Major General Ernest N. Harmon

Organic Units Integral to the Division:

Combat Command A
Combat Command B
41st Armored Infantry Regiment
66th Armored Regiment
67th Armored Regiment
17th Armored Engineer Battalion
82nd Armored Reconnaissance Battalion
142nd Armored Signal Company
2nd Armored Division Artillery
      14th Armored Field Artillery Battalion
      78th Armored Field Artillery Battalion
      92nd Armored Field Artillery Battalion
2nd Armored Division Trains
      2nd Ordnance Maintenance Battalion
      Supply Battalion
      48th Armored Medical Battalion

Assignments and Attachments to Higher Units:

July 18, 1944: VII Corps (First Army)
August 2, 1944: XIX Corps (First Army)

August 7, 1944: VII Corps (First Army)
August 13, 1944: XIX Corps (First Army)
August 18, 1944: V Corps (First Army)
August 19, 1944: XIX Corps (First Army)
August 28, 1944: XV Corps (First Army)
August 29, 1944: XIX Corps (First Army)

2nd Infantry Division
"Second to None Division"

Commanding General:
Major General Walter M. Robertson

Assistant Division Commander:
July 4, 1944: Colonel James A. Van Fleet
August 1, 1944: Brigadier General James A. Van Fleet
September 5, 1944: Colonel John H. Stokes Jr. (Acting)

Organic Units Integral to the Division:

9th Infantry Regiment
23rd Infantry Regiment
38th Infantry Regiment
2nd Reconnaissance Troop (Mechanized)
2nd Engineer Combat Battalion
2nd Medical Battalion
2nd Division Artillery
    15th Field Artillery Battalion (105mm Howitzer)
    37th Field Artillery Battalion (105mm Howitzer)
    38th Field Artillery Battalion (105mm Howitzer)
Special Troops
    702nd Ordnance Light Maintenance Company
    2nd Quartermaster Company
    2nd Signal Company

Assignments and Attachments to Higher Units:

April 14, 1944: V Corps (First Army)
August 1, 1944: V Corps (First Army)
August 17, 1944: XIX Corps (First Army)
August 18, 1944: VIII Corps
    (Assigned to First Army, attached to Third Army)

September 5, 1944: VIII Corps (Ninth Army)

3rd Armored Division
"Spearhead"

Commanding General:
September 15, 1943: Major General Leroy H. Watson
August 7, 1944: Brigadier General Maurice Rose
September 5, 1944: Major General Maurice Rose

Organic Units Integral to the Division:

Combat Command A
Combat Command B
36th Armored Infantry Regiment
32nd Armored Regiment
33rd Armored Regiment
23rd Armored Engineer Battalion
83rd Armored Recon Battalion
143rd Armored Signal Company
3rd Armored Division Artillery
    391st Armored Field Artillery Battalion
    67th Armored Field Artillery Battalion
    54th Armored Field Artillery Battalion
3rd Armored Division Trains
    3rd Ordnance Maintenance Battalion
    Supply Battalion
    45th Armored Medical Battalion

Assignments and Attachments to Higher Units:

February 8, 1944: XIX Corps (First Army)
July 15, 1944: VII Corps (First Army)
August 1, 1944: VII Corps (First Army)

4th Armored Division

Commanding General:
January 11, 1944: Major General John Wood

Organic Units Integral to the Division:

Combat Command R
Combat Command A
Combat Command B
8th Tank Battalion
35th Tank Battalion
37th Tank Battalion
10th Armored Infantry Battalion
51st Armored Infantry Battalion
53rd Armored Infantry Battalion
25th Cavalry Recon Squadron (Mechanized)
24th Armored Engineer Battalion
144th Armored Signal Company
4th Armored Division Artillery
    22nd Armored Field Artillery Battalion
    66th Armored Field Artillery Battalion
    94th Armored Field Artillery Battalion
4th Armored Division Trains
    126th Ordnance Maintenance Battalion
    4th Armored Medical Battalion

Assignments and Attachments

April 20, 1944: XV Corps (Third Army)
July 15, 1944: VIII Corps
    (Assigned to Third Army, attached to First Army)
August 1, 1944: VIII Corps (Third Army)
August 13, 1944: XII Corps (Third Army)

4th Infantry Division
"Ivy Division"

Commanding General:
January 28, 1944: Major General Raymond O. Barton
September 18, 1944: Brigadier General Harold W. Blakeley

Assistant Division Commander:
January 28, 1944: Brigadier General Henry A. Barber
July 9, 1944: Colonel George A. Taylor
August 1, 1944: Brigadier General George A. Taylor

September 19, 1944: Brigadier General James A. Van Fleet (Acting)

Organic Units Integral to the Division:

8th Infantry Regiment Infantry Regiment
22nd Infantry Regiment
4th Reconnaissance Troop (Mechanized)
4th Engineer Combat Battalion
4th Medical Battalion
4th Division Artillery
    29th Field Artillery Battalion (105mm Howitzer)
    42nd Field Artillery Battalion (105mm Howitzer)
    44th Field Artillery Battalion (105mm Howitzer)
    20th Field Artillery Battalion (155mm Howitzer)
Special Troops
    704th Ordnance Light Maintenance Company
    4th Quartermaster Company
    4th Signal Company

Assignments and Attachments to Higher Units:

February 2, 1944: VII Corps (First Army)
July 16, 1944: VIII Corps (First Army)
July 19, 1944: VII Corps (First Army)
August 1, 1944: VII Corps (First Army)
August 22, 1944: V Corps (First Army)

5th Armored Division
"Victory Division"

Commanding General:
February 23, 1944: Major General Lunsford E. Oliver

Organic Units Integral to the Division:

Combat Command R
Combat Command A
Combat Command B
10th Tank Battalion
34th Tank Battalion
81st Tank Battalion
15th Armored Infantry Battalion

46th Armored Infantry Battalion
47th Armored Infantry Battalion
85th Cavalry Recon Squadron (Mechanized)
22nd Armored Engineer Battalion
145th Armored Signal Company
5th Armored Division Artillery
    47th Armored Field Artillery Battalion
    71st Armored Field Artillery Battalion
    95th Armored Field Artillery Battalion
5th Armored Division Trains
    127th Ordnance Maintenance Battalion
    75th Armored Medical Battalion

Assignments and Attachments to Higher Units:

June 31, 1944: (Third Army)
August 1, 1944: XV Corps (Third Army)
August 24, 1944: XV Corps
    (Assigned to Third Army, attached to First Army)
August 26, 1944: XV Corps (First Army)
August 29, 1944: V Corps (First Army)

5th Infantry Division
"Red Diamond Division"

Commanding General:
December 15, 1943: Major General S. LeRoy Irwin

Assistant Division Commander:
December 15, 1943: Brigadier General Alan D. Warnock

Organic Units Integral to the Division:

2nd Infantry Regiment
10th Infantry Regiment
11th Infantry Regiment
5th Reconnaissance Troop (Mechanized)
7th Engineer Combat Battalion
5th Medical Battalion
5th Division Artillery
    19th Field Artillery Battalion (105 Howitzer)

46th Field Artillery Battalion (105 Howitzer)
50th Field Artillery Battalion (105 Howitzer)
21st Field Artillery Battalion (155 Howitzer)
Special Troops
705th Ordnance Light Maintenance Company
5th Quartermaster Company
5th Signal Company

Assignments and Attachments to Higher Units:

July 13, 1944: V Corps (First Army)
August 1, 1944: (Assigned to Third Army, attached to First Army)
August 4, 1944: XX Corps (Third Army)

6th Armored Division

Commanding General:
February 22, 1944: Major General Robert W. Grow

Organic Units Integral to the Division:

Combat Command R
Combat Command A
Combat Command B
15th Tank Battalion
68th Tank Battalion
69th Tank Battalion
9th Armored Infantry Battalion
44th Armored Infantry Battalion
50th Armored Infantry Battalion
86th Cavalry Recon Squadron (Mechanized)
25th Armored Engineer Battalion
146th Armored Signal Company
6th Armored Division Artillery
    128th Armored Field Artillery Battalion
    212th Armored Field Artillery Battalion
    231st Armored Field Artillery Battalion
6th Armored Division Trains
    128th Ordnance Maintenance Battalion
    76th Armored Medical Battalion

Assignments and Attachments to Higher Units:

July 25, 1944: VIII Corps (First Army)
August 1, 1944: VIII Corps (Third Army)
September 5, 1944: (Ninth Army)
September 16, 1944: (Third Army)
September 20, 1944: XII Corps (Third Army)

7th Armored Division
"Lucky Seventh"

Commanding General:
June 13, 1944: Major General Lindsay M. Silvester

Organic Units Integral to the Division:

Combat Command R
Combat Command A
Combat Command B
17th Tank Battalion
31st Tank Battalion
40th Tank Battalion
23rd Armored Infantry Battalion
38th Armored Infantry Battalion
48th Armored Infantry Battalion
87th Cavalry Recon Squadron (Mechanized)
33rd Armored Engineer Battalion
147th Armored Signal Company
7th Armored Division Artillery
    434th Armored Field Artillery Battalion
    440th Armored Field Artillery Battalion
    489th Armored Field Artillery Battalion
7th Armored Division Trains
    129th Ordnance Maintenance Battalion
    77th Armored Medical Battalion

Assignments and Attachments to Higher Units:

July 30, 1944: (First Army)
August 11, 1944: (First Army)
August 5, 1944: (Third Army)
August 10, 1944: XX Corps (Third Army)

September 25, 1944: XIX Corps (First Army)

8th Infantry Division
"Pathfinder Division"/"Arrow Division"

Commanding General:
July 12, 1944: Brigadier General Donald A. Stroh
August 30, 1944: Major General Donald A. Stroh

Assistant Division Commander:
February 15, 1944: Brigadier General Nelson M. Walker
July 12, 1944: Col Cyrus H. Searcy
July 26, 1944: Col Charles D. W. Canham
September 1, 1944: Brigadier General Charles D. W. Canham

Organic Units Integral to the Division:

13th Infantry Regiment
28th Infantry Regiment
121st Infantry Regiment
8th Reconnaissance Troop (Mechanized) Engineer Combat Battalion
8th Medical Battalion
8th Division Artillery
    43rd Field Artillery Battalion (105 Howitzer)
    45th Field Artillery Battalion (105 Howitzer)
    56th Field Artillery Battalion (105 Howitzer)
    28th Field Artillery Battalion (155 Howitzer)
Special Troops
    708th Ordnance Light Maintenance Company
    8th Quartermaster Company
    8th Signal Company

Assignments and Attachments to Higher Units:

July 1, 1944: VIII Corps (First Army)
August 1, 1944: VIII Corps (Third Army)
September 5, 1944: VIII Corps (Ninth Army)

9th Infantry Division
"Hitler's Nemeis"

Commanding General:
November 27, 1943: Major General Manton S. Eddy
August 19, 1944: Major General Louis A. Craig

Assistant Division Commander:
July 20, 1944: Brigadier General James E. Wharton
August 12, 1944: Brigadier General Kenneth Buchanan
September 17, 1944: Colonel James S. Rodwell

Organic Units Integral to the Division:

39th Infantry Regiment
47th Infantry Regiment
60th Infantry Regiment
9th Reconnaissance Troop (Mechanized)
15th Engineer Combat Battalion
9th Medical Battalion
9th Division Artillery
    26th Field Artillery Battalion (105mm Howitzer)
    60th Field Artillery Battalion (105mm Howitzer)
    84th Field Artillery Battalion (105mm Howitzer)
    34th Field Artillery Battalion (155mm Howitzer)
Special Troops
    709th Ordnance Light Maintenance Company
    9th Quartermaster Company
    9th Signal Company

Assignments and Attachments to Higher Units:

November 25, 1943: VII Corps (First Army)
August 1, 1944: VII Corps (First Army)

28th Infantry Division
"Bloody Bucket Division"/"Keystone Division"

Commanding General:
October 18, 1943: Major General Lloyd D. Brown
August 13, 1944: Brigadier General James E. Wharton

August 14, 1944: Brigadier General Norman D. Cota
September 26, 1944: Major General Norman D. Cota

Assistant Division Commander:
October 18, 1943: Brigadier General Kenneth Buchanan
August 31, 1944: Brigadier General George A. Davis

Organic Units Integral to the Division:

109th Infantry Regiment
110th Infantry Regiment
112th Infantry Regiment
28th Reconnaissance Troop (Mechanized)
103rd Engineer Combat Battalion
103rd Medical Battalion
28th Division Artillery
    107th Field Artillery Battalion (105 Howitzer)
    109th Field Artillery Battalion (105 Howitzer)
    229th Field Artillery Battalion (105 Howitzer)
    108st Field Artillery Battalion (155 Howitzer)
Special Troops
    728th Ordnance Light Maintenance Company
    28th Quartermaster Company
    28th Signal Company

Assignments and Attachments to Higher Units:

April 14, 1944: XX Corps (Third Army)
April 24, 1944: (Third Army)
July 26, 1944: XIX Corps
    (Assigned to Third Army, attached to First Army)
July 30, 1944: XIX Corps (First Army)
August 1, 1944: XIX Corps (First Army)
August 28, 1944: V Corps (First Army)

29th Infantry Division
"Blue and Gray Division"

Commanding General:
July 22, 1943: Major General Charles H. Gerhardt

Assistant Division Commander:
October 13, 1943: Brigadier General Norman D. Cota
August 31, 1944: Colonel Leroy H. Watson

Organic Units Integral to the Division:

115th Infantry Regiment
116th Infantry Regiment
175th Infantry Regiment
29th Reconnaissance Troop (Mechanized)
121st Engineer Combat Battalion
104th Medical Battalion
29th Division Artillery
    110th Field Artillery Battalion (105mm Howitzer)
    111th Field Artillery Battalion (105mm Howitzer)
    224th Field Artillery Battalion (105mm Howitzer)
    227th Field Artillery Battalion (155mm Howitzer)
Special Troops
    729th Ordnance Light Maintenance Company
    29th Quartermaster Company
    29th Signal Company

Assignments and Attachments to Higher Units:

June 14, 1944: XIX Corps (First Army)
August 1, 1944: XIX Corps (First Army)
August 12, 1944: V Corps (First Army)
August 19, 1944: VIII Corps
    (Assigned to First Army, attached to Third Army)
September 5, 1944: VIII Corps (Ninth Army)
September 21, 1944: XIX Corps (First Army)

30th Infantry Division
"Old Hickory Division"

Commanding General:
February 22, 1944: Major General Leland S. Hobbs

Assistant Division Commander:
February 22, 1944: Brigadier General William K. Harrison

Organic Units Integral to the Division:

117th Infantry Regiment
119th Infantry Regiment
120th Infantry Regiment
30th Reconnaissance Troop (Mechanized)
105th Engineer Combat Battalion
105th Medical Battalion
30th Division Artillery
      118th Field Artillery Battalion (105 Howitzer)
      197th Field Artillery Battalion (105 Howitzer)
      230th Field Artillery Battalion (105 Howitzer)
      113th Field Artillery Battalion (155 Howitzer)
Special Troops
      730th Ordnance Light Maintenance Company
      30th Quartermaster Company
      30th Signal Company

Assignments and Attachments to Higher Units:

July 15, 1944: VII Corps (First Army)
July 28, 1944: XIX Corps (First Army)
August 4, 1944: V Corps (First Army)
August 5, 1944: VII Corps (First Army)
August 13, 1944: XIX Corps (First Army)
August 26, 1944: XV Corps
      (Assigned to Third Army, attached to First Army)
August 29, 1944: XIX Corps (First Army)

35th Infantry Division
"Sante Fe Division"

Commanding General:
May 26, 1944: Major General Paul W. Baade

Assistant Division Commander:
May 26, 1944: Brigadier General Edmund B. Sebree

Organic Units Integral to the Division:

134th Infantry Regiment
137th Infantry Regiment

320th Infantry Regiment
35th Reconnaissance Troop (Mechanized)
60th Engineer Combat Battalion
110th Medical Battalion
35th Division Artillery
    161st Field Artillery Battalion (105 Howitzer)
    216th Field Artillery Battalion (105 Howitzer)
    219th Field Artillery Battalion (105 Howitzer)
    127th Field Artillery Battalion (155 Howitzer)
Special Troops
    735th Ordnance Light Maintenance Company
    35th Quartermaster Company
    35th Signal Company

Assignments and Attachments to Higher Units:

May 5, 1944: XV Corps (Third Army)
July 8, 1944: XIX Corps
    (Assigned to Third Army, attached to First Army)
July 27, 1944: V Corps
    (Assigned to Third Army, attached to First Army)
August 1, 1944: V Corps
    (Assigned to Third Army, attached to First Army)
August 5, 1944: (Third Army)
August 6, 1944: XX Corps (Third Army)
August 9, 1944: VII Corps
    (Assigned to Third Army, attached to First Army)
August 13, 1944: XII Corps (Third Army)

79th Infantry Division
"Cross of Lorraine Division"

Commanding General:
April 17, 1944: Major General I. T. Wyche

Assistant Division Commander:
April 17, 1944: Brigadier General Frank U. Greer

Organic Units Integral to the Division:

313th Infantry Regiment
314th Infantry Regiment
315th Infantry Regiment
79th Reconnaissance Troop (Mechanized)
304th Engineer Combat Battalion
304th Medical Battalion
79th Division Artillery
    310th Field Artillery Battalion (105mm Howitzer)
    311th Field Artillery Battalion (105mm Howitzer)
    904th Field Artillery Battalion (105mm Howitzer)
    312th Field Artillery Battalion (155mm Howitzer)
Special Troops
    779th Ordnance Light Maintenance Company
    79th Quartermaster Company
    79th Signal Company

Assignments and Attachments to Higher Units:

July 1, 1944: VIII Corps (Third Army)
August 1, 1944: VIII Corps (Third Army)
August 3, 1944: XV Corps (Third Army)
August 24, 1944: XV Corps (Third Army)
August 26, 1944: XV Corps (First Army)
August 29, 1944: XIX Corps (First Army)
September 7, 1944: XV Corps (Third Army)

80th Infantry Division
"Blue Ridge Division"

Commanding General:
July 7, 1944: Major General Horace L. McBride

Assistant Division Commander:
July 7, 1944: Brigadier General Owen Summers

Organic Units Integral to the Division:

317th Infantry Regiment
318th Infantry Regiment
319th Infantry Regiment

80th Reconnaissance Troop (Mechanized)
305th Engineer Combat Battalion
305th Medical Battalion
80th Division Artillery
    313th Field Artillery Battalion (105mm Howitzer)
    314th Field Artillery Battalion (105mm Howitzer)
    905th Field Artillery Battalion (105mm Howitzer)
    315th Field Artillery Battalion (155mm Howitzer)
Special Troops
    780th Ordnance Light Maintenance Company
    80th Quartermaster Company
    80th Signal Company

Assignments and Attachments to Higher Units:

June 11, 1944: XII Corps (Third Army)
August 1, 1944: XII Corps (Third Army)
August 7, 1944: XX Corps (Third Army)
August 8, 1944: XV Corps (Third Army)
August 10, 1944: XX Corps (Third Army)
August 17, 1944: V Corps
    (Assigned to Third Army, attached to First Army)
August 23, 1944: (Third Army)
August 26, 1944: XII Corps (Third Army)

82nd Airborne Division
"All-American Division"

Commanding General:
December 9, 1943: Major General Matthew B. Ridgway
August 27, 1944: Brigadier General James M. Gavin
October 18, 1944: Major General James M. Gavin

Assistant Division Commander:
December 9, 1943 to August 26, 1944: Brigadier General James M.
    Gavin
August 26, 1943 to December 13, 1944: [vacant]

Organic Units Integral to the Division:

325th Glider Infantry Regiment
504th Parachute Infantry Regiment

505th Parachute Infantry Regiment
307th Airborne Engineer Battalion
80th Airborne Antiaircraft Artillery Battalion
307th Airborne Medical Company
82nd Parachute Maintenance Battalion
782nd Airborne Ordnance Company
407th Quartermaster Company
82nd Airborne Signal Company
82nd Airborne Division Artillery
    319th Glider Field Artillery Battalion
    320th Glider Field Artillery Battalion
    376th Parachute Field Artillery Battalion
    456th Parachute Field Artillery Battalion

Assignments and Attachments to Higher Units:

June 6, 1944: VII Corps (First Army)

June 19, 1944: VIII Corps (First Army)

July 13, 1944: (Ninth Army)

August 12, 1944: XVIII Airborne Corps (First Allied Airborne
    Army)

September 17, 1944: British I Airborne Corps
    (First Allied Airborne Army)

83rd Infantry Division
"Ohio Division"

Commanding General:
June 1, 1944: Major General Robert C. Macon

Assistant Division Commander:
May 27, 1944: Brigadier General Claude B. Ferenbaugh

Organic Units Integral to the Division:

329th Infantry Regiment
330th Infantry Regiment
331st Infantry Regiment
83rd Reconnaissance Troop (Mechanized)
308th Engineer Combat Battalion
308th Medical Battalion

83rd Division Artillery
    322nd Field Artillery Battalion (105 Howitzer)
    323rd Field Artillery Battalion (105 Howitzer)
    908th Field Artillery Battalion (105 Howitzer)
    324th Field Artillery Battalion (105 Howitzer)
Special Troops
    783rd Ordnance Light Maintenance Company
    83rd Quartermaster Company
    83rd Signal Company

Assignments and Attachments to Higher Units:

June 25, 1944: VIII Corps (Third Army)
July 1, 1944: VII Corps
    (Assigned to Third Army, attached to First Army)
July 15, 1944: VIII Corps
    (Assigned to Third Army, attached to First Army)
August 1, 1944: XV Corps (Third Army)
August 3, 1944: VIII Corps (Third Army)
September 5, 1944: VIII Corps (Ninth Army)
September 10, 1944: (Ninth Army)
September 21, 1944: XX Corps (Third Army)

90th Infantry Division
"Alamo Division"/"Tough Hombres"

Commanding General:
June 13, 1944: Major General Eugene M. Landrum
July 30, 1944: Brigadier General Raymond S. McLain
September 22, 1944: Major General Raymond S. McLain
October 15, 1944: Brigadier General James A. Van Fleet

Assistant Division Commander:
February 2, 1943: Brigadier General Samuel P. Williams
July 31, 1944: Brigadier General William G. Weaver

Organic Units Integral to the Division:

357th Infantry Regiment
358th Infantry Regiment
359th Infantry Regiment

90th Reconnaissance Troop (Mechanized)
325th Engineer Combat Battalion
315th Medical Battalion
90th Division Artillery
  343rd Field Artillery Battalion (105mm Howitzer)
  344th Field Artillery Battalion (105mm Howitzer)
  915th Field Artillery Battalion (105mm Howitzer)
  345th Field Artillery Battalion (105mm Howitzer)
Special Troops
  790th Ordnance Light Maintenance Company
  90th Quartermaster Company
  90th Signal Company

Assignments and Attachments to Higher Units:

June 19, 1944: VIII Corps
  (Assigned to Third Army, attached to First Army)
July 30, 1944: (Assigned to Third Army, attached to First Army)
August 1, 1944: XV Corps (Third Army)
August 17, 1944: V Corps
  (Assigned to Third Army, attached to First Army)
August 25, 1944: XV Corps (Third Army)
August 26, 1944: XX Corps (Third Army)

94th Infantry Division

Commanding General:
August 11, 1944: Major General Harry J. Malony

Assistant Division Commander:
August 11, 1944: Brigadier General Henry B. Cheadle

Organic Units Integral to the Division:

301st Infantry Regiment
302nd Infantry Regiment
376th Infantry Regiment
94th Reconnaissance Troop (Mechanized)
319th Engineer Combat Battalion
319th Medical Battalion
94th Division Artillery

301st Field Artillery Battalion (105mm Howitzer)
356th Field Artillery Battalion (105mm Howitzer)
919th Field Artillery Battalion (105mm Howitzer)
390th Field Artillery Battalion (155mm Howitzer)
Special Troops
794th Ordnance Light Maintenance Company
94th Quartermaster Company
94th Signal Company

Assignments and Attachments to Higher Units:

July 27, 1944: XIII Corps (Ninth Army)
August 28, 1944: XIII Corps (Ninth Army)
September 23, 1944: (Ninth Army)

101st Airborne Division
"Screaming Eagles"

Commanding General:
May 31, 1944: Major General Maxwell D. Taylor

Assistant Division Commander:
September 15, 1943: Brigadier General Don F. Pratt
August 1, 1944: Brigadier General Gerald J. Higgins

Organic Units Integral to the Division:

502nd Parachute Infantry Regiment
327th Glider Infantry Regiment
401st Glider Infantry Regiment
101st Parachute Maintenance Battalion
326th Airborne Engineer Battalion
326th Airborne Medical Company
81st Airborne Antiaircraft Artillery Battalion
101st Airborne Division Artillery
321st Glider Field Artillery Battalion
377th Parachute Field Artillery Battalion
907th Glider Field Artillery Battalion
Special Troops
801st Ordnance Company

426th Quartermaster Company
101st Signal Company

Assignments and Attachments to Higher Units:

July 15, 1944: (Ninth Army)
August 12, 1944: XVIII Airborne Corps
    (First Allied Airborne Army)
September 18, 1944: British XXX Corps
    (First Allied Airborne Army)
September 21, 1944: British I Airborne Corps
    (First Allied Airborne Army)
September 23, 1944: British VIII Corps
    (First Allied Airborne Army)

SOURCE NOTES

Epigraph page:

* Province, Charles M.: *The Unknown Patton* (Hippocrene, 1983)

* Grassi, Captain Daniel G.: In *Quartermaster Professional Bulletin* (Summer 1993)

Prologue:

* *The New York Times* (June 6, 1944)

Chapter 1

* Churchill, Winston, quoted in *The New York Times* (June-July 1944)

* SHAEF communique (July 6, 1944)

* Eisenhower, Dwight D.: *Crusade in Europe* (Doubleday, 1949)

Patton & Fortitude

* Province, Charles M.: *The Unknown Patton* (Hippocrene, 1983)

* Province, Charles M: *The Unknown Patton* (Hippocrene, 1983)

* Patton, General George S. Jr.: *War as I Knew It* (1947)

* US Army Center of Military History: Army Historical Program Strategic Plan (US Army Center of Military History, Fort Lesley J. McNair, 2001)

* Patton, General George S. Jr.: *War as I Knew It* (1947)

* Province, Charles M: *The Unknown Patton* (Hippocrene, 1983)

* Eisenhower, Dwight D.: *Crusade in Europe* (Doubleday, 1949)

Forging Ahead
* Associated Press (July 10, 1944)

* *The New York Times* (July 11, 1944)

* *The New York Times* (July 11, 1944)

* Middleton, Drew: *The New York Times* (July 16, 1944)

* Province, Charles M.: *The Unknown Patton* (Hippocrene, 1983)

* Stimson, Henry: Radio broadcast (July 25, 1944) (quoted in *The New York Times*)

* Goguen, Raymond: *History of the 329th Infantry Regiment* (US Army, 1945)

July 20 Plot
* Hitler, Adolf: Radio address (July 1944) (quoted in *The New York Times*)

Chapter 2

* Eisenhower, Dwight D.: *Crusade in Europe* (Doubleday, 1949)

7/25
* Carter, President Jimmy: Remarks at the Matt Urban Medal of Honor Ceremony (July 19, 1980)

7/28
* Blumenson, Martin: *Breakout and Pursuit* (US Army Office of Military History, 1961)

Chapter 3

* Province, Charles M.: *The Unknown Patton* (Hippocrene, 1983)

* Patton, General George S. Jr.: *War as I Knew It* (1947)

* Patton, General George S. Jr.: *War as I Knew It* (1947)

8/1
* Province, Charles M.: *The Unknown Patton* (Hippocrene, 1983)

* Patton, General George S. Jr.: *War as I Knew It* (1947)

* Blumenson, Martin: *Breakout and Pursuit* (US Army Office of Military History, 1961) ("Take Brest" quote)

8/3
* Gabel, Dr. Christopher R.: *The 4th Armored Division in the Encirclement of Nancy* (Combined Arms Research Library, Command & General Staff College, 1986) (Quoting Hanson W. Baldwin, *Tiger Jack* [a biography of John S. Wood], 1979)

8/4
* Blumenson, Martin: *Breakout and Pursuit* (US Army Office of Military History, 1961)

* Blumenson, Martin: *Breakout and Pursuit* (US Army Office of Military History, 1961)

8/8 (Brittany)
* Grow, Major General Robert W.: Headquarters, 6th Armored Division Memorandum (August 8, 1944)

8/9 (Loire)
* Hamilton, Major Edward: Quoted by United Press International (August 9, 1944)

8/12 (Hill 317)
* Eisenhower, Dwight D.: *Crusade in Europe* (Doubleday, 1949)

Chapter 5

8/12

* Leclerc, Brigadier General Jacques: Radio address (August 14, 1944) (Quoted in *The New York Times*)

8/15

* Eisenhower, General Dwight D.: SHAEF Communiqué (August 15, 1944)

* Chandler, Senator Albert: Speaking in Congress (August 15, 1944) (Quoted in *The New York Times*)

* *The New York Times* (August 15, 1944)

* Associated Press (August 15, 1944)

* McVane, John: NBC Radio Broadcast (August 16, 1944) (Quoted in *The New York Times*)

* Patton, General George S. Jr.: *War as I Knew It* (1947)

8/16

* Kluge, F.M. Gunther von: Suicide note to Adolf Hitler, August 16, 1944 (Quoted in Blumenson, Martin: *Breakout and Pursuit* (US Army Office of Military History, 1961)

8/20

* Medal of Honor Citation for John Druse Hawk: US Army Center of Military History

* Associated Press wire report (Quoted in *The New York Times*) (August 20, 1944)

8/21

* Province, Charles M.: *The Unknown Patton* (Hippocrene, 1983)

* Bradley, Omar Nelson: *A Soldier's Story* (1951) (Quoted by Blumenson, Martin: *Breakout and Pursuit* (US Army Office of Military History, 1961)

* Province, Charles M.: *The Unknown Patton* (Hippocrene, 1983)

Chapter 6

8/22
* Eisenhower, Dwight D.: *Crusade in Europe* (Doubleday, 1949)

8/25
* Hitler, Adolf: Query to Generaloberst Alfred Jodl (August 25, 1944). Quoted in Collins, Larry and LaPierre, Dominique: *Is Paris Burning?* (Simon & Schuster, 1965)

8/26
* Collins, Larry and LaPierre, Dominique: *Is Paris Burning?* (Simon & Schuster, 1965)

Chapter 7

8/21-8/25
* Patton, General George S. Jr.: *War as I Knew It* (1947)

8/26
* Province, Charles M.: *The Unknown Patton* (Hippocrene, 1983)

8/28
* Patton, General George S. Jr.: *War as I Knew It* (1947)

8/29
* Province, Charles M.: *The Unknown Patton* (Hippocrene, 1983)

* Gabel, Dr. Christopher R.: *The 4th Armored Division in the Encirclement of Nancy* (Combined Arms Research Library, Command & General Staff College, 1986) (Quoting Hanson W. Baldwin, *Tiger Jack* [a biography of John S. Wood], 1979)

* Patton, General George S. Jr.: *War as I Knew It* (1947)

Chapter 8

9/1

* Falkenhayn, General Erich von: Letter to Kaiser Wilhelm II (December 25, 1915)

* Pershing, General John J.: Comments to reporters (September 1, 1944)

Chapter 9

Red Ball Express

* Anders, Dr. Steven E.: "POL on the Red Ball Express" in *Quartermaster Professional Bulletin* (Spring 1989)

* Eisenhower, Dwight D.: *Crusade in Europe* (Doubleday, 1949)

* Pyle, Ernie: Dispatch from the Western Front (August 1944) (Quoted by Dr. Steven E. Anders in the Quartermaster Professional Bulletin, Spring 1989)

* Bradley, General Omar Nelson: Communique of August 27, 1944 (Quoted by Dr. Steven E. Anders in the Quartermaster Professional Bulletin, Spring 1989)

8/3

* German-Controlled Radio Brussels: Broadcast, September 3, 1944 (Quoted in *The New York Times*)

* Friedreich, General Hans: Announcement over German-Controlled Radio Brussels, September 3, 1944 (Quoted in *The New York Times*)

A "Ghost" Story

* Carter, President Jimmy: Remarks at the Matt Urban Medal of Honor Ceremony (July 19, 1980)

9/6

* Churchill, Winston: Memorandum to General Dwight Eisenhower (June 17, 1944)

* Eisenhower, Dwight D.: *Crusade in Europe* (Doubleday, 1949)

9/10
* Cole, Hugh M.: *The Ardennes: Battle of the Bulge* (US Army Center of Military History, 1965)

9/11
* Gabel, Dr. Christopher R.: *The Lorraine Campaign* (Combined Arms Research Library, Command & General Staff College, 1985)

9/13
* Headquarters, 5th Armored Division: *Report After Action Against Enemy, September 1944* (November 28, 1944)

* Abrams, Colonel Creighton: Quoted by Dr. Christopher R. Gable in *The Lorraine Campaign* (Combined Arms Research Library, Command & General Staff College, 1985)

* Province, Charles M.: *The Unknown Patton* (Hippocrene, 1983)

* Medal of Honor Citation for Edgar Lloyd: US Army Center of Military History

Chapter 10

* Aulock, Colonel Andreas von: Official pronouncement (August 1955) (Quoted in Blumenson, Martin: *Breakout and Pursuit* (US Army Office of Military History, 1961)

Chapter 11

* *The New York Times* (September 13, 1944)

* *The New York Times* (September 13, 1944)

A Plan for Market Garden
* Browning, Lieutenant General Frederick Browning: Comment to

Field Marshal Montgomery (Quoted in Major General Roy E. Urquhart: *Arnhem*, 1958)

A Bridge Too Short, A Cup Half Full
* Eisenhower, Dwight D.: *Crusade in Europe* (Doubleday, 1949)

9/25
* Patton, General George: *US Third Army Letter of Instruction* (September 25, 1944)

* Province, Charles M.: *The Unknown Patton* (Hippocrene, 1983)